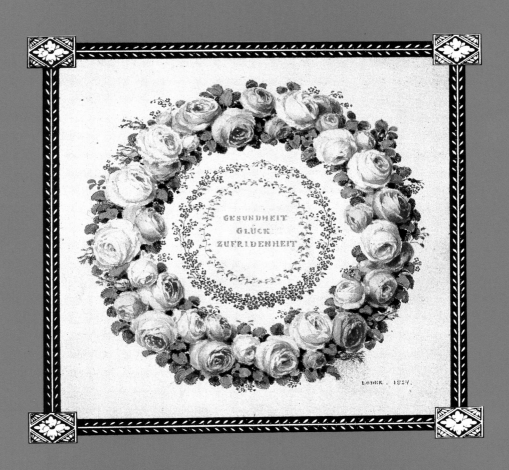

# Viennese Watercolors
## of the Nineteenth Century

Jakob Alt. *The Artist with his Son Rudolf and a Companion.*
*Looking Toward the Dachstein Mountains.* c. 1825. Lithograph.
Graphische Sammlung Albertina (Ö.K. XIX, Vol. II, fol. 33).

Walter Koschatzky

# VIENNESE WATERCOLORS
# of the Nineteenth Century

Harry N. Abrams, Inc., Publishers, New York

Illustration on the endpapers:
Matthäus Loder. *Greeting Card* ("Good health, good fortune, contentment").
1823. Private Collection.

Library of Congress Cataloging-in-Publication Data

Koschatzky, Walter.
    Viennese watercolors of the nineteenth century.
    Translation of: Österreichische Aquarellmalerei.
    Bibliography: p.
    Includes index.
    1. Watercolor painting, Austrian-Austria—Vienna.
2. Watercolor painting—19th century—Austria—Vienna.
I. Title.
ND1945.V53K67    1987        759.36′13        87-1202
ISBN 0-8109-1375-5

A Times Mirror Company

Printed and bound in Austria

# Contents

# INTRODUCTION

The art of watercolor painting reached a very special peak in nineteenth-century Vienna, the capital of the Austrian Empire and residence of its Hapsburg emperors. Painting in watercolors did not begin in that century, of course, nor was Vienna where it originated. On the contrary, dissolving pigments in water, the most obvious method of creating colored pictures, was the very earliest method of painting used.[1]

When paper came into widespread use in Europe in the fourteenth century, revolutionizing the possibilities of both drawing and painting, a whole new world opened up for watercolor painting in particular—with enormous implications. All mediums (pencil, pen, and brush) now found new ways of creating, on paper, linear or two-dimensional figures for the purpose of making an artistic statement, and those new ways gave rise to fresh objectives.

By the end of the medieval period two very different techniques of watercolor painting had emerged. One technique used dense, opaque paint to model highlights and depths and to produce an effect of solidity and corporeality. The other used relaxed, transparent brushstrokes; and the areas of color were pale enough to allow the paint underneath—and even the paper itself —to show through, which tended to produce floating, delicately luminous effects.[2]

The difference is fundamental. In the former, opaque technique (known in England as *body color*) a painting is always built up layer by layer, beginning with the darkest color and lightening progressively. The final "highlights" are achieved with applications of an opaque white pigment called Chinese white. This is why body color is said to be painted from dark to light and how, as its name suggests, it is able to produce a vividly three-dimensional, almost palpable image. In the other technique, termed transparent watercolor, the lightest tone available to the artist is the white of the paper he leaves unpainted. He starts with the palest shades, the thinness of the watercolor medium allowing him to lay down transparent areas of color one on top of another with a wet brush. This process, sometimes known as "glazing," has the effect of modifying the colors that show through the various layers (yellow seen through blue, for instance, looks green). The dark-er sections are painted next, and finally a few powerful blacks are laid on to provide the deep shadows. In other words, the watercolorist works from light to dark, exploiting the transparency of his well watered-down pigments. It is this transparent technique alone that is properly termed "watercolor painting."

Transparent watercolor produces an entirely different effect from opaque body color, despite the fact that both use exactly the same ingredients: pigment, water, and a bonding agent (usually gum arabic). The difference lies solely in the density of the wash. Pure watercolor is capable of conveying more than a subject; it can convey atmosphere, intangible vibrations, and a kind of reality that transcends the physical realm. This is because of the ways in which the light that the white ground reflects shines through the transparent layers of paint to produce the sort of glowing, extraordinarily delicate nuances of color that the glazing process makes possible.

The scientific term for this modification of super-imposed colors is additive mixing. Straightforward mixing in water is incapable of producing such tints; that method (subtractive color-mixing) invariably has the effect of "killing" colors by giving them a duller, grayer look. So it can safely be said that the big problem in body-color painting is how to achieve brightness: that technique does not permit glazing, and the mixed colors it employs tend to become murky and to lose their luminosity.

Artists attempted, particularly in the eighteenth century, to overcome this difficulty by adding a little Chinese white to all their body colors, which lightened them. Works painted in such "pastel tones" possess a character all their own. The opaque manner of water-color painting with Chinese white added came to be known generally as *gouache* (or, even more recently, poster paints) and completely dominated the Rococo period. In fact, the subsequent history of watercolor painting is the story of a gradual emancipation from gouache and the emergence of a lighter, freer type of work using transparent paints. This development culminated in a number of truly brilliant high points of pure watercolor painting in the first half of the nine-teenth century, after which the two techniques (opaque and transparent) were used in conjunction before eventually almost dying out toward the end of the century.

For the artists, there was more involved, of course, than technique alone. The choice of a particular medium is never accidental, nor will it be governed by, say, an advance in terms of materials, although obviously the latter—special brushes, for example, or paints, or suitable paper—must be to hand. The crucial factor is the artist's desire, an aspiration. This "artistic aspiration," which is certainly not explicable in terms of any rational act of volition, means that the originality of the paintings of a given period is one of the clearest expressions of the place that period occupies in the history of the human psyche.[3] That in turn is a product of everything the artist, his patrons, and ultimately all the members of a particular generation are for and against in their lifetime. It is in this sense that we speak of the "vital consciousness" of an age.

Artistic aspiration is defined in three stages: firstly by a given set of circumstances, secondly by the altering and overcoming of those circumstances, and thirdly by the goal achieved (the "vital consciousness" mentioned above) as a contribution toward a new and better view of the world and its problems.

Underlying all this is the fundamental problem of the ambivalence of the human situation: man is both determined—that is to say, bounded by time and place—and free, in other words, capable of acting creatively, with discernment, and in an organized manner. In fact, of course, man is obliged to act thus, since in the very exercise of his freedom of choice he is conforming to a law imposed upon him. In his novel *Kindred by Choice*, Goethe has Charlotte say, "As life draws us along we believe that we are acting on our own initiative, choosing what we do and how we take our pleasure; but, of course, if we look more closely, it is simply the intentions and inclinations of the age that we are compelled to coexecute."[4]

Properly speaking then, the questions that will concern me here are these: what "intentions of the age" did this great flowering of watercolor art in nineteenth-century Vienna reflect; what were the conditions that led up to this high point; what course did this blossoming of watercolor painting take, and who were the artists who used their freedom to attain such heights?

Some things that artists do call for great intellectual effort and a slow process of maturing. Certain works of art need to be constantly altered and improved before they achieve their final form. Buildings, sculptures in marble or bronze, large-scale murals, mosaics, and paintings on panel are all examples of this. But the rule does not apply to drawings, and it certainly does not apply to watercolor paintings.

The watercolorist's spontaneous manner of working directly on paper, using the simplest of means (its very simplicity makes watercolor one of the most demanding of artistic activities), is uniquely capable of capturing his thoughts and feelings as an artist—that is to say, as the person who, more than any other in his day, has a special capacity for apprehending the present and anticipating the future. The artist, in other words, has the ability to "discover" reality and to bring his spontaneously encoded version of the truth to the attention of his fellow men—always supposing that they are equipped with the requisite powers of perception.

At which point I must state quite categorically that anyone contemplating such pictures in the belief that art is some kind of entertainment, a diverting embellishment of everyday life, is very wide of the mark. Art never was and never should be any such thing. The function of pictorial art has always been to reveal, convey, and propagate a deeper understanding of a particular worldview or conception of life.

Such spontaneous pictorial records, directly mirroring artists' conceptions of an age, are of truly inestimable value. I am reminded of the passage in Hegel's *Aesthetics* in which he speaks of "the miracle ... of the whole mind passing directly into the skill of the hand."[5] It follows that nothing whatever—no document, no historical or sociological interpretation, no list of dates and events—can say the things about an age (its worldview, and the joys, fears, and hopes that informed it) that these works are capable of conveying, small and sketchily executed though they often are. It is this quality that can elevate a simple watercolor sketch to the status of a key witness to its time—invaluable and unforgettable. Nor is that all: the depth and eloquence of the emotion that engendered the watercolor may make such a painting extremely important artistically—not so much in terms of any striking artistic skill or effect but, because, being filled with a certain tension in its internal structure, it is able to put that emotion across.

All of this I believe to be particularly true as regards the nineteenth century—a fascinating period in which ends and beginnings, legacy and renewal, expectation and disappointment are as inextricably bound up with one another as are the problems of conservation and change, adaptation and resistance. Today, perhaps more urgently than ever before, we are in a position to examine what all this means to us: progress, for example, which much of the nineteenth century idealized; the rise of the technological sciences; the whole relationship between reason and nature; and finally the conflicting demands of industrialization and Humanism.

The history of the Austrian Empire may well have reached something of an apogee during this period—in terms of its geographical hegemony, its internal organization, the power it wielded at the heart of Europe (where it acted as both bridge and bulwark simultaneously[6]), and the almost unprecedented cultural aura of which it formed the nucleus—a fact that is only now beginning to be understood fully and appreciated.

At this period in history Vienna, the "Imperial Capital and Residence," was indeed one of the brightest jewels in the world's cultural crown. However, the city did not achieve that status overnight, and together we must go back a little in time to discover how it came to do so.

J. C. Brand
1722–1795

J. M. Schmuzer
1733–1811

F. A. Brand
1735–1806

V. Janscha
1743–1818

C. Schütz
1745–1800

L. Janscha
1749–1812

J. Ziegler
1749–1802

F. H. Füger
1751–1818

M. v. Molitor
1759–1812

F. Runk
1764–1834

J. Abel
1764–1818

J. A. Koch
1768–1839

C. P. Schalhas
1767–1797

B. Wigand
1770–1846

J. Gauermann
1773–1843

J. Knapp
1778–1833

C. Russ
1779–1843

J. Kniep
1779–1809

J. Mössmer
1780–1845

J. Rebell
1787–1828

J. Alt
1789–1872

J. N. Hoechle
1790–1835

M. M. Daffinger
1790–1849

F. X. Petter
1791–1866

M. Loder
1791–1828

J. A. Heinrich
1794–1822

T. Ender
1793–1875

P. Fendi
1796–1842

A. W. Rieder
1796–1880

F. G. Waldmüller
1793–1865

J. Fischbach
1797–1871

J. N. Passini
1798–1874

J. Kuwasseg
1799–1859

F. Loos
1797–1890

E. Gurk
1801–1841

J. Höger
1801–1877

J. Kriehuber
1800–1876

J. Gerstmeyer
1801–1870

J. E. Teltscher
1801–1837

F. Barbarini
1804–1873

A. Schindler
1805–1861

R. Theer
1808–1863

J. Danhauser
1805–1845

F. Gauermann
1807–1862

L. Russ
1809–1864

R. Alt
1812–1905

L. Fischer
1813–1872

M. Krafft
1812–1885

J. F. Treml
1816–1852

E. Stöckler
1819–1893

C. Schindler
1821–1842

A. von Bensa
1820–1902

A. v. Pettenkofen
1822–1889

F. Alt
1821–1914

J. Selleny
1824–1875

C. Goebel
1824–1899

A. Schönn
1826–1897

A. Romako
1832–1889

L. Passini
1832–1903

S. L'Allemand
1840–1910

E. J. Schindler
1842–1892

A. Greil
1841–1902

R. Raschka
b. 1847

E. Charlemont
1848–1906

1740

1780

1790

1792

1835

1848

1916

Maria Theresa

Joseph II

Leo-pold

Francis I (II)

Ferdinand I

Francis Joseph I

Chronological Table of the Artists Discussed from 1750 to 1900

Jean-Etienne Liotard. *Archduchess Marie Christine Painting with Watercolors.* 1762. Crayon and red chalk. On loan from the Gottfried Keller Foundation; Musée d'art et d'histoire de Genève, Geneva (1947–38).

# I  THE REFORMS OF MARIA THERESA AND HER SON JOSEPH II

Maria Theresa, born in 1717 as the eldest daughter of Emperor Charles VI, inherited her father's crown when he died unexpectedly in October, 1740, at the age of only fifty-five. (Her succession had been provided for by the so-called Pragmatic Sanction.) It became apparent immediately that a radical reorganization of the Austrian Empire was urgently necessary—and also that the young empress was a woman of outstanding gifts. She had a lucid understanding of governmental structures and of the demands of a new era, and she was inspired by an unshakable vision of a powerful, well-ordered multinational empire. All this was coupled with a rare ability to make vigorous, often quite intuitively motivated decisions. There was an irrational element in her makeup, the kind of "lucky streak" that successful leaders ought always to possess.

Maria Theresa's real greatness, however, lay in her maternal, humane, almost familiar attitude to the peoples of her realm; it formed the basis on which she arrived at her political decisions. At the same time she owed much of her success to her knack of placing the most outstanding advisers (Bartenstein, Haugwitz, Liechtenstein, Kaunitz) in the right job at the right time —and to her ability to listen closely to what those advisers said.

The so-called Theresian Reforms (which began in 1746) set out to make fundamental changes in all areas of the administration and political leadership of the monarchy, and the empress had to challenge powerful interests to push them through. In this she received crucial support from the loyal nobility, from a civil service that could be relied on implicitly to do its job, and from an officer corps that selflessly represented its empress and Austria in every garrison throughout the empire. Together these provided the requisite solid foundation for developments, the true importance of which would be inadequately conveyed by reeling off a list of individual measures affecting the administration, fiscal law, the army, or by mentioning, say, the centralization of power and the abolition of serfdom.

What really mattered was something quite different, something that lay behind the facts: an idea—or rather an ideal—of human dignity, tolerance, and humanity. That was what fostered Maria Theresa's Austria. That was what informed its sustaining attitude toward life and the world, an attitude characterized for generations to come by prudence, understanding, and consideration for others—though also (there is no ignoring the fact) by a certain fatalism.

Part of the outlook that that ideal molded for at least two centuries (I personally believe its effects are still visible today) was a powerful commitment to an active, critical concern with culture. There was in Austria an awareness, at least, of the meaning and value of the arts and a feeling for the kind of education required to foster them. Maria Theresa herself was a trained opera singer and had worked as such before and even after her marriage. She, and perhaps to an even greater extent her children (all accomplished musicians), furnished the perfect model for those characteristically Viennese pursuits of domestic music-making and enthusiastic attendance at the opera.

The political significance of the Theresian Reforms for Austria and for what proved to be a sound and smoothly functioning heart of central Europe over two centuries need not concern us here.[1] On the other hand the cultural awareness of the period and its effect on the development of the arts must constitute my starting point.

Maria Theresa, though persuaded of the almost providential nature of her task, was not in the least given to any kind of strutting Baroque self-glorification. On the contrary, she repeatedly displayed very human and often quite self-critical traits. She wondered, for example, whether her decisions and reforms would adequately provide for a better future for her empire and would effectively benefit mankind, or whether the ill-tempered impatience of her son and heir Joseph would place all her achievements in jeopardy. Disappointment and resignation were very much the empress's lot in later years, for many of her fears regarding Joseph II proved eminently justified.

When plans were put forward in Vienna for founding an Academy to embrace all branches of the arts and sciences, it was suggested that the celebrated German writer Gotthold Ephraim Lessing (1729–81) should be asked to head it. Lessing himself was very ready to give up his "ghastly circumstances" in Wolfenbüttel in the duchy of Brunswick,[2] and the fact that his wife Eva König owned a silk mill in Vienna constituted a further reason for moving to the city. In the spring of 1775 Lessing even had talks with the relevant authorities in Vienna. These came to nothing, although, as he wrote to his brother Karl, he had been given "the very finest of receptions everywhere."[3] Indeed, Lessing's arrival in Vienna was reported in all the city's newspapers, and when his tragedy *Emilia Galotti* was performed in his honor, the audience accorded him repeated ovations. The authorities, however, decided against the project: the founding of an Academy of Sciences, they felt, should be "deferred until better days."[4] (In fact it had to wait for another seventy years.)

Lessing was eventually received by Empress Maria Theresa—and she sent him on his way with a rather remarkable observation: "I believe I take his meaning," the empress said. "I am aware that good taste is not making any great headway. I just wish he would tell me whose fault that is. I have done all that lay within my wit and power to do. But I often think to myself: I am a mere woman, and there is not a great deal a woman can accomplish in such matters."[5] On that score she was undoubtedly mistaken. Maria Theresa was living proof of what a woman could accomplish in such matters, for she ushered in a new era of incomparable splendor. In addition to all her political, legal, financial, and humanitarian reforms she laid the groundwork for a flowering of the arts that was soon to give Austria a leading role on the international cultural stage.

In his *Oxford History of Music* Sir William Henry Hadow, whose view is certainly not clouded by local prejudice, makes this very clear. "If I had to cite the three greatest artistic periods in the history of the world," he writes, "I should name Periclean Athens in first place, Elizabethan England in second place, and in third place, without a doubt, Vienna in the second half of the eighteenth century and the first quarter of the nineteenth."[6] For a whole host of reasons that conviction has never been brought to the attention of—and is certainly not shared by—the world at large.

Firstly there was the political position that Austria occupied among the European powers in the nineteenth century. With nationalism rampant in every country in Europe, objective judgments were scarcely possible. Moreover, Austria also faced enemies within: many nationalist forces were at work within this multinational empire; repeatedly defeated in war, Austria was eventually scorned, derided from within its own ranks. Then there was the country's collapse into economic insignificance, which was aggravated by the total superiority of the victorious Allied powers after the First World War. Reduced to the status of an impoverished minor power, Austria temporarily lost all sense of identity and feeling of self-assurance.

This situation scarcely warranted a separate cultural self-awareness, let alone one with any claim to inter-

national attention. The conspicuous Austrian fatalism—as embodied in the old plague song, *"Ach du lieber Augustin,"* with its chorus of "Dear old Augustine, it's all over for you"—turned into pessimism and the kind of destructive self-criticism of Austrian abilities and achievements exemplified by Karl Kraus's mammoth Expressionist drama, *The Last Days of Mankind*.

Real and imagined inferiorities eventually led Austrians to admire all things foreign, which opened the door to every kind of outside influence. The resultant lack of an independent identity reduced Austria's chances of recognition even further. Finally, the poverty of the interwar and postwar years meant only limited and not particularly attractive opportunities for Austrian authors to publish. With international interest already at a low ebb, Austrian artistic achievements proceeded to fall into total oblivion, locked in a downward spiral of diminishing interest and lack of demand.

Today, I am glad to say, the situation has changed radically in many respects. Austria's artistic self-confidence has soared to fresh heights; there has been a huge increase in international interest, and the number of Austrian publications as well as their quality has substantially increased. One thinks of the field of contemporary literature, of recent international successes scored by Austrian artists, of exhibitions that have traveled all over the world, and of the greatly enhanced reputations now enjoyed by Austrian painters such as Egon Schiele, Gustav Klimt, Oskar Kokoschka, and by turn-of-the-century art. Developments in the musical world come to mind too—the Vienna State Opera, the Vienna Philharmonic, the Salzburg Festival—as well as the successes of certain Austrian books, including a number of monographs about artists, which have had a perceptible influence on the art market.

Nevertheless, it took the academic world decades to outgrow a tendency to look down its nose at the nineteenth century. For a long time Vienna's art historians showed a marked disinclination to accept Austrian artists of the period as valid research subjects. That, too, has changed as a result of the pioneering work of such modern scholars as Bruno Grimschitz, Heinrich Schwarz, and Fritz Novotny. Yet even now the reputation of watercolor painting in Austria—and particularly in Vienna—is very much less glorious than it ought to be. The time has come to set the record straight.

## FRENCH INFLUENCES

In Austria and throughout Europe, the eighteenth century was clearly dominated by the example of France, which governed people's way of life, their manners, and their language, as well as key areas in the arts. How far that dominance was more than merely alleged need not concern us here. What is certain is that the French constantly laid claim to a position of artistic superiority, and the upper classes of Austrian society were prepared to concede that claim.

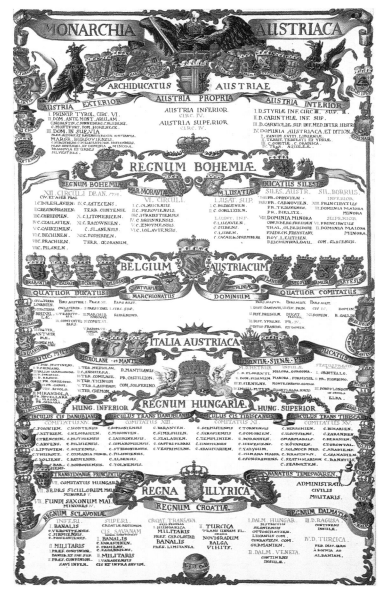

1   Charles-Joseph Roettiers. *The Austrian Monarchy.* 1769          2   Charles-Joseph Roettiers. *Systematic Index.* 1769

When Voltaire was asked his opinion of Prince Eugene of Savoy, the highly successful army commander who had defeated the Turks and—after having left France in disappointment—had achieved great renown in the service of the Austrian emperor, the author replied that the prince was doubtless to be admired for having collected art in a country where art counted for nothing.[7] Let us take another example. In 1809 few things aroused such intensity of feeling in Vienna against the French occupation as the enforced removal to Paris of the paintings in the Imperial Art Gallery. In fact, the man appointed by Napoleon to oversee the operation, Dominique-Vivant Denon (1751–1825), director of the Musée Napoléon, unwittingly contributed in no small degree toward stimulating cultural awareness among the Viennese. Even in 1815, after the Battle of Waterloo, the fall of Napoleon, and the collapse of his plans to assemble the world's greatest works of art in the Louvre, strident demands for the immediate return of the paintings were initially refused by the French on the grounds that spoils of war had always been regarded as legitimately acquired. Military pressure eventually persuaded them to change their minds, and the paintings were returned to Vienna. Questioned on the matter, Denon shrugged and said: "Let them take them [the paintings] all away again, but they lack the eyes to see them properly. France will always prove, through her superiority in the arts, that these masterpieces were better here than anywhere else."[8]

Maria Theresa's chancellor, Prince Wenzel Kaunitz-Rietberg (1711–94), was a particular admirer of France. His entire policy had been based on diplomatic efforts to achieve a *renversement des alliances* (change in alliances), abandoning Austria's traditional agreements with the maritime powers in favor of a pact with France. On May 1, 1756, this was achieved.

Since Kaunitz's appointment as chancellor in 1753, he had also been in charge of foreign policy; thus he was able to exert crucial influence on not only political but also cultural developments, particularly since, by this time, he was the empress's closest confidant. Enlightened (he was an enthusiastic subscriber to Diderot's *Encyclopédie*), liberal, and retaining impressive intellectual powers until the last, Kaunitz more than anyone else molded the image of the Theresian era.[9] As Austria's envoy to the French court, Kaunitz had secured the support of the influential Madame de Pompadour for better political and cultural relations between the two countries. On June 9, 1786, he wrote about her to the empress: "It is her enthusiasm and wisdom alone that we have to thank for all that has so far happened between our two courts."[10]

When Vienna wished to commission an encyclopedic book with plates for the education of Maria Theresa's youngest son, Archduke Ferdinand (b. 1754), it seems the Viennese court could furnish no artist good enough to be entrusted with the work. The prince's tutor Philipp von Rottenberg had drawn up an overall structural plan for the book, and it provides an almost unique survey of the contemporary state of knowledge, a rare compendium of the political and intellectual worldview of the mid-eighteenth century.[11]

Possibly through Madame de Pompadour, who was considered to be his particular patroness at the Parisian court, Charles-Joseph Roettiers, a member of France's Académie Royale and a highly respected master of drawing, painting, and copperplate engraving in Paris, was finally employed to do the job.

The execution of the book's ninety-nine teaching plates—today one of the treasures of the Austrian National Library's manuscript collection[12]—is truly superb and does indeed show what a huge margin separated the Frenchman from any comparable non-French artist of the period.

Incidentally, the plate entitled *The Austrian Monarchy (Monarchia Austriaca)*, though artistically unexceptional, bears witness to the sheer size of Maria Theresa's empire: the total of fifty-eight hereditary territories, domains, and titles gives some idea of the vast reach of Hapsburg power. Those states included the original Austrian crown lands with Vienna at their center, Inner Austria (comprising Styria, Carinthia, and Carniola), the "forelands," Bohemia, Silesia, the Netherlands, Luxembourg, Milan, Florence, Pisa, Jerusalem, and Venetia, Hungary, Serbia, Bulgaria, Bosnia, Croatia, Dalmatia, and Transylvania, to mention only the most important.

This book's three volumes—a smaller, less elaborate version of which is in the Joanneum in the Steiermärkisches Landesmuseum in Graz, clearly brought there by its founder, Archduke John—present a virtually complete picture of the age and its value concepts. In addition to the classification of the monarchy's territories, there is, for instance, the *Bilanx Austriaca*, a system of securing a foreign-policy equilibrium through distribution of alliances, and *Religio* as the basis of all order. *Politica* shows the way in which all classes and estates work together, while *Ratio* depicts the philosophy of soul, body, and God; of man and nature and ontological concepts. *Ethica universale*, together with various other systems, forms part of an understanding of the position of man in creation and society. The plates—*Ars militaris* is an example—that offer a breakdown of the various sections in the army and the naval forces and the way in which they work together are of enormous interest. They depict the hierarchy of all military ranks, from clerk and runner right up to marshal, the different branches of the armed forces, and finally the goal of a peaceful life under God's protection.

Roettiers's artistic achievement in the opaque watercolor paintings in this work is quite outstanding and may be seen as the prelude to an indigenous development in Vienna. The book was officially presented to the fifteen-year-old Archduke Ferdinand at Schönbrunn Palace on December 31, 1769. Not much is known about its effectiveness as a teaching aid: history remembers Ferdinand as the least gifted of the imperial princes, and his later career was undistinguished.

## THE VIENNA ACADEMY

In 1749, Jacob Matthias Schmuzer entered the "old" Vienna Academy (founded about 1692 by Peter Stindel and since 1726 under the direction of Jacob von Schuppen) to train in a variety of skills, including copperplate engraving. So greatly did he distinguish himself that he was brought to the attention of the empress, who arranged for Schmuzer to continue his training in Paris under the highly respected German painter and teacher, Johann Georg Wille. Wille championed a Dutch style of landscape painting that opted decisively for the reality of nature and against the "composition of beautiful parts" advocated by the German Neoclassicist Anton Raphael Mengs (1728–79). Wille's decision proved crucial as far as developments in Vienna were concerned.

Recalled to Vienna in 1766, Schmuzer immediately launched a renewal in art education. He founded a drawing and engraving school that was based on Wille's ideas from the outset. In fact, Schmuzer cited them in his application for permission to set up such a school, a document that begins with the often-quoted words: "Since drawing is the soul of all the arts, I am of a mind to open a school for drawing in Vienna."[13] He went on, "It is necessary to combine with this indoor school some landscape drawing from nature. There the student learns in the full light of day how to combine areas in the distance with the second and third [back]grounds. There it is possible, above all, to explain the light of the sun and, through reflection, the effect of shade. Mr. Wille, my esteemed teacher, has become what he is largely as a result of his practicing incessantly this type of drawing, and he bids all his pupils do the same. Since, however, unlike in France, it is not permitted here to walk where one will in the countryside, I must respectfully request… written permission for myself and my pupils to draw from nature such landscapes as, for the purposes of art, I find suitable."[14] Here, clearly, are the roots of the later flowering of watercolor landscape painting.

However, despite permission being promptly granted at the highest level on July 14, 1766, things did not at first proceed entirely without incident. The most celebrated mishap was the arrest, in 1769, of the school's professor of landscape drawing, Franz Edmund Weirotter (1730–71), together with three of his pupils, when he tried to draw the waterfall at Gaming. From then on, Prince Kaunitz saw to it that students and professors were issued with "passports," and the authorities were instructed "to provide for the requisite advancement of their work."[15]

The fact that the chancellor had placed himself (on July 1, 1766) at the head of Schmuzer's new school as its *Protector* (patron) indicates the importance that that influential statesman attached to promoting the arts. The appearance of a plan to amalgamate the old Academy with Schmuzer's new school—already progressing by leaps and bounds—drew a serious declaration of principle from the chancellor.

Maria Theresa had asked Kaunitz for an expert opinion, and this he duly delivered on May 25, 1770. It is probably one of the most remarkable cultural monuments of its day. Kaunitz began by describing in general terms the advantages that might accrue to the nation from the arts. He took as his example France under Louis XIV: "Men such as Poussin, Lebrun, Girardon, Mansard, and the other great masters of art, by improving taste and training able pupils, brought the nation more lasting benefit than all the generals—Condé, Turenne, Vauban, and the rest—put together."[16] It was a pointed thing to say to an empress whose pride lay not least in her military leaders, men of the stature of Daun and Laudon.

Kaunitz went on to point out the physical and financial strains that France had been placed under, despite all the expansion consequent upon its military successes. He suggested that the country would have been reduced to impoverishment and even collapse had it not become "the proud mistress of all other nations in the domain of art and taste."[17] Unsparing in his criticism of existing conditions, Kaunitz argued at length the need for education, "because genius is powerless without the appropriate study, that is to say, without a considered philosophical understanding of the beauty of nature."[18] The chancellor concluded:

> The furtherance of the fine arts in a state is an important object of concern for the wise ruler: cities will not only be embellished but also enriched by the same; quite apart from the travelers who visit such cities in order to view the works held there, young artists will often come from abroad to learn or to achieve greater perfection in their art. Foreigners place commissions, and good taste spreads to the mechanical and craft trades as well. Entirely new branches emerge, and industry receives a stimulus. There is thus no better way for a ruler to promote the welfare of his nation and to earn the gratitude of posterity than for him to kindle or introduce the fine and liberal arts therein and to improve them, support them, and help them to gain acceptance.[19]

Shortly afterward, it was decided to amalgate the "old" Academy with Schmuzer's school, and hurried efforts were made to enlist the most qualified persons as professors. It was all done with the *placet* of the empress, who noted on the official document establishing the Academy, "[I] now await the sole good effect of the insight and supervision of the prince, whom [I] shall gladly back in all matters."[20] A new era had begun.

At the Vienna Academy the "patron" threw himself into a frenzy of activity; he first produced a detailed statute of organization, laying down guidelines for developing the different subjects. Five departments were set up, and an academic council and a secretary were appointed (the latter job going to Baron Joseph von Sonnenfels, a key figure in the Viennese Enlightenment). The professors were given assistants, and provision was made for the admission of honorary members.

3   Friedrich Heinrich Füger. *Archduchess Marie Christine and Duke Albert Showing Their Art Treasures.* 1776

The newly organized drawing class may be regarded as the starting point of a crucial development as far as this book is concerned. (It is interesting to note in passing that there were dissensions among the professors from the outset, obliging Kaunitz to take repeated steps against "lack of cooperation" and "a deliberately fostered spirit of partisanship."[21])

Meanwhile the new approach to art was reflected in a striking change of policy with regard to scholarships. The consequences of that change were to prove momentous. Hitherto Paris and London had been considered virtually the only suitable places for artists to receive further training abroad (Venice, influential for a while, was now quite forgotten). Kaunitz began to point artists in a new direction: Rome. The respected Viennese portraitist Anton Maron (1733–1808) had been advocating such a change for some time ("send the young artists to Italy"), but few people had listened to him. The Austrian chancellor now argued that artists would acquire a "solid" education there, learning "after the example of Antiquity... noble simplicity, truth, a quiet greatness... in particular correct drawing, the nature of the truly beautiful...."[22]

Kaunitz's adoption of the concept coined by the German painter Adam Friedrich Oeser (1717–99), "noble simplicity and quiet greatness," signified a deliberate break with the Baroque era. The concept had already been taken up by the German responsible for creating the Neoclassical movement in the arts, Johann Joachim Winckelmann (1717–68) in his *Thoughts on the Imitation of Greek Works in Painting and Sculpture* (published in 1755), and it marked the official acceptance of a new cultural age.

Needless to say, this new worldview lay behind the changes. The classic Baroque political idealism of Austria had modeled itself on the concept of the *imperium*. It was this imperial ideal, this function of the universal ruler that Austria was destined to fulfill as the hub of the Holy Roman Empire of the German Nation.

This ideal had been clearly expressed in such buildings as the church of St. Charles Borromeus in Vienna (the Karlskirche) or, a little way upstream from the city, in Klosterneuburg. Vienna saw itself as the legitimate heir of Rome, and art was supposed to give visible expression to this legacy, as had been the case during the reign of Maria Theresa's father Charles VI. The situation now was quite different, however. The whole of Europe was being swept by a tidal wave of enthusiasm for another kind of antiquity—the ideal exemplar of human and political virtue.

One painter, Jacques Louis David, a Frenchman, was to unleash a revolution. The works of Greek antiquity (known only through copies done by the Romans) had been the object of attention in artistic circles in Europe since 1748, the year of the official discovery of Pompeii. But the change in the climate of opinion did not become fully apparent until 1784, when David exhibited his *Oath of the Horatii* in Rome. All the virtues for which David's generation of Neoclassicists yearned

were enshrined in exemplary form in this painting. The German painter Johann Tischbein (1751–1829) reported from Rome: "If ever a painting created a stir, this was it. For days on end there was almost a procession: kings and queens arrived to view it; cardinals and prelates, monsignori and parish priests, wealthy citizens and workingmen all came flocking."[23]

Kaunitz's reorientation met with the approval of Empress Maria Theresa. An increase in the number of scholarships to Rome was accepted, and several applicants were promptly selected. Gottlieb Nigelli, Franz Zauner, Hubert Maurer, and Friedrich Heinrich Füger were among the first.

Füger's selection was anything but a matter of course. There was even talk at the Academy of an "exceptional favor and of a noteworthy testimonial recognizing his great talent as well as his diligent application."[24] (We shall see what was meant in a moment.) Be that as it may, in the late summer of 1776 the young Füger left for Rome as a "pensioner." Seven years later he was recalled to take charge of the Vienna Academy. In that position Füger consummated the great change that occurred in Austrian art.

## JOSEPH II AND NEOCLASSICISM

The year 1780 represented a turning point in Austrian history. Maria Theresa's death brought a whole era to an abrupt end, leaving the way open for one that was to be radically different. The new age was undoubtedly molded by the figure of Emperor Joseph II (1741–90), who had long urged, with great impatience, that the principles he had framed be put into practice. His impatience had sparked off the rows with his mother. The empress had appealed to him over and over again while he was her coregent (1765–80), in tones of near despair. "You show too much your aversion to time-honored custom," she wrote to her son on Christmas Day, 1775, "too much your overly liberal views on private and public morality. You worry me: I tremble for the future."[25]

That Joseph's goals were inspired by the loftiest ideals is not in any doubt; they deserve all our admiration. His pursuit of them, however, was doomed to failure—because of the shortness of his life and reign, because of the indolence of humanity, which has always had more time for its own advantage than for high ideals, and lastly (something Joseph could do even less about) because of events in France in and after 1789. The French Revolution made crystal clear what horrors inevitably accompany so drastic a change in the fundamental structure of society and how rapidly things can get out of control.

Joseph had little contact with art. His preoccupations lay elsewhere. What he wanted were changes in the concept of the common good and the removal of deep-rooted prejudices. His goals were equality before the law and education to combat superstition. Reason alone was supposed to guide the individual and the commun-

THE REFORMS OF MARIA THERESA AND HER SON JOSEPH II

ity. Freedom of speech and thought were supposed to prevail, and religious intolerance was to be overcome. The emperor wanted to improve agriculture and industry in order to increase the prosperity of all. He wanted to liberalize trade, encourage population growth, facilitate settlement, and relieve the worst poverty with a social building program (exemplified by the new General Hospital in Vienna). Extensive parks and recreation areas were to make the inhabitants of the city healthier. The Prater and the Augarten—spacious imperial lands adjoining the Danube—where thrown open to the public. Finally, he wanted political relations between nations and among the European powers to proceed along entirely new lines. And all this was supposed to happen at once.

Joseph II was in for a disappointment. Moreover, he could not understand the resistance he encountered: "I love all men without exception or qualification, and I prefer the man who thinks well and conducts himself honestly above the man whose only merit is that he numbers princes among his ancestors."[26] These were courageous words, and they commanded respect.

No less an authority than Goethe reported in the *Tiefurter Journal* around this time:

The latest items of literary news from the capital of our country [note that Goethe regarded Vienna as the capital of Germany!] announce with one voice that the dawn of a most beautiful day is in the process of breaking there, and though we find ourselves at some remove from those regions, we are inclined, even so, to give credence to the same. For surely no host of savage sun worshipers could greet the arrival of the Queen of Heaven with greater fervor, with fiercer joy and delight thrilling through every limb, than our Viennese exhibit—albeit in a similarly rough-and-ready manner—in honor of the first rays of a blessed reign by Joseph II. We wish him and them a most beautiful day.[27]

There is no doubt that Joseph, with his ideas—and even more with his manner and way of setting about things—did not always make friends, particularly among the great and powerful. Nor did he endear himself to the ladies when he interfered in trifling matters, for instance, on September 20, 1787, when he banned the use of makeup, laying down heavy penalties for any infringement.

A far graver point against the emperor was the abolition of so many monasteries. That move had been idealistically motivated at the start; in reality it led to monstrous abuses, with irreplaceable artistic and cultural treasures being squandered, or simply destroyed. Joseph made repeated references to "junk" and—in the case of Hradčany Castle in Prague—"second-hand goods" that, he felt, "ought to be gotten rid of."

As an innovator, Joseph II was of course all the more sympathetic to Academism and its ideas that the arts could be taught and learned and that their objective was clearly the "enlightenment and education of mankind."[28] Yet, before very long, that was precisely what provided the point of departure for mounting opposition on the part of the younger generation of art students. In the Romantic climate of the *Sturm und Drang* (Storm and Stress) years, they were preoccupied with freedom, genius, and creative autonomy. In 1815 Joseph Anton Koch, who had quit his native Tyrol and the Stuttgart Academy in that spirit and turned his back on the teachings of the Academy in Vienna, gave devastating expression to his feelings in his usual earthy manner: "Like a swarm of maggots emerging from a spoiled cheese, a countless host of artstock [as in livestock; *Tr.*] comes crawling out of these art academies."[29] Ultimately, then, Joseph II's reforming endeavors met with failure even in this field. As we shall see, the peaks of artistic achievement reached over the next few decades were, for the most part, not the work of academically trained artists.

Where the emperor's frantic efforts did have some lasting effect, though, was in the social process that started to become apparent during his brief, ten-year reign. That process—the rise of the middle classes and the advent of the Industrial Age—was not confined to the Austrian Empire; nevertheless, the Josephine reforms did play a special part in it. Finally, if the whole of Europe at this time, with its rulers and its courts, is taken into consideration, an even greater respect for Joseph's principles emerges along with regret for what proved to be their futility. "Any realm over which I preside," he had said once, "must be governed by my principles. In it prejudice, fanaticism, partisanship, and slavery of the spirit must be suppressed; and each of my subjects made able to enjoy his natural freedom."[30] In fact, the basic moral and intellectual stance later dubbed "Josephinism," rather than the emperor's reforms as such, crucially shaped the cultural and intellectual history of Austria from that time on.[31]

It is impossible to understand the subsequent development of Austrian art without some knowledge of this background. At the heart of the Josephine approach to life were the principles of tolerance and equilibrium represented by the Greek concept of *sophrosyne* (literally, "of sound mind," prudent or reasonable). Later, when I trace the emergence of the Biedermeier phenomenon, it will become apparent that the chief impulses behind that phenomenon stemmed from this quarter. Although in the wake of events in France, which for Austria were vividly symbolized by the execution (seen rather as the murder) of Maria Theresa's daughter Queen Marie Antoinette, an antirevolutionary paralysis descended on the Austrian political scene, the typically Josephine attitude of compromise on all questions of freedom, authority, tradition, and so forth survived nevertheless.[32]

It was not an attitude shared equally by all sections of society. The higher nobility was either rigidly loyal to the emperor or—as in Bohemia or Hungary, for example—fiercely nationalist and autocratic. While some of the ordinary nobility were strongly clerical, and some highly enlightened, the class that was most pronouncedly Josephine in its outlook was the broad stratum of the upper and middle bourgeoisie.[33] This included the culturally crucial class of the monarchy's public servants, men whose whole mentality had come to be governed by the ideal of serivce and the Theresian ethos of loyalty, incorruptibility, and personal modesty.[34] Here was the source of that strain of cheerful realism in the Austrian character, a strain that found particular satisfaction in the glorious flowering of Viennese watercolor painting.

## THE BREAK WITH TRADITION

The Vienna Academy grew rapidly. It soon boasted excellent professors in all subjects, together with their assistants (kown initially as "adjuncts" and later as "correctors"), and began to attract increasingly large numbers of students.

Watercolor painting must have been practiced in the Academy's landscape department as early as 1785 or thereabouts. Johann Christian Brand even instructed a number of private pupils specifically in what he called "water painting."[35] Jacob Schmuzer had already demanded, as a matter of principle, that painters work out of doors to study problems of space and light, and it had become increasingly clear in the course of such work that adherence to the traditional method of painting in opaque gouache was no longer possible, however delightful its subtle pastel tones with their superimposed white highlights.

It was almost as if artists had suddenly become aware of a key philosophical notion: a whole is more than the sum of its parts. A juxtaposition of tangible objects no longer constituted the goal of artistic endeavor, but rather the rendition of an overall atmosphere in terms of space, air, light, and distance. From now on, all the artists who devoted more and more of their attention to the surroundings of Vienna, to the Prater, the Danube meadows, and the hills and mountains southwest of the capital—Baden, Mödling, Hinterbrühl—began by experimenting with the traditional manner of painting and then gradually found their way to transparent painting, to the technique of glazing, and to colors blended by means of wet brushstrokes.

Certain examples proved influential. One was Schmuzer's own style, which remained based on the Dutch manner of his teacher Wille. While it was topographically faithful, artistically its seventeenth-century Dutch rustic genre was somewhat alienated. It was this method that Goethe had so strongly condemned in his 1811 biography of his friend [Jacob] Philipp Hackert (1737–1807; like Schmuzer, a pupil of Wille): Goethe regarded the "mean and wretched peasant cottage with its adjoining kitchen garden and tiny orchard," which are "nervously cobbled together on a quarto sheet,"[36] as no subject for an artist in pursuit of higher objectives.

At the Vienna Academy, too, there was a parting of the ways: one school set its sights on the *veduta* (a painting or drawing of a view), trying to reproduce a particular view; the other school, more concerned with general truth, was intent on portraying the ideal behind things—an artistic objective. For a while, then, there was a split between the topographical and ideal approaches

Johann Christian Brand. *Herdsmen Resting on a Riverbank.* 1781. Gouache. Graphische Sammlung Albertina, Vienna (14.573).

Josef Abel. *Portrait of the Landscape Painter Martin von Molitor.* 1811. Oil on canvas. Sammlungen des Regierenden Fürsten von Liechtenstein. Vaduz Castle, Vaduz (1.365).

Martin Ferdinand Quadal. *Jacob Matthias Schmuzer* (sitting in the foreground at the left) *and Friedrich Heinrich Füger* (painting at the easel on the right) *with Their Colleagues and Students in the Life Class at Vienna's St. Anna Academy.* 1787. Oil on canvas. Akademie der bildenden Künste, Vienna.

4   Martin von Molitor. *Rocky Landscape with a Flock of Goats*. c. 1785

Martin von Molitor. *Lake in the Woods with Two Boats*. c. 1795. Brush and sepia. Graphische Sammlung Albertina, Vienna (6.001).

to landscape painting. The point to remember is that the heyday of achievement came later, when the two camps —ceasing to regard each other as hostile—joined in pursuit of a single objective, namely depicting an idealized reality.

The chief artist to tackle this problem was Martin von Molitor,[37] a pupil of Johann Christian Brand (his best pupil, according to Adam von Bartsch[38]). Molitor came from an impoverished background in the army aristocracy and had a crippled foot. His talent had earned him the financial backing of the empress and in 1789–95 led to Kaunitz's awarding him a scholarship "as a special favor." Eventually Molitor's work attracted a circle of connoisseurs that included Duke Albert and Archduke Charles (both of whom were responsible for the large Molitor collection in the Albertina today). The French ambassador and later commandant of Vienna, Count Andreossy, even dedicated a poem to the artist.[39] Molitor was an exceptionally influential trend-setter in his day. A contemporary, Archduke Charles's personal physician Joseph K.E. Hoser, described how Molitor's

rich culture drew a "circle of educated persons" round him, "who, while he painted, took pleasure in conversing with him about art."[40] In this way Molitor swiftly won general recognition for his characteristic fusion of ideal invention and actual observation. Even when August Schaeffer, writing in 1877, called him "the last of the Mohicans in Baroque landscape painting," he acknowledged that Molitor's works were "tastefully composed."[41] In fact, far from being the last representative of a vanished era, Molitor was the first of a new one.

When, because of his bad foot, Molitor took the young Jakob Gauermann along with him to complete a commission to paint views of the Tyrol, the consequences were far-reaching.[42] The resultant works marked the beginning of the *voyages pittoresques*, artists viewing their native landscape and discovering its beauty.

A very clear reference to Molitor's new departure can be seen in Josef Abel's portrait of the artist in the collections of the prince of Liechtenstein in Vaduz.[43] Painted in 1811—a year before Molitor's death, when he was fifty-two—the portrait looks back over the artist's life and sums up his view of art. In it Molitor is seen breaking his oil brush over a portfolio of colored papers. This corresponds to a step he had taken twelve years previously—abandoning oils—with which he had given watercolor painting a new status. As Reinhold Baumstark writes: "In Vienna, Molitor, the most important landscape painter of his generation, was chiefly committed to idealized portrayals of nature. Around 1800 he had made the decisive switch from stereotyped late-Baroque *vedute* to a new, Viennese type of idealized landscape. In fact he may be regarded as the creator of this manner—and therefore as the pioneer and precursor of a new age."[44]

It has never been satisfactorily explained why, given his sorry financial situation in 1795, Molitor did not seize the offer of a job as corrector at the Academy. His teacher Johann Christian Brand, the grand old man of Austrian landscape painting, had died, and it was proving difficult to find a successor. The council decided "to make the most able landscape draftsmen correctors" and appointed Lorenz Janscha and Molitor—"who has always been used as a helper."[45] However, Molitor refused "in order to pursue other prospects."[46] So the job went to Carl Philipp Schalhas, a man who must still be credited with a very special talent for watercolor landscape painting.[47]

Schalhas was the artist who most decisively took the step from the traditional type of foreground treatment to a new feeling for space. At the same time he introduced a whole new palette of transparent watercolors. But less than two years later—1797—Schalhas too was dead (like so many, a victim of consumption before he reached thirty). There is no doubt that Schalhas's watercolors had already shown the way things were going. However, Molitor's example, "his idealized landscapes, furnished with poetically enhanced *veduta*-like details, led to an idyllic transfiguration of the indigenous landscape"[48] that outweighes even the work of Schalhas. A fresh feeling for nature had found tangible expression.

Jacob Matthias Schmuzer. *View of the Danube*. 1791. Black crayon and watercolor. Graphische Sammlung Albertina, Vienna (14.923).

## IDEALIZED TRANSCRIPTIONS OF NATURE

As the eighteenth century advanced, the catchword "nature" acquired ever greater prominence. The problem of nature occupied a central position in the developing sciences and in philosophy after Descartes, Hume, and Rousseau, as well as in the whole of Enlightenment thinking. One authority, the French literary historian Paul Hazard, has even spoken of the "nature mania" of the period. Nature permeated the new thinking in every sphere: morality, law, religion, aesthetics, politics. People spoke of natural wisdom and of Mother Nature. Soon they were virtually equating God and nature, as in pantheism, and what they meant was the free, untrammeled growth of the "English" park, not its cropped and artificial French counterpart. Finally, citing the same catchword, people set about climbing mountains, which had hitherto been considered frightening only: they began to find the high mountains beautiful to look at, and proceeded to conquer them.

One concept may be said to have underpinned all of this: nature is a whole; its law is inner freedom. This freedom was what mankind yearned for now. The next step was seeing landscapes untouched and unadulterated by man as an embodiment of nature. In nature, in God's open country, there still lived natural human beings uninfluenced by social conventions. The goal of revolutionary ideas became the realization (or restoration) of that ideal.

In other words, what was natural was also deemed to be already free. In association with morality and ethics, the establishment of this state of nature came to signify "inner purity" as reflected in the beauty of unspoiled landscapes.

People had identified "the good" with "the beautiful" since antiquity (the *kalo-kagathia* idea). Now this was taken to mean that the aesthetic experience of viewing nature—in other words, "the beautiful"—and, by extension, the accurate, unadulterated representation of it in a work of art, were at the same time an education, indeed an elevation toward "the good."

Of course, taking pleasure in beauty (and conversely feeling aversion to ugliness) also signified an affinity in the observer with the unspoiled quality of nature. This made the artist who created such works a moral agent, in that he served to educate taste (= the beautiful = the good) by pointing the way toward nature: it was

5    Lorenz Janscha. *View of Vienna from Cobenzl.* c. 1796

Bau der Schlagbrücke bey dem rothen Thurm Thor 1780.

effect of the wars shortly to be fought right across Europe, from Belgium to Silesia, be overlooked, and the part played by the nationalist impulse inherent in the German Wars of Liberation.

Vienna took in immigrants of all nations and languages. They came from Bohemia, Moravia, Hungary, Croatia, the so-called Austrian forelands, Walachia, the Turkish provinces, Galicia, and Italy. Merchants and industrialists from Greece, Illyria, and the Orient set up shop in Vienna; Polish and Russian firms made the capital their headquarters. All these elements contributed to the image of a city that was soon bustling with commercial activity. At the same time Vienna exhibited an intellectual openness that made it quite unique.

All this must be taken into account if one wants to understand the phenomenal flowering of civilization with which Vienna greeted the new century. Indeed, it taxes the imagination to picture the full splendor and variety of early nineteenth-century Vienna: the elegance of the city's leading families, the beauty of their carriages and their superb horses, the gentlemen in their fashionable clothes, and the young ladies sparkling with that legendary Viennese charm—not to mention the enormous diversity of costume worn by Styrians and Tyrolese, Armenians and "Musulmen," Polish Jews and Bohemian peasant farmers, Moravian wet nurses and women of the *demimonde*.[58]

The figures speak a cooler, clearer language: in 1754 Vienna numbered 175,400 inhabitants; just three decades later, in 1785, there were 265,000 people living not just in the inner city within the belt of fortifications, the bastions, and the glacis (today's First District) but also in twenty surrounding *Vorstädten*, districts or suburbs.[59] The inner city was no longer capable of accommodating so many people, so that there was a rapid expansion of the districts outside the glacis, which was known as the "Esplanade" then (seventy-five years later it became the famous Ringstrasse).

Vienna had indeed become a thriving city; in the suburbs, however, rootlessness, grinding poverty, and appalling living conditions increasingly made their presence felt. Thousands saw their hopes very swiftly dwindle to nothing. A proletariat came into being; prostitution was rife, and people were forced to perform degrading tasks in their attempt to scrape together a living from the leftovers of the rich. In the context of such diversity, it was everyone's ambition to achieve something that would make him stand out from the crowd and insure him at least a modest livelihood. And in the midst of all this, a new generation of young artists emerged, with the Academy behind them, but nothing in front of them except what they could secure by their own efforts.

## JOHANN CHRISTIAN BRAND'S CLASS AT THE ACADEMY

At the Academy, drawing and the use of watercolor were both taught in the historical-rudiments class that was presided over in the crucial years from 1784 to 1818 by the history painter Hubert Maurer. Maurer's assistant Valentin Janscha came from near Radmannsdorf (now Radovljica in Slovenia) and was an accomplished watercolorist. Developments in watercolor painting, however, were the work of Valentin's brother Lorenz (or Laurenz), a member of the landscape-painting class. Lorenz Janscha, having absorbed to the full the artistic influence of his teacher Johann Christian Brand (whom he was eventually to succeed), broke completely with the latter's outmoded gouache technique and became the decisive exemplar at the Academy in the field of watercolor painting. But there had been a prelude to this.

Back in 1766, the year his Academy of Engravers was founded, Schmuzer had managed to get Franz Edmund Weirotter, an Academy student and a particularly gifted young artist from the Tyrol, recalled from Paris to become professor of landscape drawing and etching. On Weirotter's premature death in 1771, his former substitute Johann Christian Brand took over his teaching position.

Brand, as we have seen, became perhaps the most important artist in Viennese landscape painting as it moved away from the Baroque tradition toward the new realism, which fused the multitude of details present in real life into an ideal whole.[60] Brand's work in graphic art too (for example, the twenty-four-part series entitled *Viennese Street Cries* with typical figures from the everyday life in Vienna (published in 1775)) was important to the later emergence of genre art.

A whole generation of Vienna's landscape artists passed through Brand's class, for his teaching career spanned all of twenty-five years. When he died in 1795, the obvious replacement for Brand was his very much younger brother Friedrich August Brand,[61] who had substituted for his brother as "corrector" since 1776.

However, Friedrich August was actually a copperplate engraver; in fact, he is described in the records as having been "ignorant of painting."[62] It was decided that he should teach his brother's class only until such time as a worthy successor was found, and particularly since he was "often poorly,"[63] he should be given the "most able landscape draftsmen to assist him as correctors." That was a notably "Austrian" solution, for what was meant to be a provisional arrangement in fact lasted eleven years and proved thoroughly successful.

As we have seen, the first of the "correctors"—after Martin von Molitor had turned down the job—was Carl Schalhas. The second was Lorenz Janscha,[64] who had been a student at the Vienna Academy since around 1770: initially under Weirotter, then under Johann Christian Brand, for whom Janscha often substituted in later years. Thus continuity and controversy unfolded side by side and together pointed toward a new path. Eventually (in 1806), Janscha formally stepped into Brand's shoes as professor.

Lorenz Janscha was to become a watercolorist *par excellence*. Initially plunged into the refinements of the

10   Friedrich August Brand. *Langenzersdorf, near Vienna.* c. 1780

11   Lorenz Janscha. *The Roman Ruins at Schönbrunn.* c. 1785

12   Lorenz Janscha. *In Erlaa Park, Outside Vienna.* c. 1790
13   Lorenz Janscha. *The Artist Drawing in the Adlitz Rift.* c. 1800

watercolor technique through having to hand-color prints in the series published by Artaria (as Rudolf Alt was later obliged to color lithographs for his father, or—the most famous example—Turner and Thomas Girtin for Dr. Thomas Monro's series), Janscha later spontaneously evolved into the artist who did more than any other of his day to develop the transparency of palette, lightness, and atmospheric quality of the watercolor medium. Janscha can be credited with actually overcoming the traditional fashion for gouache.

Following Lorenz Janscha's death in 1812, teaching in the landscape department entered a period of stagnation.[65] Not until the war with France ended in 1815 was Josef Mössmer (who had been a pupil of Friedrich August Brand since 1796) charged with its continuance. Mössmer was and remained an adherent of the Molitor school. His influence was considerable, for he headed the landscape class until 1843. Mössmer also encouraged working outdoors, enabled artists to go on painting tours, and produced books of models. Yet he never seriously distinguished himself as an artist.

For the younger generation of realists Mössmer personified the academic "enemy."[66] So future developments, no longer receiving their impetus from the Academy, took a quite different course, influenced by those outside it—by real life—as clients, liberal artistic ideas, and the actual tasks of the day demanded.

Friedrich Heinrich Füger. *Self Portrait in Black Coat, with Hand Supporting Head.* c. 1777. Watercolor on ivory. Graphische Sammlung Albertina, Vienna (29.572).

## FRIEDRICH HEINRICH FÜGER

A minister's son from Heilbronn, Friedrich Heinrich Füger was attracted to Vienna by the reputation of the new Academy. He came to the city to continue his studies—and stayed to become the most important figure in the flowering of Austrian art that took place as the eighteenth century gave way to the nineteenth.

Born in 1751, Füger had begun his training in art at the age of twelve by attending a drawing school in Stuttgart. Disappointed with his teacher there, Nikolaus Guibal, he quit and went north to study law in Halle.[67] Füger soon took up art once again, however, under Adam Friedrich Oeser in Leipzig (Goethe's old drawing teacher). Oeser influenced Füger in the direction of the cool Neoclassicism he himself had absorbed in Bratislava under Georg Raphael Donner. It was a manner peculiarly suited to the new self-awareness of the Josephine era, and the kind of Neoclassicism that arose out of Füger's intellectual grounding and artistic ability came to constitute a distinctively Austrian style.

However, that is not what concerns me in this book. The key to the evolution in watercolor painting that I have outlined lay in a by-product of Füger's artistic work. On a visit to Dresden while he still lived in Leipzig, Füger had made the acquaintance of the English envoy Sir Robert Murray Keith and had studied Keith's collection of English portrait miniatures. The artist immediately tried his own hand at these, showing a quite exceptional talent for a watercolor technique that was delicate yet free, relaxed and at the same time meticulous. Füger was having some success with the technique even before he left Dresden. In 1774 he went to Vienna—as indeed did Keith, though on diplomatic business. Füger began to study at the Academy and was soon recommended and even introduced to Kaunitz. The chancellor, recognizing immediately that here was a very welcome newcomer to the city—intellectually as well as artistically—undertook to look after him. He began by securing a court commission for Füger that was to give him an opportunity to demonstrate his prowess.

Archduchess Marie Christine, the empress's favorite daughter, and her husband Duke Albert of Saxe-Teschen had returned at the beginning of July, 1776, from a trip to Italy that had lasted several months. During the trip they had taken possession of the collection of prints and drawings that Count Giacomo Durazzo, Austria's envoy in Venice, had been busy putting together since 1773, in accordance with his instructions. This was the basis of the present Albertina Collection, which is named after the duke.[68]

Füger's commission was to put on record the couple, on their return to Schönbrunn Palace, showing the newly imported art treasures to the empress, with the family gathered round them. The work, painted on parchment using an opaque technique of miniature painting, quickly became famous at court, as Johann Georg Meusel reported in his *Teutschen Künstlerlexikon*

14   Friedrich Heinrich Füger. *Portrait of Archduchess Maria Clementina of Austria.* 1795

15   Friedrich Heinrich Füger. *Portrait of a Young Man.* 1785
16   Carl Philipp Schalhas. *Trees and Rocks.* c. 1785

Friedrich Heinrich Füger. *"The Wedding Sacrifice," Portrait Study of a Lady.* c. 1788. Brush and ink. Graphische Sammlung Albertina, Vienna (24.228).

(*Dictionary of German Artists*), published two years later.[69] Füger's reward for this proof of his talent was a scholarship to Rome. In his years there, however, he showed no inclination to bow to the strict discipline of Roman-style Neoclassicism. As he wrote to his old teacher Guibal on March 30, 1779: "In Rome it is now a sin to possess genius and human understanding, and it is particularly dangerous to allow people to notice that one has come equipped with such."[70]

Kaunitz remained convinced of Füger's talent and in 1783 recalled him to Vienna as vice-principal of the Academy with the right to succeed the school's aged and sickly principal Caspar Sambach in due course;[71] which he did in 1795.

Füger promptly undertook a comprehensive reorganization of the school and embarked on a period of vigorous artistic activity. This constituted his principal official contribution and achievement. In addition, however, he personally instructed talented pupils in oil and in watercolor painting in a kind of "private academy" in order—as a petition of 1784 puts in—to demonstrate "the proper preparation of the pigments,

the mixing of the same, their treatment, and good use of color."[72]

Füger's mastery of the watercolor miniature was such that he is today regarded as one of the all-time greats in this genre. Leo Schidlof, a prominent expert in London, even called him "one of the greatest masters that ever lived."[73] In his own day, however, this aspect of his talent earned Füger very little renown. A young Swiss traveler Johann Heinrich Landolt, visiting Vienna in the summer of 1786, made the following highly significant entry in his journal: "[Füger] paints what he wants to here and enjoys it. He earns the most money with portrait miniatures in watercolors. For a half-figure he charges 24 ducats; with a bit of landscape or something else in the picture, 30 ducats. What a pity that, for the sake of such trifles, Füger neglects his true field, which is large-scale history painting. In Vienna, of course, such things find fewer admirers than do portrait miniatures, which is why he is obliged to do as the Romans did with their vestals and bury his talent alive."[74] Today the reply to Landolt's Neoclassicist concern is that Füger's immortality is in fact due to his skill with watercolors and to his portrait miniatures.

What was special about the way Füger painted? The answer probably lies in what he himself referred to as his "impatient hand," which "never wanted to settle down to a laborious, painstaking imitation in the manner of other painters."[75] Füger worked with relaxed crisscrossed brushstrokes—often in what might be called an impressionistic manner, in that he laid down his colors in dabs and splashes in a manner he had devised very early. Rather than set one dot of color beside another, Füger painted wet and used broad strokes (notwithstanding the small format), going very much further in this direction than the English models he had adopted. A whole generation took its cue from Füger's unique touch with the brush.

With these three elements—a search for real life, an artistic ideal, and free brushwork—all the conditions for a new awakening of watercolor art seemed to be present. Not quite; two further elements were necessary to the renewal of watercolor painting: the new vital consciousness, and the role of patron and client.

## The Transformation of the "Voyages pittoresques"

Given the social structure of the time, the largest patrons remained the imperial court and the nobility. They were soon joined by the up-and-coming middle class, which combined a pronounced sense of realism and entrepreneurial spirit with a proud awareness of their capital city. Precisely this new prosperity of Vienna, with its beautiful buildings and streets, its pulsing life and unique individuality, now became a topical subject.

The newly established publishing houses, encouraged by the freedoms allowed them under the Josephine reforms, were quick to appreciate this state of affairs and

Carl Schütz. *View of the Kohlmarkt in Vienna.* 1786. Pen and watercolor. Graphische Sammlung Albertina. Vienna (28.634).

began to issue print series of the sort pioneered by the Swiss: etchings, reproduced in outline and hand-colored on the basis of watercolor originals, after the manner of Johann Ludwig Aberli (1723–86). Both elements—the original and the hand-coloring—proved crucial steps in the development of watercolor painting.

The first Viennese licence to practice the art trade had been granted in 1770 to two cousins, Carlo and Francesco Artaria from Blevio on Lake Como. From 1775 their premises were "At the Sign of the Three Messengers" in the Kohlmarkt, and from 1789 in the house known as "The Angelic Salutation" in the same street.[76] The importance of the Artaria cousins in terms of cultural history cannot be rated too highly, particularly since they soon assumed a key role in the field of music publishing as well. Their introduction of the technique of engraving, on zinc plates, notes on a musical staff (1778), a technological revolution in music publishing, served as a basis for launching a catalogue that the names of Haydn and Beethoven were to make famous.

In the visual arts the Artaria cousins' most important project was the colored set of *Views of Vienna (Wiener Ansichten)*, which was such a resounding success that the house of Artaria has not looked back since. As *ve-*

*dute* of Old Vienna, these prints—known after their authors as the "Schütz-Ziegler-Janscha series"[77]—were never outdone. Two pupils of Schmuzer and Brand, Carl Schütz from Ljubljana and Johann Ziegler from Saxony, agreed to collaborate in 1778 in order to "represent the finest and most beautiful parts of the magnificent royal-imperial capital city of Vienna and its suburbs, including those lying beyond the lines [of fortification]".[78] The "advance announcement of [subscriptions for] painted and engraved prospects of Vienna" already appeared in the *Wiener Zeitung* on February 13, 1779. This provides an exact date for the watercolors on which the engravings were based—and which are considerable rarities today. Potential subscribers were assured that "the artists mean to spare no effort in selecting the finest and most interesting views, sketching them from nature as faithfully as possible, executing them in a pleasant and tasteful manner, and taking every care to use good-quality paper and obtain a clean impression." It was expressly stated that they intended to proceed "along the lines of the Neapolitan and Swiss regions painted by Johann Ludwig Aberli and Caspar Wolf [that is to say, using the method that Schütz was mainly responsible for bringing to Vienna]."

An immediate start was made on the first watercolors —the view of Belvedere Palace (Pl. 17). Understandably though, the execution of the first thirty-six prints took until April, 1784. Even that represented a very

17   Carl Schütz. *Belvedere Palace, Vienna.* 1784

substantial achievement on the part of the painters and engravers concerned. The series was an immediate success, which encouraged the publisher and the artists to extend and continue it. At this point the Janscha brothers, Valentin and Lorenz, both employed at the Academy and both of Slovenian origin like Schütz, were also called in.

Lorenz in particular increased the artistic input of the series substantially, contributing the approach to landscape that he had acquired from Johann Christian Brand. Moreover, extending the series to include the more distant environs of the city gave a big boost to the walking tours that young artists now began to undertake: Janscha's use of color provided them with their model.

The full set—eventually fifty-seven prints—was completed in 1798, and the original watercolor working drawings, in their rich profusion, probably qualify as the crucial practical step toward the subsequent masterly achievements of this branch of art in Vienna.

The success of the Artaria undertaking sparked off a host of similar publishing projects. A rival firm Franz Xaver Stöckl, which began trading in the nearby Seitzerhof in 1782, expanded the series with additional views of the environs of Vienna.

The young Ferdinand Runk, who had come to Vienna from Freiburg im Breisgau, was already making a living in this way in 1785. Runk was to prove a tower of strength to many other German artists who came to Vienna seeking their fortune, and in that alone he made a major contribution to the development of watercolor landscape painting. Living at 24 Laimgrube an der Wien, Runk was next-door neighbor to Jakob Gauer-

mann, who came to Vienna in 1798, and Runk took him particularly under his wing. It was through Runk that Gauermann arrived at a momentous idea: applying the objective realism used in city (or suburban) *vedute* to the Alpine landscape in general and to the lives, dress, and working methods of its inhabitants (those whom Archduke John was to call "the healthier people untouched by the spirit of the age").[79] Runk was also responsible for putting his compatriot Gauermann in touch with John, the "Styrian prince," in whose service a wide variety of work was soon available.

A further development in the landscape *vedute* was undertaken by Joseph Eder, whose publishing house in the Graben was founded in 1789. Eder added views from the Tyrol to his series, and again Runk was charged with their execution. The "passport" that the Academy issued to the artist for this purpose still exists: "The Royal-Imperial Academy of Art has no objection to granting Ferdinand Runk of Freyburg, landscape painter, his request for permission to sketch landscape subjects in the Tyrol."[80]

The extension of such publishing projects to cover the Alpine regions and their inhabitants had a great deal to do with Archduke John of Austria (1781–1859). Through a combination of inclination and education —the young man's tutor in the years 1792 to 1804 was the forceful and influential Swiss scholar Johannes von Müller—this son of Emperor Leopold II and brother of Francis I (his title as emperor of Austria; as the last Holy Roman emperor he was Francis II) had acquired a view of the world in which nature, the Alpine regions, and a loyal and simple life-style were crucial elements.[81] Archduke John's earliest known diary entry on the subject speaks for itself. On a trip into the mountains around Mariazell, in the autumn of 1796, the fifteen-year-old archduke wrote (in French): "I found a land encircled by high mountains containing broad and

Valentin Janscha. *Driving Red Deer and Wild Boar in the Danube Meadows.* c. 1780. Watercolor and gouache. Graphische Sammlung Albertina, Vienna (14.718).

Ferdinand Runk. *Schlattingbach Falls and Watermill, near Murau.* c. 1800. Watercolor. Graphische Sammlung Albertina, Vienna (7.064).

beautiful valleys and magnificent Alps, extensive glaciers, and, to borrow a term, *Alpenhirten* [Alpine shepherds], as they are called in Switzerland."[82]

In 1801, with the enemy armies of France advancing alarmingly on Austria, John was assigned the very urgent task of fortifying the Alpine passes in the Tyrol. The inventory of mountains, roads, and settlements that he had drawn up is something more than a product of nature worship as an artistic pastime; it also does much more than simply flesh out the general staff's maps of the area. For John, publicizing the beauties of the nature he now so enthusiastically experienced on his trips up remote valleys and over passes at the foot of magnificent mountain landscapes came to represent a conscious and very important contributory factor in the spiritual mobilization of Austrian patriotism.

Runk's pictures of the Tyrol launched the process. Increasingly, "general attention"[83] came to be directed at the Alpine regions and their bold inhabitants, whose resistance to the invading French became a shining model of the general fervor of Austrian patriotism and a symbol of all the national virtues. This in turn created and stimulated the demand for views of the Alpine landscape. Watercolor painting had found a new function.

In 1803 the publisher Tranquillo Mollo, who had left Artaria to start his own firm, launched himself on the market with a series of prints of the Salzburg region by Wilhelm Friedrich Schlotterbeck (1777–1819). The remarkable, deeply bitten aquatint technique employed by this artist produced some startling effects. This series of Salzburg views made a great impression on the German Romantics, prompting them to make Salzburg the goal of their expeditions. As a result, many a German watercolor of the Austrian mountains has its roots in Schlotterbeck's series. For the Austrian Romantics, however, it was a different matter.

Two years earlier, on May 26, 1801, Josef Schreyvogel had founded an Agency for Art and Industry (Kunst- und Industriecomptoir) that was to prove far ahead of its time. He promptly solicited the services of the already well-known artist Martin von Molitor for some pictures of the Tyrol. Molitor in turn enlisted the help of the young Jakob Gauermann. (According to Gauermann's diary, the real reason why he was taken on was because of Molitor's game leg.) What in fact came out of the journey was something quite different than just a series of *vedute*. This encounter between the two generations that these artists represented caused the transition from *vedute* of idealized nature with staffage to realistic landscape paintings, artistically rendered. The latter went into an artistic sphere far beyond the traditional "views" found in the *voyages pittoresques*. Of course, watercolor—with its freedom, its directness, and

*Wiener Freywillige. 1797.*

*Erstes Corps. | Studierende. | Handelsstand. | Acad.-Künstler. | Zu Pferde. | Landständische.*

Unknown artist. *Uniforms of the Vienna Volunteers in 1797* (left to right: First Corps, Students, Tradesmen, Academy Artists, Mounted, Gentry). 1797. Colored copperplate engraving. Graphische Sammlung Albertina, Vienna: "Wiener Historische Blätter (Viennese Historical Prints)."

its sheer manageability—was a particularly suitable medium for this new purpose.

All too swiftly, however, Vienna was engulfed by the war. The many new beginnings that the reforms of Maria Theresa and Joseph II had inspired were violently interrupted. Artists were exempt from military service in Austria—certain sources are inclined to attribute the huge increase in enrollments at the Academy to this fact—but this did nothing to diminish the patriotic fervor of art students. In 1797, before the turn of the century, such Neoclassicist-inspired emotions had led to scenes bordering on high comedy when the call to arms went out. Carl Russ described one such scene: "All the students from all departments of the Academy were assembled in the great Hall of Antiquities. On the raised modeling platform stood the professors: Schmuzer, the Nestor of the Academy, Jakobi [Jacobé], Vinzenz Fischer, Martin Fischer, the anatomist and sculptor, the grave-faced Maurer, the fiery Lampi, the battle-breathing Kauzig [Franz Caucic], and at their head the splendid, stately Füger reading the call to arms with all the emotion his sonorous voice could command. Hundreds of voices clamored excitedly in response as we firmly clasped hands, vowing to live and die for the sacred cause of house and home, for country and emperor—vying with one another in our ardor to write our names in the ranks of passionate defenders of the fatherland; the solemn faces of our good professors ran with tears. Oh sacred moments, never shall I forget you!"[84]

# II  The War Years and the Congress of Vienna

The future Emperor Francis (1768–1835) was the son of Grand Duke Leopold I of Tuscany and the eldest grandson of Maria Theresa (who had somewhat unconventionally announced his birth during a performance at the Court Opera House by shouting gaily from her box, "Poldi's had a little boy!"). Francis arrived in Vienna in 1784, aged sixteen, to have his education completed and to be prepared for the throne—tasks that his uncle Emperor Joseph II intended to oversee personally in conformity with his principles.

In Vienna young Francis found the outward circumstances of the late Rococo age (and it was in this setting that Carl Schütz portrayed Joseph's first meeting with his future wife Elizabeth, in front of the Belvedere.[1]) Very soon, however, Francis was to be caught up in a whirlwind of change, as world events and personal tragedies crowded in upon him: the death of his dear wife in premature childbed, tragically coupled with the fatal illness of Joseph II, the ill-starred campaigns against the Turks, events in France as the revolution broke out and began to run its course, and the threat to the lives, as well as the eventual execution, of the French king and Queen Marie Antoinette (who was his aunt). His father, who succeeded Joseph II as Leopold II, was probably the most enlightened ruler of his day and a man who looked forward to a more humane, more rationally ordered future and felt a deep aversion for militaristic power politics in any shape or form. Leopold found himself forced into the position of threatening France with war—at which critical juncture he suddenly and quite unexpectedly died. All Leopold's efforts to re-introduce a measure of calm after his predecessor's over-hasty reforms were thus brought to an abrupt halt, and his twenty-four-year-old son was catapulted onto the imperial throne in an extremely difficult situation.

As if that had not been enough, France's revolutionary army chose this auspicious moment to violate an Austrian frontier and invaded the Netherlands. That was the beginning of more than twenty dramatic years of war, a war that was to be characterized by heavy losses and that repeatedly, for one reason or another, took a disastrous turn for Austria. Struggles for supremacy, conflicting interests, and political equivocation

among his allies dogged young Emperor Francis as much as the poor leadership, miscalculations, and military shortcomings on his own side. Although all these factors and more undoubtedly played their part, two must be seen as crucial. One was Napoleon's superiority as a military commander and the myth to which it gave rise; the other was the character and personality of Emperor Francis himself.

The emperor was an extremely able, shrewd, and sensible man. He was deeply—perhaps too deeply—convinced of the duties and responsibilities implicit in his divine right. He was equally convinced—perhaps somewhat wishfully—that he was a plain and simple "people's emperor," and his concern for justice for all, while it eventually and quite rightly earned him the surname "Francis, the Good," cost him dearly in terms of loss of charisma. Francis's greatest weaknesses were a tendency to place his faith in stubborn persistence (coupled with a gnawing distrust that was clearly not unrelated), and his dull and somewhat arid belief that the state was a machine that could be controlled simply by faultless administration.[2] These weaknesses were also what motivated the counterforces ranged against "legitimacy." Heinrich Drimmel has very aptly pointed out that the emperor's guiding ethos was his desire simply "to weather Napoleon."[3] It was a lot to expect, and yet at the same time, it was too little.

Still, the contention often voiced that France represented the new (liberté, égalité, fraternité) and Austria the old, in the shape of hidebound tradition, can be exposed as one of the biggest lies in history. For one thing, in Napoleon's empire the watchwords of the revolution had become mere "empty shells" and no longer carried any weight.[4] For another, the nation that the reforms of Maria Theresa and Joseph II had turned into one of the most progressive in Europe can hardly be dismissed as an incarnation of the obsolete.

From the Austrian viewpoint, this was a battle against the destruction of all values, the annihilation of all order; Austria was fighting for its life. This lent the campaigns a special degree of intensity that affected the entire nation. It also gave rise to a new sense of national frustration, composed of historical, religious, and moral elements—though of course no one could then have predicted the catastrophes to which the moves and counter-moves, the arrogance and mutual hatred of the various national camps would one day lead. All this transformed the outward forms and manifestations of life— and with them the subject matter of art.

France had appealed to Roman antiquity as a symbol of its national empire, ascribing to itself the virtues of courage, loyalty, and love of country exemplified in Jacques-Louis David's painting *The Oath of the Horatii*. (Napoleon had even commissioned toga-like state robes.) Austria, for its part, looked to its German forebears and took the medieval ideal of chivalry coupled with the artistic notion of Gothic beauty and fervor as its models. Almost overnight, as it were, these ideals superseded the classical themes on which the academies in particular had been ringing endless changes.

Laxenburg Palace to the southeast of Vienna was the architectural embodiment of the new Austrian ideal. It was a favorite resort of the emperor and his family, replete with crenelated towers, balconies, and romantically embellished halls, courts, and tiltyard, surrounded by atmospheric lakes and parklands that perfectly reflected the new mood. The "Germanic" character was now being compared and contrasted with everything "foreign." Mirrored in it was Austria's own medieval past, considered the source of all good. Historians, writers, dramatists, and poets spoke with one voice.

The chilvarous poems of Johann Baptist von Alxinger, for example, met with an enthusiastic reception. In 1806 the emperor's second wife (another Maria Theresa, 1722–1807) took the advice of the writer Karoline Pichler and introduced old German dress for functions at the Franzensburg.[5] The ladies of Vienna promptly followed suit, and the whole fashion scene underwent a rapid transformation. Many of the por-

traits Füger painted in these years show examples of full pleated ruffs. Karoline Pichler, writing in 1808, had this to say about the shift in the *Zeitgeist* (spirit of the time): "The enormous changes and the violent destruction produced a diametrically opposed trend, and hearts and minds turned more firmly and affectionately toward the old familiar things. Since the plague of doubt was widely recognized as being harmful, the faith of our fathers, the fatherland, and the customs and history of the fatherland increasingly became cherished notions in which storm-tossed spirits sought refuge."[6]

## THE ROMANCE OF CHIVALRY

Matthäus Loder is a prime example of an artist who has fallen into undeserved oblivion.[7] Loder was born in Vienna, though his father, a paperhanger from Eichstätt in Bavaria, had been one of the many immigrants who flocked to the city during the 1770s. Loder showed early promise and was admitted to the Academy at the age of thirteen. Described as a "needy pupil,"[8] he was awarded one of the top scholarships in recognition of his exceptional talent. The scholarship ran until 1805 and effectively underwrote his training. An extremely hard worker, Loder took advantage of the wealth of opportunities available to him. He illustrated many of the pocketbooks, calendars, and playing cards with which Vienna's publishers enjoyed such success in those years; his gift for minute detail fitted him superbly for such commissions. He also worked as a stage designer and as a designer of festive decorations, and one day—the exact date is not known—Loder was appointed drawing teacher to the emperor's daughter Marie Louise. (Even in Paris, after she became empress of France as Napoleon's wife, Marie Louise continued her training under Jean-Baptiste Isabey. Incidentally, this led to Isabey's being commissioned to visit Vienna

Johann Nepomuk Hoechle. *The Imperial Family in Laxenburg Park.* 1807. Watercolor. Graphische Sammlung Albertina, Vienna (22.684).

18    Matthäus Loder. *Twelve Designs for Playing Cards.* c. 1818

19   Matthäus Loder. *View of Vienna.* c. 1810

20   Matthäus Loder. *Banquet in a Baronial Hall.* c. 1807–8

in 1812 to paint a picture of the imperial family.) Back in Vienna after the fall of Napoleon, Marie Louise was to remember Loder, her Viennese drawing teacher.

Meanwhile—around 1807—Loder had painted a series of pictures in the old German style.[9] These had so successfully confirmed his reputation that he had been able to leave the Academy at last, give up his scholarship, and get married.[10] (Archduke John once referred to the couple, who were later to attend him for more than a decade, as "a model of love and devotion."[11])

M. T. Wietersheim sees Loder's watercolor *Banquet in a Baronial Hall* as the high point of these old German works. It is indeed an exceptional work, as proven by the fact that Duke Albert of Saxe-Teschen acquired it for his Albertina Collection. The delicacy of detail is astonishing, and yet the overall effect—the treatment of space and light—is one of quiet, composed beauty. With this piece of Austrian Romanticism Loder reached a personal pinnacle of achievement.

There was, however, absolutely no question in Vienna of the kind of Romantic movement that characterized the German art of the period. The German artist Philipp Otto Runge, writing in 1802, could speak emotionally of "when the sky above teems with countless stars, the wind whistles through the vastness of space, the wave breaks with a roar in the far reaches of the night, and above the forest, the firmament is flushed with red as the sun illuminates the world . . .";[12] Vienna, with its strong grip on reality, could make little of such raptures. The Austrian author Franz Grillparzer felt that "the fact that the Germans attach so high a value to this seesawing reverie, this imageless, nonconceptual sentience," was quite plainly "the nation's undoing."[13]

Therefore, the romance of chivalry did not occupy even Loder for long. Other commissions soon came his way, very different commissions that were firmly anchored in real life. Yet even in these Loder never lost his delicate, delightful rapport with his subject, the quality that gives his works a timeless charm and will always raise Loder, as a watercolorist, far above the great majority of his contemporaries.

## THE FRENCH OCCUPATION

Though fierce while it lasted, the siege of Vienna, in the early days of May, 1809, during which Napoleon's army bombarded the fortifications, was of only brief duration. Grillparzer's description is typical: "I had been unable, during the siege, to refrain from joining the student corps, which was manning a section of the walls. As the guns thundered without interruption all night, shells flew through the air in all directions, and fires raged in various parts of the city, my father, who thought I was exposed to all those bullets, could not contain his anxiety. Next morning, after the surrender of the city, my weeping mother appeared on the bastion. . . . She begged me to come straight home and satisfy my father that I was still alive."[14]

In the early hours of May 13, even the fortified inner city of Vienna was obliged to surrender. The army corps commanded by the French marshals André Masséna and Jean Lannes marched in and occupied the imperial capital. An unprecented nadir had been reached. Austrian troops beating a hurried retreat from their rout at Regensburg (Ratisbon) failed to reach Vienna in time, let alone to defend it. They took up positions in a broad arc around the city—a difficult task—made even more difficult by the treacherous nature of the terrain between the many arms of the Danube.

In Archduke Charles the Austrians had a very experienced army commander. In fact, of all the Allied military leaders, Charles was possibly most nearly a match for their brilliant opponent in terms of breadth of vision and strength of resolution. Now, however, events had taken the very turn that had prompted Charles, as commander-in-chief, to advise against war even before it was declared: Austria's army was outclassed by the French military machine, with its modern equipment and modern methods of command, as he had warned. The opportunity of defeating Napoleon still lay far in the future. But the war party had had its way; and now, following a chain of defeats, heavy losses suffered in incessant rearguard actions, and finally the occupation of the imperial capital, the situation was nothing short of disastrous. Discipline and morale appeared to be in tatters and the monarchy on the verge of collapse.

Charles knew that if there was one thing that could still motivate the Austrians, one last emotional opportunity for the battered army, it was an engagement in the immediate vicinity of the nation's capital. Accordingly he urged that Napoleon should be forced into a decision there and then.

Napoleon for his part welcomed a showdown. His situation was growing daily more difficult. He knew very well that, while he could probably defeat the Austrians as long as they were on the run, this would be difficult in a few days's time when the relieving armies —particularly the one Archduke John was leading on forced marches back from Italy, where it had scored notable successes at Sacile and Pordenone—joined forces to oppose him.

Both sides began to make feverish preparations. Napoleon forced a number of bridgeheads and made an attempt to gain the far bank of the Danube unnoticed and so outflank the enemy.

Charles brought off a number of decoy maneuvers, managing effectively to deceive the French with regard to his deployment and intentions. As a result, some vanguard skirmishing around the small village of Aspern suddenly and rather unexpectedly escalated into a full-scale engagement. The main bodies of the two armies clashed head-on and began to surge back and forth, each side alternately gaining and losing the advantage in rapid succession.

The events of that Pentecost Sunday (May 21, 1809) and more particularly of the decisive following day, the seesawing of attack and counterattack, make a fascinat-

21   Johann Nepomuk Hoechle. *The Battle of Aspern.* 1809

ing story, though it is one I cannot go into in detail here.[15] Suffice it to say that the fighting that raged around the church and churchyard of Aspern during those two spring days was characterized by an almost unprecedented vehemence, with both Napoleon and Archduke Charles finding themselves in the very front line several times. Something that had never happened before happened at Aspern. In a decisive encounter between two major armies, the hitherto undefeated Napoleon was taken on by an evenly matched opponent and beaten. Charles won the day; and under cover of darkness, the French army retreated from the field. Napoleon, of course, regained the upper hand a mere six weeks later when he defeated the Austrian army soundly at Wagram. Nevertheless, Aspern had shattered a myth and inspired the belief that Austria would one day recover from the shame of the Peace of Schönbrunn.

It goes without saying that the most momentous decisions the respective commanders made during the two bloody days of the Battle of Aspern (each army suffered over 20,000 dead) depended on their ability to see what the other side was up to. Consequently the French, who held Vienna, were jealously guarding all the city's observation posts. Yet in the midst of all this frantic activity a young artist, Johann Nepomuk Hoechle, sat painting a watercolor. Just nineteen years old, Hoechle had recently completed his training under Füger and was anxious to record the dramatic events taking place before his eyes.

The resultant work, *The Battle of Aspern*, is perhaps one of the most unusual in the entire Albertina Collection. It is accompanied by a statement, handwritten by the original owner, which surely requires no comment:

This drawing was made from nature with the aid of a telescope by Joh. Höchle Jr. from a vantage point in Heiligenstadt in Pentecost week, 1809. The work was progressing well when a troop of French arrived and surrounded the artist, whom they accused of being a spy. (At the time, every tower in the city and in the suburbs was controlled and guarded by the enemy lest the movements of the army be revealed.) The sanctions of martial law were immediately proclaimed to apply to him. A circle formed, and three men stepped forward to shoot him. He was given a handkerchief with which to blindfold himself. Amazingly, he retained sufficient presence of mind at this point to begin haranguing the commanding officer. Fortunately he spoke perfect French, and he berated the officer for being about to murder an artist who, dedicated to battle painting, was availing himself of this rare opportunity to exercise his talent, with no ulterior motive. He demanded to be taken before Hulin, the commandant of the city, so he could prove that he was the son of the court painter to H.M. the Emperor. He relied, he said, on the notorious fair-mindedness of the French to grant him this just request, and his punishment, in so far as he

deserved any, should be ordained only by a higher instance and not there on the street, etc. In short, anyone who knew him will be familiar with his modesty and refinement. These advantages, together with a ringing eloquence inspired by his predicament, proved his salvation. The officer ordered him to fall in, and he was taken before the commandant of the city, who found his statements to be true and released him with a caution. Fortunately, no one asked him for the drawing, which he had hidden in his sachel and which he handed in person to the undersigned together with the foregoing (rather more circumstantial) verbal report by the artist.
Anton Gräffer.

This inscription on the painting in the Albertina has saved this dramatic incident from oblivion.


## DIRECTIONS IN WATERCOLOR ART

Already in this first decade of the new century, watercolor painting in Vienna was beginning to move in what were clearly divergent directions. These were dictated by the kinds of commission available at the time, by the changing nature of society and of the clientele for art, and perhaps most of all by the individual characters of the artists themselves. Most watercolor work was still *landscape painting*,[16] but other tasks that increasingly fell to the medium were *flower painting*, for which the manufacturing class at the Academy (aimed at Vienna's porcelain industry) provided the highest qualifications, as well as *portrait painting*, which had acquired a characteristically Viennese flavor since the example of Füger, and finally the *portrayal of scenes*, at first historical for the most part.

In watercolor landscape painting at least five groups of artists need to be distinguished:

1) the painters whom Archduke John began to appoint in 1802 to make a record of the Alpine regions;

2) the academic tradition that, after Lorenz Janscha was taken ill in 1808, was represented mainly by Josef Mössmer;

3) an imported German Romanticism, impressively pursued in Vienna chiefly by Johann August Heinrich. Heinrich lived in the city from 1812 to 1818; (With the exception of the Olivier brothers and Julius Schnorr von Carolsfeld, none of whom worked much in watercolor, all the other Germans of this school who came to Vienna, whether drawn by the excitement surrounding the founding of the Brotherhood of St. Luke patron saint of the arts, or *Lukasbrüder*, traveling for study purposes, stopped in the city only briefly, never became assimilated, and so have no place in my survey.)

4) the powerful Tyrolese artist Joseph Anton Koch, who lived in Rome (and quite specifically repudiated Vienna, where he lived from 1812–15[17]). But Koch must be included here because of his standing as a renewer and because his influence on the young gives

22   Joseph Rebell. *View of Lake Como.* 1811

Josef Mössmer. *View of Tyrol Castle.* 1809. Watercolor with ink outlines drawn on
top. Graphische Sammlung Albertina, Vienna (14.832)

Joseph Anton Koch. *Oberhasli in the Bernese Alps.* Between 1792 and 1795. Watercolor and gouache with white highlights.
Akademie der bildenden Künste: Kupferstichkabinett, Vienna (6.580).

Peter von Hess. *Joseph Rebell at his Easel in Subiaco.* 1817. Pencil. Graphische Sammlung Albertina, Vienna (5.473).

Joseph Rebell. *Wooded Landscape "Selve della Diana Scitica."* 1812. Brush and sepia. Private collection, Munich.

him a special place; ("What is the point of all this concentrating on bits and pieces in art, this mechanical copying of hands and feet, and trees and snakes, this laborious drawing from nature, all for the purpose of cobbling together a poorly composed mosaic?... Let the creating mind absorb an item, the tiniest detail, and from deep within itself pour forth the whole universe in a single casting, lit by the sheet-lightning of idealizing imagination."[18])

5) lastly Joseph Rebell who, after training in Vienna under Michael Wutky, went to Italy in 1809 and lived there quite successfully until 1824, when he returned to Vienna, though Emperor Francis had appointed him to succeed Füger as early as 1819. In the few years at the end of his life that Rebell spent working in Vienna, his brilliant landscapes, drenched in light, provided probably the most powerful impulse toward further developments in watercolor.

With these five distinct groups of artists, watercolor painting in Vienna was evolving along what had become a very broad front.

## THE EARLY PAINTERS BY APPOINTMENT TO ARCHDUKE JOHN

Archduke John had made his first trip into the mountains around Mariazell as an adolescent in 1796. Just four years later—in 1800—he was given the task of reconnoitering the Tyrol for military purposes. His mandate covered fortification, defense, and the mobilization of the inhabitants. For John the notion of a *Landwehr* (local militia) became a prime objective. His brother Charles had military and organizational objections to the concept, and Emperor Francis was actually hostile to it: in the latter's eyes any idea of arming the people was highly suspect, and politically the prospect of losing control of such a force was extremely disquieting. John, however, stuck to his plan and even received permission to put it into effect in Styria.

This was the beginning of John's long love affair with that province, from which sprang everything that followed: the topographical and statistical research, the recording of dress, customs, and commerce, and even the idealistic hope of improving the lives of all Styrians by founding an educational institute at Graz.

In 1801 John was detained in Salzburg and the Tyrol, but the following year he made a start on his objectives in Styria.[19] Initially it was the iron industry in the Mürz Valley and the adjoining valleys that concerned him. But after climbing the Schneeberg, visiting the monastery of Neuberg, and then in 1803 exploring the Hochschwab range and the Dullwitz, such excursions came to mean more to him and laid the foundations of his deep and abiding affection for the province of Styria. John turned to the Vienna Academy in search of a suitable young artist to accompany him on his travels and record certain views; he chose Johann Kniep.

Johann Kniep. *High Valley in the Tauern Mountains.* 1807–8. Watercolor. Private collection (E. J. 3).

Even the first two expeditions before war intervened produced some notable works. Then John, appointed Deputy War Minister, toured the southern Alps through Carniola and Lombardy as far as Switzerland. Kniep went with him, and an extensive collection of watercolors resulted. The fighting and the Austrian defeat in 1805 brought a major hiatus. John withdrew from public life, purchased Thernberg Castle, and devoted himself to other pursuits.

The survey program resumed in 1807 with an inventory of Carinthia and the frontier regions of Carniola and Friuli. In the late autumn of that year John again traversed Upper Styria from the town of Aussee to the Lungau Valley, pushing on as far as Heiligenblut and returning by way of the Seetaler and Stub Alps. A similar trip was undertaken in 1808, but shortly after war broke out once more, and John assumed heavier responsibilities. The crisis and defeat of 1809 followed, and in his bivouac one day, the archduke received a letter from his secretary, Johann Gebhard. "The good young man Knipp *[sic]* died on July 30," Gebhard wrote, giving as the reason the artist's "dismay at the unfortunate turn taken by political events and difficulty in seeing very far into a gloomy future."[20]

Kniep's oeuvre is limited in scope because his life was so tragically cut short. Yet he is an artist who must not be overlooked. The earliest mention of his name dates from 1802, when Friedrich August Brand, his teacher, asked that he and Josef Mössmer be nominated for scholarships: "In the school I look after there are two exceptional talents. They are Johann Kniep and Joseph *[sic]* Mössmer.[21] The first has aged and impoverished parents, while the second is a fatherless orphan. The indigence of both—the only food they can afford is bread—is holding them back in the pursuit of their skill and hampering their education."[22] Interestingly, Archduke John always chose his painters by appointment with an eye to their social circumstances, and this doubtless played a part in Kniep's case, too. But the young man also fulfilled all John's artistic expectations. The record of his death describes him as "landscape painter to H.R.H. Archduke John."

Kniep's achievement may have been curtailed, yet the initial step he took, namely looking for the beauty of the country in the real mountains, represented a solid advance for landscape painting. No imagined ideal, no "cobbling together of beautiful components," as Jacob Gauermann had put it in his diary in reference to the theory of Anton Raphael Mengs (1728–79), no invention were necessary here. It was enough to apprehend reality with one's eyes open and to reproduce it with a sympathetic understanding. That is why Kniep is so important—from the first inklings he gleaned from drawing the contours in views by Carl Schütz (for whom Kniep worked as a colorist) to his eventual mastery of the intangible quality of his impressions of nature as he captured atmosphere in his paintings.

Following the death of Kniep and the appalling political disappointments of 1809, an almost despairing John withdrew even further from public life. He did go on with his botanical work of studying the Alpine flora scientifically, enlisting the services of the talented Johann Knapp as a flower painter at Schönbrunn. But then the archduke turned back to what the historian Joseph von Hormayr had urged on him as a new function for art, namely the creation of *Leit-Bilder* (exemplary images) from Austria's history. What was needed now, John felt,[23] was not another landscape painter but someone who, having studied history, looked to his own past and not to antiquity: "What has come down to us from the Greeks is divine—but it is dead—whereas we—we are alive, and it is the living who are right!"[24]

In 1808 or 1809, Kniep had already recommended his friend Carl Russ for such work, and indeed Russ now took over the place on John's staff that Kniep's death had left vacant. Russ recorded his first meeting with his new employer as follows: "Summoned by the archduke to the imperial citadel. He smiled at my Asiatic reverences—asked me if I had read this or that author on our national history and was good enough to fetch me the relevant books from his reference library. 'Read diligently,' the good archduke said as he handed me a sheet of paper, 'here is an essay on nine compositions.'"[25]

Archduke John duly appointed Russ to his staff in 1810 and immediately took him along on a trip through the Alpine regions and on a visit to the health resort of Rohitsch Sauerbrunn. It seems that relations between the two were soon on an almost friendly basis, John noted in his diary during that visit that he and his painter had stayed up discussing Greeks, Romans, Germans, and universal laws until late at night. Russ's testimony exists also, "What a life [I led] at the archduke's side; his wide-ranging culture and his astonishing knowledge of history, geography, mineralogy, chemistry, botany, geognosy, and mining aroused my enthusiastic astonishment."[26]

On the other hand, Gebhard, the archduke's secretary, left a record of how much the enthusiasm of the

Carl Russ. *A Styrian Farmer and his Wife from Passail.* 1813. Watercolor. Private collection (E. J. 63).

painter Russ and his endless accounts of the Roman past got on the nerves of the entire retinue.[27] So it is easy to imagine what a shock Archduke John must have given his history painter when he completely changed the nature of the latter's employment, as indicated in the archduke's diary entry for June 24, 1810: "My painter [i.e. Russ], since he is to sketch the regional costumes...." Painting the everyday dress of provincial peasant farmers was a task that may well have struck this master of historical painting as highly unusual and indeed hardly worthy of his art. However, Russ performed it with painstaking care and enormous skill, producing the thirty-five watercolors of Styrian dress that are among the most valuable existing sources for the study and preservation of what are still the most handsome of Austria's regional costumes.[28]

Carl Russ left the archduke's service in 1818, after he was appointed curator of the Imperial Art Gallery in the Belvedere, a post he held until his death in 1843.

## The Defeat of Napoleon

The history of the world took a dramatic turn during the four days of the Battle of the Nations, fought near

Leipzig on October 16 to 19, 1813.[29] Numerous defeats —Abukir, Trafalgar, Aspern, the Tyrol, Moscow, the Berezina, Spain—had nibbled away at Napoleon's forces but left his power intact and his reputation as a general undiminished. This time, however, things were different.

Austria had spared no efforts to mobilize a mighty force, and both Field Marshal Prince Karl Philipp Schwarzenberg and his chief of staff, Count Joseph Radetzky, were leaders of above-average military ability. So was Field Marshal Gebhardt Blücher, commander of the Silesian army. Moreover, for the first time, the balance of forces was in the Allies' favor: Napoleon, with rather more than 200,000 men and 114 batteries, faced over 361,000 men and 165 batteries. The battle became a bloody massacre. Barely 50,000 of the more than 400,000 Frenchmen Napoleon had originally brought with him recrossed the Rhine, while the Allies left 53,834 dead on the field at Leipzig, 15,418 of them Austrians. The victory over Napoleon was complete, however.

What had made that victory possible was the political maneuvering that preceded the engagement. Count Clemens Metternich had at last managed to put together the alliance that had eluded the opponents of Napoleon until then; that had allowed the Frenchman to proceed on the "divide and rule" principle to defeat those opponents separately and individually. One is still moved by the words that Prince Metternich (a grateful emperor had conferred the title on him at Leipzig on October 20, 1813) uttered in 1855, toward the end of his life, on the occasion of the forty-second anniversary of the Battle of the Nations: "May God in his mercy so enlighten men that they embrace no causes that will lead to carnage."[30] Such was indeed the state of affairs that that great man's masterly policy had preserved for decades by then. But as Metternich spoke that sentence his time was almost at an end, and the march of events, moving rapidly toward fresh wars, had clearly acquired an unstoppable momentum.

Before leaving the battlefield at Leipzig, the three victorious monarchs resolved to lay the foundations of a permanent order in Europe at a congress of all the powers. Austria, having borne the brunt of the battle, was to act as host, and its capital offered the ideal venue. First, however, three important events took place: the Allies' entry into Paris (March 31, 1814), the signing of the Treaty of Paris (May 30, 1814), and the triumphal reception that Vienna accorded to Emperor Francis (June 16, 1814), for which an arch of triumph was erected near the Corinthian Gate (Kärtnertor), close to where the Opera House now stands, and an extensive program of festivities was planned. In the words of one contemporary:

Vienna has never seemed dearer nor more beautiful to me than on that day that made up for so much suffering and allowed so many misfortunes to be forgotten in that it celebrated the rebirth of Austria's political might and national greatness. The streets bedecked with lights and hung with row on row of sumptuous decorations; the pathways strewn with grass and flowers, a hundred thousand men and women milling about in smart new clothes, the sparkling uniforms of the civic guard.... [The emperor's] nature seemed unchanged and found expression in the same old way; the same affability, the same gravity holding in check a deeply felt joy, the same blend of dignity and modesty discernible in his features—an involuntary smile came to my lips as the poem being recited by the leader of the no less inevitable choir of "white-robed virgins" clearly so embarrassed the man in whose hand lay the fate of millions—the monarch who had but lately quit the scene of tremendous events—that, bowing politely, he kept waving his hand in a gesture like that of someone warding off dense clouds of incense.[31]

The city was caught up in an unprecedented mood of elation. This became even more intense when the Congress of Vienna opened in mid September, 1814 (although the subsequent massive price increases on all consumer goods soon tempered the delight of the local populace). Kings, rulers, potentates, and representatives of two hundred states and a variety of associations were invited and duly arrived with their courts, diplomatic corps, retinues, and servants.

The splendor (as well as the sham) almost defy the imagination, as do the attendant problems of accommodation, protocol, and supply. Hopes were high. An accountant in the service of the emperor—Matthias Perth by name—wrote thoughtfully in his diary on January 21, 1815:

From what afflictions have we had to be delivered, what deeds have had to be done, and what sacrifices made to the tranquility of this world before we have come together, after twenty-two years of woe, in freedom and peace before God. What upheavals have the years of terror wrought upon this earth; what streams of blood have they tapped and drawn from this source alone. Praise be, that terrible time is over and a new age dawns. Yet whether it will be a brighter and a happier one does not depend on this or that individual success. [It depends on] whether we are all become wiser for the experience and better for the suffering—that is the only question.[32]

On September 25, Czar Alexander I of Russia and King Frederick William III of Prussia met at the Vienna city boundary near the bridge to Tàbor, where they were received by the emperor and escorted into the city. The congress went into session. At first no such spectacular successes as had perhaps been expected were forthcoming. People seemed more interested in having a good time than in making progress on the diplomatic front: hence, when asked how the congress

Johann Nepomuk Hoechle. *The Carrousel in the Court [Spanish] Riding School.* 1814. Watercolor, pen and ink. Graphische Sammlung Albertina, Vienna (22.667).

was going (*"Ça marche, le congrès?"*), Prince de Ligne's famous punning reply: *"Le congrès ne marche pas, il danse, ce qui fait que rien ne transpire que ces messieurs"* (*marcher* = to make progress/to walk; *transpirer* = to transpire/to sweat).

In fact, of course, the Congress of Vienna was of enormous importance in three crucial respects.[33] It achieved an unprecedented reorganization of European political relations, the most striking success being a stable balance of power and several decades of peace. It adopted the Vienna Regulations, an international legal convention that for an unbroken period of more than a hundred years provided a civilized framework of rules for diplomatic relations. And it gave a tremendous boost to the city itself, enhancing its self-esteem, bringing Vienna a new awareness of itself, and preluding a distinctively Viennese *Lebensfreude* (delight in living). Above all, the last is what paved the way for the ensuing Biedermeier era.

The festivities associated with the congress, which ran from September, 1814 to June, 1815, were characterized by splendor and conducted in an atmosphere of freedom, elegance, and charm that can have had few parallels before or since. Ever more ingenious ways were found of providing the city's important guests and the Viennese themselves with the most exciting and imaginative entertainment. Theatrical and operatic performances, formal and fancy-dress balls, sleigh rides, firework displays, a recital on twenty pianos with each instrument played four-handed, and Beethoven's mammoth concert in the Redoutensaal (the ballroom of the Spanish Riding School) followed one another in a ceaseless round of revelry.

The high point in many people's estimation was the *Karussell* (carrousel) that took place in the Spanish Riding School on November 23, 1814. In the presence of all the leading figures of the congress and more than 2,500 invited guests, twenty-four gentlemen of Austria's high nobility, dressed as medieval knights, staged a magnificent display on horseback. A tournament, a quadrille, and a contredanse made up the program. Standard-bearers, heralds, and twenty-five equerries formed their escort. Each rider was assigned a favored lady, all of whom were dressed in the four colors of the quadrille: Hungarian in emerald-green costumes, Polish in crimson, old French in blue, and Austrian in black. All the costumes were made of velvet and trimmed with lace and precious stones beyond price. These couples afterwards led the 2,500 similarly costumed guests in to a gala banquet in the Redoutensaal.

Then suddenly the magic was all over. Like a bombshell the news reached Vienna on March 5, 1815, that

25   Johann Adam Klein. *Mounted Uhlans at Emperor Francis I's Entry into Vienna.* 1814

23   Johann Nepomuk Hoechle. *Emperor Francis Welcoming Czar Alexander and King Frederick William Outside Vienna.* 1814 (1833)
24   Johann Nepomuk Hoechle. *Emperor Francis I Entering Vienna Through the Carinthian Gate.* 1814

Napoleon had left the island of Elba and landed at Cannes on March 1, with 900 men; he was advancing rapidly northward from Lyons, and troops were flocking to his banner.

The Congress of Vienna reacted with surprising speed and unanimity, executing a formal ban that virtually amounted to a joint declaration of war on March 13. The delegates hurried to complete their proceedings; indeed, it is possible that Napoleon's Hundred Days provided the spur for a number of agreements that the congress would not otherwise have reached. Be that as it may, by June 9 it was possible to initial the Final Act and wind up the congress of Vienna with all the treaties completed. Six hundred thousand men drawn from all the congress powers now stood ready to launch a concentrated assault on France.

Napoleon, however, had no intention of waiting to be attacked. Staking everything on a single card, he marched into Belgium and routed Blücher's Prussian army at Ligny. Then he turned his attention to the British army under Wellington, unaware that Blücher and his deputy Gneisenau were still operational. As a result, the Prussians were able to come to Wellington's aid at Waterloo and set the seal on the final defeat of the *perturbateur du monde*, as the congress had officially described Napoleon.

Johann Nepomuk Hoechle. *The March over the Vosges Mountains.* 1815. Watercolor, pen. Graphische Sammlung Albertina, Vienna (22.694).

Meanwhile the huge Allied army was in full advance. Led by the emperor, Crown Prince Ferdinand, and Prince Metternich, it crossed the Vosges Mountains in July, encircled Paris, and forced the French to surrender. The long years of war were finally at an end, a whole epoch of history now lay in the past, and the era of glorious empire gave way to the less flamboyant but far happier Biedermeier era.

## JAKOB GAUERMANN BECOMES PAINTER BY APPOINTMENT TO ARCHDUKE JOHN

Meanwhile the developments in various directions taken by painting had continued—if somewhat sporadically due to the war and to people's fears regarding the future in general and the French occupation in particular. "What's to become of me, a poor painter?" Jakob Gauermann scribbled in his diary in May, 1809.[34] Soon afterward he received a visit from Napoleon's agent, Dominique-Vivant Denon, who had recently—on May 11—shipped off to Paris the 400 masterpieces in the Imperial Art Gallery. Denon was accompanied by Alexandre L. Delaborde (1774–1842), and the two men suggested to the terrified Gauermann that he should go to Paris himself. The painter confided in his diary: "So you're pleased that Director Denon and Mr. De la Borde called on you, praised your work, talked to you about going to Paris, bought some pictures and ordered more? That is entirely natural and laudable, for one does not live by bread alone, and unless a man love honor and fame he will never achieve anything very great or beautiful."[35]

After mature reflection Gauermann turned the offer down, feeling, as a family man, that too much uncertainty attached to it. Something did come of the meeting, though: Gauermann agreed to collaborate on a book by Delaborde to be entitled *Voyages pittoresques en Autriche* (which eventually appeared in 1821–2 with aquatints after Gauermann's originals.)

But—in 1811—at the first sign of a break in the war, Archduke John became anxious to resume the work begun by Johann Kniep. The Academy artist Ferdinand Runk recommended Gauermann and submitted some of his work for inspection. It found favor, and the artist was commissioned to embark on a series of *Styrian Prospects.* Gauermann also received immediate orders to accompany John on his next tour to revisit the Lake of Schwarzen in the valley of the Sölk, which had made an extraordinary impression on the archduke during a visit in September, 1810. Gauermann was now to record this sight as the first in the series. John's application to the appropriate department for the issue of police passes (a copy of which is in the dossier in the Akademie der bildenden Künst, Metternich Archives) provides the first clear account of the archduke's objective:

I am sending you my clerk Binner to ask you to make out police passes for the painters Russ, Gauermann, and Viethinghof, and the mineralogist Mohs. They are directed to tour Styria and Carinthia, collecting fresh materials for the regional description on which I am currently engaged. I have already written to Count Bissingen to ask him to issue the necessary orders to the relevant administrative departments in order that these men shall not lack the often essential backing of the authorities. I have given them a request to the same effect, drawn up by myself, but the police pass is the most important thing and the surest warrant of the authenticity of their mission. I beg you, therefore, to be so good as to issue the same, provided that no other obstacles obtain of which I may be unaware.

With the further request that you rest assured of my especial esteem, I remain yours most sincerely,
John—Vienna, June 1, 1811.

Gauermann delivered the requested view of the Lake of Schwarzen at the end of August, 1811, and from then on he produced a steady stream of such large-format watercolors. Each year he made an extended trip through Styria to record views of the province using his distinctive technique. Gauermann began with a delicately stippled contour drawing in pen, done *in situ*, to which he added detailed notes on the colors. The actual watercolor was neatly painted back in his studio. This was the tried and tested method, the one Gauermann had been taught, and a perceptibly stiff, overworked effect was the inevitable result. But Gauermann's love of nature was deep and genuine, as witness Baron Joseph von Hormayr: Gauermann, he wrote in 1821, toured with the archduke "in order to make a thorough study of every aspect of nature in those mountains and of their inhabitants, with his deep capacity for feeling, his sense of beauty, and his versatile intelligence."[36] The *Styrian Prospects* series was finally completed in 1818. The sixty-two large watercolor paintings still form the nucleus of the landscape section of the Archduke John Collection.

When Carl Russ resigned as painter by appointment, also in 1818, the archduke gave the position to Jakob Gauermann. With a salary of 200 gulden a month, it represented an excellent and guaranteed employment, yet Gauermann's output now began to decline rapidly. He kept fairly busy at first, working on a number of projects including the decorations of the Brandhof, the country house that Archduke John acquired in that same year. The first phase of restoration included stained-glass windows with portrayals of rustic life. The designs and their execution by Gottlieb S. Mohn were completed in 1822.

Gauermann's private circumstances, however, increasingly got in the way of his artistic work and prevented him from traveling. Through his marriage to a foster-daughter of the Viennese piano manufacturer Anton Walter he had come into a small farm in Miesenbach, near Gutenstein, a town about 50 kilometers southwest of Vienna. As the children grew up, their father's presence during the summer months became indispensable (the family continued to winter in Vienna). Consequently Gauermann saw less and less of the archduke, and relations between them gradually wore thin. This had a depressing effect on the artist who, after battling with endless self-reproaches, decided that his mission in life was to further the talent of his son Friedrich by teaching him everything he knew.

Eventually Jakob came to believe that it was through Friedrich's career that his own life had found its fulfill-

ment. Until his dying day, Jakob Gauermann continued to feel for "his" archduke all the affection of the early years, coupled with unforgettable memories of the mountain tours they had shared. This was despite the fact that for a time after 1816 he had felt deeply hurt and insultingly passed over in favor of the other, new painter by appointment Matthäus Loder, who was constantly in Archduke John's company and able to accompany him on his travels. Perhaps the falling-off in Jakob Gauermann's output did have something to do with these circumstances after all, for what an artist creates is governed by his whole being and essentially dependent on it.

However, during those very years in which he was particularly preoccupied by his personal problem of having to live in the country and feeling cut off from his patron and from the capital with all its artistic impressions, Jakob Gauermann clearly immersed himself once again in the freedom and purity of life in nature.

The result was a wealth of pictures portraying resting herdsmen, Alpine dairymaids, and the bold, free existence of the huntsman. When viewing his work, one can almost hear the lines from the didactic poem *Die Alpen* (1729; "The Alps") by the Swiss poet Albrecht von Haller:

> Seek, then, you mortals, to improve your state,
> Use what art has devised and nature bestowed upon you.
> ...
> Nature's disciples, you still know golden days!
> Albeit no poet's domain of fabled splendor;
> For who records the outward show of feigned conceits
> When virtue prompts delight and poverty is blest?
> ...
> How blessed who, like you, with home-bred oxen
> Plows the now dead earth of his own fields,
> Who loves his state and never longs to better it;
> Bliss is too poor by far to add to his well-being.[37]

The fact that the poem was published in Vienna in 1817 makes it an even more likely source of inspiration for the artist.

However, a very much clearer source was Archduke John's own love of nature, as illustrated in one of his finest diary entries:

A feeling for nature is a rare commodity. Seclusion is such a splendid thing. One is restored to oneself. And then the contemplation of nature! What comfort, what illumination! How one is set free from all the mire of the world, how moved to serious work, inspired to great endeavors! There I feel capable of achieving and of producing much that the city had nipped in the bud....

What a contrast, when I look out of my window [in the city] and, gazing toward my mountains, think about my life, between my life here and amid those mountains. Here everything is subject to constraints and formalities that cannot be overthrown, that have

26   Jakob Gauermann. *Pastoral Scene.* 1817

27   Jakob Gauermann. *Pürgg at the Foot of the Grimming.* 1816

to be; but that to one who has seen nature and lived in it—one who knows it—become increasingly intolerable. Nothing but noise, vain activity, amusement, empty striving, enjoyment, heartlessness, self-indulgence, envy, and low trickery. The good is forgotten, stifled in the mire. A hollow, wretched existence in this so-called wide world, no fresh air; nothing of all that makes nature so lovely. Everything [is] artificial; everything small, so many things dead! How far removed from my mountains, where the creator has inscribed the simplest laws with simple lineaments, laws of which everyone becomes aware when his heart returns to simplicity....

The Alps towering in great majesty, the splendor of our evergreen forests. The air is free; everything in it is free; we ourselves are free. This quietness and calm partakes of greatness. I walk over mountain and valley, and I think and plan. A calm lies over these regions that must appeal to all who have any feeling for the grandeur of nature. Here all thought of the wide world, all care disappears. A man breathes freely and believes himself free. Closer to his Creator, he is caught up in contemplation of nature on a grand scale and filled with a divine emotion. I sat down on a grassy slope above my hut, for it was a fine evening, and watched the return of the animals, each detachment with its bells. The sound of those bells, the lowing, and the different sound of the sheep bells all combined to form a marvelous whole.[38]

Johann Adam Klein. *The Artists Ernst Welker and Johann Christoph Erhard "in the Pulpit" in the Park at Aigen, near Salzburg.* 1818. Watercolor, pen and brush in brown, with traces of pencil. Stadtgeschichtliche Museen, Nuremberg (Norica 37).

## THE GERMANS DISCOVER SALZBURG

Under the Napoleonic empire there had been powerful political reasons for the influx of German artists into Austria. Now a quite different element emerged.

In the case of the painters Ferdinand and Friedrich Olivier, two brothers, it was undoubtedly their clear commitment to German Romanticism as an intellectual movement that had brought them from Dessau to Vienna in 1811, when Vienna was the last focus of everyone's hopes of eventually overthrowing French domination. A further factor had been the presence in Vienna of Friedrich Schlegel, the acknowledged leader of the Romantic school. Shrewdly exploiting Schlegel's reputation, Metternich had taken him into the service of the Austrian government in the hope that he would contribute toward mobilizing opposition to the French among intellectuals. Indeed, when Schlegel began his course of lectures on the philosophy of history in Vienna on February 27, 1812, he drew a fascinated and enthusiastic audience of the highest caliber. At one lecture no fewer than twenty-nine princes were present in the hall, and the circle of Schlegel's admirers included the German author Joseph von Eichendorff and the Austrian politician Theodor Körner.

Vienna had been the center of the Romantic movement then, but that had been in wartime. The advent of peace opened up entirely new prospects more suited to realism. This became immediately apparent in artistic terms as well and even affected the work of many German Romantics. Just as the discerning artist Johann August Heinrich had become engrossed in the tissue of forces that constitute the beauty of a landscape, a whole generation now discovered the simple, authentic beauty of the Austrian mountains. Bruno Grimschitz, celebrating Heinrich's landscapes, spoke of the uniqueness of "this new self-surrender, without preconceptions, to the scene as it appeared," a surrender that was "grounded in and sanctified by an idealized emotion deepened by religious awe."[39]

The Congress of Vienna had passed resolutions regarding Salzburg that, as it happened, offered artists in particular fresh opportunities of gaining access to the beauties of nature. (I say "as it happened" because this eventuality can hardly have been uppermost in the minds of men like Talleyrand, Castlereagh, Metternich, Wellington, and Gentz.) The romantics flocked to Salzburg to work in this loveliest of cities and its surroundings.

Johann Adam Klein from Nuremberg had not shown any conspicuously Romantic leanings during his first stay in Vienna from 1811; in fact, his work had been characterized by a fresh, true-to-life realism. But on his second visit to Austria, when together with his painter friends from Germany Johann Christoph Erhard, Ernst Welker, and the brothers Friedrich Philipp and Heinrich

28  Jakob Gauermann. *Archduke John Climbing the Hochwildstelle.* 1819

Johann August Heinrich. *Romantic Wooded Landscape.* c. 1812. Pen and wash, Chinese white on blue paper. Graphische Sammlung Albertina, Vienna (24.293).

be more "cosmopolitan" (*weltbürgerlich*; nowadays we would say humane) than science and art? "The pure affinity of the mind," Metternich continued in his speech, "elevated above every material circumstance, reaches out over time and space."[43] The study of the arts, the feeling for everything great and beautiful, represented he felt the nation's true wealth and an inseparable part of its renown. He also felt that furthering the Academy would enable Austria to offer her sons and grandsons "the things we still seek beneath foreign skies."[44] Here, in embryo, was the conflict that was to lead to so many problems in the future: the conflict between the cosmopolitanism of the Enlightenment and the nationalist aspirations of the nineteenth century, which sought to drive out everything foreign.

Enthusiasm for and involvement in the arts were surprisingly widespread around this time. In 1821 F.H. Böckh's handbook gave the names and addresses of no fewer than 715 artists living in Vienna[45]—most of them, of course, destined for oblivion.

Reinhold, he toured Salzburg and the Salzkammergut in the summer of 1818,[40] Klein was filled with a most delicate sensitivity to the beauty of the mountains.

Important though this was, it was in fact less crucial than the final victory over the idea of "composing" nature. (Grimschitz rightly speaks of Klein as ushering in this next phase of development.[41]) From now on artists were driven by purely artistic concern to discover the world as it really was and not as they, or anyone else, thought it should be.

## METTERNICH AS CURATOR OF THE ACADEMY

The attraction of the Vienna Academy remained undiminished, especially after Metternich accepted the post of curator on August 30, 1810 and launched a major revival of the institution amid some important changes of personnel. Schmuzer died in 1811, followed shortly afterward by Lorenz Janscha in 1812, by Sonnenfels (as secretary, the intellectual driving force of Josephinism), Hohenberg, and Nobile. Zauner retired in 1815, and Füger's death in 1818 drew a line under an era that was now finally at an end.

Undeterred by his enormous political and governmental responsibilities, Metternich devoted himself to the Academy with surprising vigor and headed it for thirty-seven years. He immediately introduced new statutes, prompting Joseph von Hormayr to say that "the true rebirth of the arts among us dates from the year 1812, when on February 12, a holy day for all Austrians,"[42] the new measures were brought in: teaching plans, better prizes, scholarships, new members, and much else besides. The chancellor took the opportunity to stress the importance of promoting the Academy in future, since an art college contributed to a civilized society like nothing else. Metternich asked what could

## JAKOB ALT DECIDES TO STAY IN VIENNA

The magnet of the Academy had attracted to Vienna in 1810, Jakob Alt, a twenty-year-old art student from Frankfort. Later, it was said that he had actually been on the way to Italy to continue his studies there. Be that as it may, Alt decided to look for accommodation in Vienna[46] and found it in Vienna's "artists' quarter" in the Alser district, with the young widow of a goldsmith and engraver named Franz Rudolph, who had died after little more than a year of marriage.

The young woman, Maria Anna *née* Schaller, from Gresten in Lower Austria, was also twenty. As a widow she found herself in difficult circumstances, and she sought to ward off the worst poverty by letting rooms. Love blossomed swiftly between the—as tradition has it—extremely pretty landlady and the German art-student who was her lodger; the couple were married on November 12, 1811. It was to be an exceptionally happy marriage. In 1871, still hale and hearty, Jakob Alt and his wife celebrated their diamond wedding anniversary, and when they died it was within weeks of each other. The Alts had a total of seven children, the first of whom—a boy—was born on August 28, 1812. He was named Rudolf Franz.

Marriage and the responsibility of a family brought a fundamental change in Jakob's circumstances. There was no question of his continuing his studies, especially since the dramatic inflation of 1811 had cost the young couple all their savings—as it had for so many of their contemporaries. Jakob Alt had to start earning a living. He tried to apply all the knowledge of traditional brush technique and gouache style acquired from his Frankfort teacher Johann Baptist Beer to Viennese *vedute* along the lines of the series Schütz and Ziegler had published with Artaria. The initial results were modest and brought him little success. Refusing to accept

Jakob Alt. *Idealized Landscape.* 1817. Gouache over pencil. Graphische Sammlung Albertina, Vienna (4.941).

defeat, Alt continued his experiments to find fresh solutions and new commissions. About 1816 he hit upon some attractive solutions of his own. In 1817 Alt took up "ideal" landscape once again, though with a somewhat antiquated use of gouache and an altogether obsolete mood of bucolic idyll. Then he made a fresh departure (it was a year of general upheaval): he went walking in the Salzkammergut and painted a number of views of its most beautiful lakes. His use of whitish opaque paints (the method he had learned in Frankfort) remained virtually unchanged. His staffage was still stiff; he continued to build up his space in neatly horizontal compartments, but a start had been made. With his large watercolor *The Spinner at the Cross*, with its view of Vienna,[47] Jakob Alt created his first masterpiece.

There could be no more striking example of the revolutionary atmosphere of the time than this contrast within the one year, 1817. Just as Alt was trying hard to imitate the idealized models of Claude Lorraine, with mythological staffage, by using classical flute-playing herdsmen set amid an imaginary Roman countryside as a sort of self-affirmatory boost to his ego—to show that an artist could paint even without an Academy training —the complete antithesis suddenly took possession of his brush. The reality of the Austrian landscape, peopled with peasant farmers in their provincial costume (all still highly idealized), comes over almost as a protest. Possibly this was a result of Alt's search for something new, but it is also possible that he could not avoid accepting the new demand as regards subject matter.

Once again Jakob Alt had taken a step in the direction of the new art of watercolor; however, something else

secured his livelihood. In that same year Alt began to collaborate closely with Adolf Kunicke (who happened to be a neighbor of his in the Alser district) on works for the Lithographic Institute, an up-and-coming publishing house founded by Aloys Senefelder. The outcome of their collaboration was *The Danube from its Source to the Black Sea*, a series of 264 lithographs that appeared between 1818 and 1826 and proved to be the publisher's greatest success.[48] Jakob Alt did watercolor sketches from nature for this series—which loosened up his style enormously—and executed the sketches on stone. Young Rudolf Alt accompanied his father for drawing practice and before long was actually assisting with the project, principally by hand-coloring the endless prints with watercolors. For Rudolf the incalculably valuable result of all this labor was a subsequent skill with the brush that often bordered on the miraculous.

Both directly and indirectly, therefore, Jakob Alt made a decisive contribution to Austrian art, for "the Austrian [i.e. the Styrian] approach resides in the organic transformation of the problem of landscape,"[49] and the work of Jakob Alt implies the switch to a purely painterly world. In fact very few additional impulses were required to accomplish the change to realism in the 1820s. They were to be found, on the one hand, in the radiant paintings of Joseph Rebell (who was recalled to Vienna from Rome in 1819), and on the other hand in the paintings Thomas Ender created in Brazil, which were available to all artists in the Imperial Court Library in Vienna from 1820.

THOMAS ENDER'S JOURNEY TO BRAZIL

The Enders, too, were among those emigrants drawn to Josephine Vienna from abroad. Johann Ender

29   Jakob Alt. *View of the Lake of Traun.* 1817
30   Thomas Ender. *View of Oberdöbling, near Vienna.* 1814

31   Thomas Ender. *View from the Corcovado, near Rio de Janeiro.* 1817–18
32   Thomas Ender. *The Austrian Chamberlains on Their Way to São Paolo.* 1818

(1752–1816) had come from Frankenstein in Silesia (now Zabkowice, Poland), leaving his job there as a cutler in the family workshop in search of a higher standard of living. (Incidentally, Ender's ancestors had left the Valais region of Switzerland not long before that and immigrated, by way of Vorarlberg, the westernmost province of Austria, to Silesia, where they had improved their lot very substantially.)

Vienna failed to live up to Johann's expectations, however. Working as a junk dealer, he never managed to rise above the direst poverty. He had married very young (at the age of twenty-four), but his wife died, leaving him with children. Therefore, he married again (in 1790), and on November 3, 1793, twin sons were born: one was named Johann after his father, and the other Thomas after his godfather.

The second marriage was a troubled one, and the twin brothers grew up in grim domestic circumstances. Both showed a talent for art, much to their father's displeasure, though in the end he did nothing to prevent them from entering the Academy together on April 23, 1806—at the age of twelve. There they became assiduous students in the historical-rudiments class.

For the past thirty years this class had been headed by the religious Neoclassicist Hubert Maurer (1738–1818), who became one of the principal targets of the critical displeasure of the *Lukasbrüder*, a group of Romantic students led by Johann Friedrich Overbeck, one of the founders of the Nazarener group of artists.

Although the young Ender twins took no part in the controversy, it was soon evident that there was to be a parting of the ways for them too. This occurred in 1810, when Thomas transferred to Lorenz Janscha's landscape class to train as a landscape painter and Johann continued under Maurer (and subsequently under Franz Caucic) to train as a history painter. Later Johann actually specialized in portrait painting, in which he gained a reputation that at times completely overshadowed that of his brother.

In 1812, thanks to Metternich's new ideas, more money became available for students who wanted to go on walking tours in order to work from nature. This was to be an important step toward the new fashion for realism.

For Thomas Ender this marked a turning-point in his life. He quickly completed his first studies in the immediate environs of Vienna, and they were an instant success. In 1810 he already carried off the first prize for "landscape drawing," while his fellow student Ferdinand Georg Waldmüller won the other prize for "figure drawing." "This greatly encouraged me to work at my landscape drawing," Thomas Ender admitted later. "I now began to study nature in the environs of Vienna, particularly the Prater. I spent all day every day in the open air, returning to the city only in the evening."[50]

The Ender brothers's first study trip took place in the same year. It took them to the Schneeberg region to the southwest of the capital, a region that epitomized the romantically wild mountain landscape in its most extreme form for a whole generation of artists from Molitor to Loder and from Gauermann to Janscha. Thomas's twin brother Johann recorded his impressions of the trip in his diary: "We had to cross a number of mountains at the start in order to reach Muckendorf, where the impressive waterfall is to be found. We had the pleasure of seeing this by the most magnificent moonlight, which effectively banished the memory of all the exertions that had gone before."[51]

Thomas Ender's teacher Lorenz Janscha died on April 1, 1812. Once again the Academy found itself with a staffing problem, as it had following Brand's death in 1795. The decision was made to replace Janscha with Josef Mössmer, who had long functioned as Janscha's deputy and had had considerable responsibility for the students' training. As an artist, however, Mössmer was of little importance—a lifelong imitator, neither rejecting nor living up to the example of Molitor. Understandably, therefore, his appointment was only provisional at first.

This was all most unsatisfactory as far as the students' education was concerned, and one result was that Thomas Ender began increasingly to seek his own way, studying in the magnificent art collections that Vienna had to offer, notably the Imperial Art Gallery, and also in the Imperial Court Library. The library's famous keeper Adam von Bartsch gave Ender some useful instruction.

In oil painting Ender's models were clearly the Dutch realists, who fascinated him. But nothing is known of how or through whom he gained the kind of experience with watercolor that lies behind his *View of Oberdöbling, near Vienna*, for example, painted in 1814. One thing alone is clear: no one in Austria at that time possessed a comparable degree of mastery in terms of transparency, treatment of light, and atmosphere. The date on the painting explodes all the theories to the effect that it was encounters in Gibraltar, Brazil, or Italy that schooled Thomas Ender in the perfection of contemporary English watercolor painting, for no such encounters took place until years later.

One fact was probably of fundamental importance, namely that Ender had removed himself from all the constraints and copying of the Academy environment and had made himself largely independent. It can safely be assumed that Adam von Bartsch had plenty of opportunity and sufficient knowledge to advise Ender and to gain admittance for him to—for example—the collections of Duke Albert of Saxe-Teschen (i.e. the Albertina) or of the prince of Liechtenstein. Thomas Ender was the first to make this break, an all-important step in the development of watercolor painting. That is why Rudolf Alt said later that, for him and for the "youth" of his day, Ender had been the *non plus ultra*.[52]

Around 1815 Thomas Ender was doing a lot of work for Viennese publishers, hand-coloring sets of engravings. Once again a clear connection can be established between this kind of early drudgery and a later, masterly command of the watercolor brush. In that year

Ender's name was put forward for the top scholarship of 150 gulden, in special recognition of his talent. That scholarship enabled him to travel farther afield—to Salzburg, for instance, which had recently become rather more accessible: "In 1816 I spent five months drawing from nature in the Salzburg mountains, venturing as far as the Tyrolese frontier—a land rich in picturesque images that so stimulated me with its magnificent mountain scenery that I believe that it was here I first learned to see nature."[53]

Ender was so pleased and so encouraged with his successes that, in 1817, he even competed for the Academy's big landscape-painting prize—and he won it. His painting was duly placed on exhibit and attracted universal attention, which in turn moved Prince Metternich to extend his personal protection to this promising young artist and to seek to use his influence on Ender's behalf. In a matter of weeks the prince received his first opportunity to do so.

The artist himself described the events that followed in the fragment of autobiography he wrote in later years: "Also in that year [1817] the natural history expedition was dispatched to Brazil on the occasion of the marriage of the Austrian Princess Leopoldine to D[om] Pedro. A painter was to be taken along. I have always felt a great urge to travel, and such a journey could not but strike me as a most delightful prospect. I applied and was really most fortunate in that, Prince Metternich having liked my recent Salzburg sketches so much, I was given the post of painter to the expedition primarily as a result of his patronage."[54]

Politically, Brazil was of enormous interest to the Austrian chancellor in several respects. A cardinal objective in his eyes was supporting the monarchical principle as such. Secondly, establishing relations with Brazil might bring Austria many advantages, not least in the economic sphere. And thirdly, creating a counterweight to British power accorded with one of the permanent goals of Austrian policy.

A former Portuguese colony, Brazil had been made a kingdom in it own right in 1815. Through Crown Prince Dom Pedro it would become linked again with its former mother country in a personal union. Metternich saw the marriage of a daughter of Emperor Francis I to Dom Pedro as a political move of potentially global importance. Francis withheld his approval for a long time—less as a statesman than as a father. (Indeed, Leopoldine was destined to become one of history's tragic figures. She endeavored obediently and conscientiously to fulfill her role, behaving in exemplary fashion and with great dignity, while suffering shame and scorn at the hands of a completely inhuman husband who eventually drove her to her death.)

Toward the end of March, 1817, four ships stood ready to make the Atlantic crossing. In Livorno two Portuguese battle ships waited to convey Leopoldine herself, who had been married *per procurationem* in Vienna's church of the Augustinians on March 13, 1817, and whom Prince Metternich now accompanied in person, together with her immediate retinue, on the overland journey to the port of embarkation. In Trieste two Austrian frigates, *Austria* and *Augusta*, prepared to transport the members of the expedition and their mass of equipment to Rio de Janeiro.

Brazil was a vast and almost unexplored country; one of the most valuable aspects of the entire undertaking was thought to be that a scientific expedition comprising leading experts in zoology, botany, geology, and mineralogy was to accompany the archduchess. The expedition was considered a major contribution to civilization on Austria's part—not the least in that an artist was attached to it to make a record of Brazil's flora and fauna as well as of the country's landscape, people, and way of life. In fact, Ender's work constitutes a historical document of quite unique importance as far as Brazil is concerned.

This is not the place for a detailed account of the events and findings of the expedition itself,[55] though I must pay admiring tribute to the selfless dedication with which Johann Natterer and Johann Emanuel Pohl completed their colossal research program. This was underlined by the vast body of material collected, brought back to Vienna, and assembled in a special Brazilian Cabinet in the Imperial Court Library, as well as by the impressive publication of the expedition's results.

Regrettably, the senseless vandalism unleashed by the Revolution of 1848 was responsible for a fire that started in Joseph's Platz and reduced the entire Brazilian Collection to ashes; it might have destroyed the whole Imperial Court Library, together with such adjacent buildings as the palace of Duke Albert (home of the Albertina Collection). By great good fortune these were spared. So—almost by accident—were the volumes containing Thomas Ender's watercolor paintings. (Waldmüller had insisted on showing these matchless examples of the watercolorist's art to his students at the Academy, and thus they were preserved for posterity.[56])

On March 28, 1817, Thomas Ender set out from Vienna to join the other members of the expedition aboard the *Austria*. The voyage was marked by a series of dramatic incidents. Just out of Trieste, heavy storms destroyed the ship's superstructure and sails and obliged it to limp into Pula. Further repairs necessitated weeks of delays in Malta, Gibraltar, and on the island of Madeira; during none of this time was Ender idle.

At sea he painted life abroad the *Austria*, the ship's accommodation, the scientists reading or suffering from heat exhaustion, the sailors making music or catching fish, and over and over again the maze of the rigging against the snow-white sails and the blue southern sky.

Possibly in Gibraltar, something remarkable happened for the first time: Ender discovered a fresh dimension of color and light and a new fluency of style that made use of relaxed, transparent brushstrokes such as had never been seen before in Austrian watercolors. What sparked this change? Perhaps the availability of English Whatman papers, or new colors of the kind

English watercolorists had long been using, or even an encounter with artists working in accordance with the principles of the English Watercolour Society? No answers have been found. However, what came of this new dimension later, after Ender's return to Vienna, was of crucial importance. To the new generation of artists, Thomas Ender and his watercolors came to represent an ideal model.

After ninety-two days at sea, the Austrians reached Rio de Janeiro on July 14, 1817. The Portuguese ships bringing Archduchess Leopoldine had not yet arrived, so at first the expedition was delayed in Rio with nothing to do.

Ender, however, set to work immediately, sketching and painting indefatigably in Rio itself and in the vicinity. He ventured farther afield, climbed the Corcovado, and depicted the harbor, the life of the natives, the business premises and the elegant haciendas of the wealthy merchants.

The country's new queen finally arrived and was received with due pomp and ceremony. The expedition then set out to penetrate deep into the interior, and its appalling hardships began.

Ender painted and painted, producing a continuous pictorial record of a kind that is quite unique. He had already painted 130 watercolors between Trieste and Rio; he painted a further 652 on the actual expedition —that is to say, between July, 1817 and May, 1818. To these another 71 watercolors and 244 sketches must be added, which he gave to Prince Metternich on his return (in 1951 they were sold by private owners and returned to Brazil). But if the quantity is amazing, the quality is even more so. Ender was working very freely, without hesitation or second thoughts. The watercolors are not uniformly successful: haste, fatigue, and the heat all left their mark. But many of them have to be classed among the very finest achievements in watercolor painting.

In the end, the enormous strain of jungle and mountain travel, aggravated by poor camping conditions, proved too much for Ender's health. Whereas the other members of the expedition were able to rest at the end of each long journey on foot or on horseback, the painter's work began at that point. It was a life of constant overexertion: "I soon felt the ill effects," Ender was forced to admit. "A state of such enervation, physical and moral, took hold of me that I simply lay there exhausted and could neither stand nor walk. A trip to the foot of the Bird Mountains, where I bathed in the cold river morning and evening, restored my strength a little."[57] The Prussian Consul-general von Langsdorf having offered to put him up in his house in Mandioca, Ender remained behind to recuperate, but eventually he had to return to Rio. Then he accompanied the gentlemen of the court—the "Austrian chamberlains"—on their ride to São Paolo. There Ender's strength completely failed him in the intolerable climate, and he was obliged to seize the first opportunity of returning home. The *Austria* was about to ship home the first consignment of the expedition's findings—rock samples, stuffed animals, plants of all kinds, and a mass of detailed reports—and Ender sailed on her on June 1, 1818. This time the voyage went according to plan, and sixty-five days later the ship tied up in the harbor at Genoa.

The extent of Thomas Ender's work exceeded all expectations, and Metternich rewarded him with a scholarship that enabled him to spend several years (until 1823) living and studying in Italy—and even to take his twin brother Johann with him.

Before leaving Vienna Thomas made an agreement with the art dealer Domenico Artaria that he would produce views of Italy for him. A revealing letter from the artist throws some light on his artistic objectives at this time.[58] Thomas wrote to Artaria on December 19, 1820, saying that the prospect of Florence he had ordered was ready at last. Ender also recalled how, when he had visited Artaria in his shop in Vienna, the dealer had been in the habit of saying so many beautiful things about Italy and about its bright, clear skies, and how he had quite rightly reproached Ender with making all his landscapes so gloomy. "Then I had never seen a clear sky; now my only ambition is to capture it in paint. As long as I remain in Italy, it is my firm resolve to do everything possible to study the graduation of colors."[59]

Thomas's brother Johann, meanwhile, was enjoying enormous success, painting portraits in Rome. He even applied for an extension of his scholarship; this was granted, and he stayed for another two years.

Thomas returned home in 1823, and not long afterward Joseph von Hormayr reported in his *Archive*: "[Ender's] admirable industry has brought back... a rich yield of 500 drawings together with 40 small and 6 large, half-finished paintings from the environs of the eternal Rome."[60]

It is clear that, while in Rome, Thomas Ender met Joseph Rebell. This is substantiated by the changes in Ender's style and by noticeable influences in the works he brought back with him.

What makes this influence even more plausible is the fact that Ender had accompanied the emperor and Prince Metternich on their trip to Rome in 1819. The party had spent more than three weeks in the city (from March 31 to April 24), during which a remarkable event had occurred: visiting an art exhibition in the Palazzo Cafarelli, Emperor Francis had been so struck by Rebell's work that he had appointed him Füger's successor on the spot (Füger having died in 1818), and summoned him back to Vienna.

Thomas Ender's experience and Joseph Rebell's skill, taken together, had wrought a great change in Viennese watercolor painting.

# III  IDEAL ART AND REALISM

## A CONFLICT OF GOALS

At this point I must pause, for art is about to take the step that gives meaning and substance to all that follows, and that makes Austria's contribution so original.

The real conflict in art had become the one between Ideal art and Realism. The philosophy that derives its values from the ideal is based on Plato's theory of Ideas. That is to say, it stems from the view that over and above each real thing there exists an Idea of that thing—an Ideal form, an archetype of all temporal reality, a thing above things, as it were, perfect and of universal validity.

From the Christian point of view, the Ideal is wholly anchored in the Creator Who is both *summum bonum* (which corresponds to Plato's supreme Idea, the Idea of Good) and, at the same time, *summum pulchrum*. However, the concretization of an Idea—namely the object in the visible, tangible world—exhibits all the shortcomings of the earthly world along with its transience. Consequently, the theory of Ideas and Ideal art have always leaned toward renunciation and transcendency and offered artistic spiritualization as the basis from which these artists hoped to rise above earthly limitations, to become the quintessence of perfection through the creation of art.

The Aristotelian counterpole to Plato's theory, which has run right through the history of civilization as a perpetual alternative, looked at things very differently. In Christian terms, this was taken to mean that, in God's creation, mankind had been given the task of mastering the real world; therefore, mankind was closest to God, and resembled Him most, when doing so. Thus man's task was to explore and grasp created reality in order to be able to perceive the general on the basis of the particular and the individual— to perceive the supramundane, the spiritual, and ultimately, the divine.

Hitherto both views of the world had been sustained to a greater or lesser extent by the fear of God. The difference had been merely one of method—deductive or inductive. Now, however, an entirely different, third view entered the picture. This change is commonly attributed to the shattering blow delivered to this kind of trust in God by the Lisbon earthquake of 1755. Such wholesale destruction and loss of life prompted the

Johann Nepomuk Passini. *Self Portrait of the Artist at Work.* 1819. Etching. Graphische Sammlung Albertina (Ö.K. XIX, Passini [the elder], fol. 1, no. 1).

question—and it was not a rhetorical one—of whether God existed at all in His omnipotence as *summum.* Either He had been unwilling to prevent the catastrophe, in which case He was not all-benevolent; or He had been unable to prevent it, in which case He was not all-powerful; or He had failed to foresee it, in which case He was not all-knowing. From then on, there was an atheistic ingredient in Enlightenment thinking that should not be ignored. In principle it fell short of being compelling, for the cool reason that drove men to investigate, measure, and improve readily cohabited with a concept of God and with the ethos of Christianity.

Indeed, as the Congress of Vienna ushered in the Biedermeier era, the aspect of Enlightenment thinking that proved chimeric was the idea that the world was a mechanism that could be understood in rational terms. Victory over a foreign power had also been a victory for faith, piety, and zeal. Particularly among Austrians it was generally recognized that the emotions bring people closer to the truth; give them love, joy, and spiritual absorption, and generally constitute man's humanity. After 1815, as the idea gained ground that the world stood on the threshold of a timeless era of peace, men turned increasingly to a view of life based on Realism. People saw life itself as a reality that must be brought into harmony with the Ideal. This reinforced their rejection of atheism, of rationalism, and in particular of the French philosopher Baron Paul d'Holbach's *homme machine* as belonging to the alien domination which they had finally overthrown.

How close to each other the contradictions lay here, and how narrow the ridge along which progress must pick its way emerge with remarkable clarity from two remarks made by Archduke John. They occur in a letter he wrote to Johann von Kalchberg, concerning the recently founded Joanneum Museum in Graz: "A Professor of Higher Aesthetics? I could wish we knew our lower aesthetics thoroughly first before we start flying so high; I have a terrible fear of the spirit of the Schlegelians—etc.... A Professor of Manufacturing to give lectures at the Museum... that is a far greater necessity for our country than the others."[1] Here was genuinely physiocratic thinking, and it was progressive and realistic.

In the diary he kept of his journey to England, Archduke John described a visit to James Watt in Birmingham on January 5, 1816. Watt had talked about the incalculable changes that his steam engine would bring in the future, and the archduke noted:

> Birmingham had been the storm center for all local popular uprisings, lootings, and disturbances because it contained the largest number of the sort of people who have no home and no country of their own, whose daily wage is all they possess, and to whom every means of increasing it must be welcome. Could anyone continue to cultivate the iniquitous hope that Austria, in order to obtain a larger number of such people,... should turn her richly compounded multination state into a manufacturing state and make of it an artificial machine based solely on money, the most ephemeral thing under the sun....[2]

This was a remarkable comment amid all the euphoria of the Industrial Revolution. The conflict between Ideal art and Realism had broken out in earnest.

## INNER HARMONY

Seen in this light, it was only logical that the Viennese painting that grew up in this period should have devoted itself wholly to the world of the visible. It was even more logical that the art of watercolor, spontaneously functioning as an avant-garde, should have been the kind of painting most immediately involved.

What was specifically Austrian about the process was the balance achieved between many, very different demands. The critic Bruno Grimschitz went to great pains to elucidate this peculiarly Austrian quality. His book on nineteenth-century Austrian drawing, published in 1927, took as its starting point the fact that "the painting of Old Vienna was devoted with the most lively originality to the visible, that is to say, to the worldview of the new bourgeois individual."[3] This corresponded to "the realistic sensuality fundamental to the Austrian character";[4] as well as according with the highly topical realism of a generation embarked upon the actual conquest of the world. This art became quintessentially Austrian precisely because it suited the Austrian character and sprang from the Austrian situation. For that very reason, of course, it remained of primarily local interest, though its perfect truthfulness came to represent a valuable enrichment of art in general. According to Grimschitz, "when the immediate world of appearances became the perfect subject matter of artistic endeavor, when realistic energies released the pictorial force of color, the sensual power of Austrian talent shaped the image of existence in abundant fullness and with radiant liveliness."[5] Grimschitz was the first critic to appreciate properly this aspect of Austrian art.

The conflict between the two demands of the early Biedermeier years—to do justice to reality without abandoning the ideal—generated a "realistic energy" that was, in fact, also idealistic,[6] namely the awareness that it took reason to develop the emotions, that the acceptance of existing hierarchies created the requisite orderly context for human existence, and that, quite simply, "life" need not be sacrificed for something other than itself—that life was a good in its own right.

The "Austrian" ingredient in all this was an attempt to turn the level-headed prudence of the Josephine ethos into the Biedermeier delight in harmony. By the time it became clear that this tendency was moving too fast and too far in the direction of resignation and dull routine, Austrian art was already well on the way to a fresh change.

A body of supremely harmonious works of art has come down to us from this era, timeless, unsurpassable works of painting, literature, and music; works that were more than simple products of the mind—they were true acts of creation, full of joy, beauty, and life.

## WIGAND'S PRECISION PAINTING

A comment about the painter Balthasar Wigand in Constant von Wurzbach's *Biographisches Lexikon des Kaiserthums Österreich (Biographical Dictionary of the Austrian Empire*, 1888[7]) is altogether typical: "Lastly I find in my notes a historical painter named Balthasar

33   Balthasar Wigand. *Vienna Seen from Grinzing.* c. 1825

Balthasar Wigand. *View from a Window Overlooking the Freyung in Vienna.* c. 1825. Watercolor and gouache. Historisches Museum der Stadt Wien, Vienna (56.380).

Balthasar Wigand. *Napoleon Leading his Troops Past Schönbrunn Palace.* 1815. Watercolor and gouache. Private collection, England.

Wigand of whom I know no more than that he was born in '1771'[8] and died at Felixdorf on June 7, 1846. His works are not mentioned anywhere, and neither Nagler nor other authorities on Austrian artists… devote so much as a syllable to this painter."[9]

Whereas little more than four decades after his death, Wigand and his oeuvre had already fallen into total oblivion, in his lifetime that oeuvre had been seen as one of the glories of Biedermeier Vienna. Now it is once again counted among the most delightful products of the art of Old Vienna. Eight years after Wurzbach's *Lexikon* was published, Wigand was rediscovered at the Congress exhibition in Vienna (1896), and in no relevant book or exhibition since 1905 has he been overlooked. Yet, as Hans Bisanz rightly observed in 1967,[10] Wigand's art still deserves to be very much better known than it is.

Wigand, whose best work was done in the decade between 1820 and 1830, had identified his artistic objective very early. Almost before he had completed his Academy training—around 1793—Wigand began to concentrate on watercolor miniature painting. His subject matter, though largely consisting of views of Vienna like those engraved by Schütz and Ziegler, also included designs of his own. These tiny works—the largest are postcard-size—were usually painted in sets to adorn fine pieces of furniture or caskets made of the choicest materials. The delicate charm of these exquisite objects was very much in keeping with the taste of the time; they also appealed strongly to the era's fondness for commemorative gifts and family albums.

Wigand's life unfolded without dramatic incident. The son of a "coffee-boiler by the Carinthian Gate,"[11] he grew up in modest circumstances, studied hard, and developed his special talent for minutely detailed painting. After spending his days in almost unimaginable industry, Wigand died, old but still poor, under the roof of his son, an employee of the Vienna-Gloggnitz Railway Company.

In his lifetime Wigand enjoyed exceptional fame and esteem. His clientele tended to be limited to the wealthiest strata of society, for the select nature of the craft objects he decorated had its price. Possibly his most beautiful work, however, was free of any such association with a craft project. This was an album of watercolors put together around 1820 as a family book for a certain Princess Lubomirska; it contained twelve gouache views of Vienna.[12] (After having belonged to English collections for many years, it returned to Vienna in 1959.)

From the technical point of view, Wigand is an interesting example of the changing times in art. He began by executing his incredibly precise pictures in dense, opaque colors, establishing their general character in cool, blue-gray tones and painting the borders first in violet and then in gray or black. Then, between 1815 and 1820, Wigand switched to warm, mellow greens, showed a predilection for green mounts as well, and used progressively less Chinese white in his paintings.

The Congress of Vienna in 1814–15 was naturally a marvelous time for Wigand with its many foreign visitors, enormous assembled wealth, and huge demand for souvenirs. Moreover, the events of the congress itself —the festivities, processions, sleigh rides, and parades —coupled with the fact that Vienna was host to all the most important figures in the contemporary world, offered him an inexhaustible source of subject matter.

There is no doubt that Wigand was an isolated phenomenon, and the scarcely explicable fluctuations of quality in works that—rightly or wrongly—bear his name will keep scholars busy for a long time. What they will need to bear constantly in mind is that, for all his professionalism and virtuosity, Wigand's greatest strength lay in the naivety that continued to characterize his work. In fact, Wigand's finest masterpieces include works that are not stunning in their perfection. Wigand lovingly idealized the reality of Vienna in his Biedermeier precision painting as no one else has done, leaving an image of an age of magical sensibility.

## THE HEYDAY OF MUSIC

Living conditions in Vienna underwent a great change in the 1820s. The conservative political order—"reactionary" as opposed to the "action" of revolution and war—saw itself as a protective, calming, countervailing force. Its policy of "holding fast to the familiar"[13] had far-reaching consequences.

The intransigence of Metternich's right-hand man Friedrich Gentz, who saw the police state as the cornerstone of human well-being,[14] together with the implementation of the system of surveillance set up by Count Joseph von Sedlnitzky, which produced an early form of the police state, were to blame for gradually freezing out social life in public. People simply retreated into the private sphere. This fostered an entirely new and different kind of zest for living and socializing in an intimate setting. Domestic music-making, dancing, and amusing conversation became increasingly fashionable and led to an unprecedented blossoming of salon life in Vienna.

It has been pointed out that the "Metternich system" aimed to encourage modest, tranquil pleasures whenever and wherever they were to be found; the only things it strove to prevent were noisy, overstimulating, and potentially riotous assemblies of large numbers of people.[15] Consequently, these years also witnessed an unprecedented craze for theatrical entertainment. At the same time there was a mushrooming of "establishments" in which orchestras played music for dancing, their repertoires soon dominated by the Viennese waltz.

An undeniable luster was added to Viennese culture at this time by the activity of Ludwig van Beethoven (1770–1827), who lived in Vienna from 1792 until his death. Few people were more deeply aware of his genius than the German Romantic author Bettina (Brentano) von Arnim. She met the composer in Vienna in May, 1810, and wrote about the encounter to Goethe, whom

Johann Nepomuk Hoechle. *Beethoven's Study in the Old Black Spaniard House.* 1827. Brush and ink with wash. Historisches Museum der Stadt Wien, Vienna (15.828).

she admired so much, at Weimar: "When I saw him I forgot the whole world—I am still a minor [she was twenty-five], but I am nonetheless right in averring what possibly no one, now, will either understand or believe, that culturally he was out in front of the whole human race. And shall we ever catch up to him? I doubt it. May he but live until the mighty and exalted riddle that inhabits his mind has ripened to its highest perfection."[16]

Beethoven's impact on Vienna and the jubilant enthusiasm that greeted each performance of one of his works must have been awe-inspiring. Almost equally awe-inspiring is the fact that the celebrated Viennese violinist Joseph Boehm (who later taught that great Beethoven interpreter Joseph Joachim) dared to perform Beethoven's late quartets—works so difficult and profound that they are considered problematical even today—at morning concerts in the first coffeehouse to open in the Prater. It was "a truly glorious yardstick of Viennese culture at that time," as R. Kralik and H. Schlitter said.[17]

Beethoven's celebrity was never more apparent than in the sheer size of the crowd that attended his funeral on March 29, 1827. The famous actor Heinrich Anschütz recited Franz Grillparzer's mourning words of obituary at the graveside, beginning: "Whoso comes after him will not be continuing, for Beethoven ceases only where art itself ceases...".[18]

Already the very next day—on March 30, 1827—Johann Nepomuk Hoechle hurried round to Beethoven's former apartment in the old Black Spaniard House, the last of the restless composer's many addresses (he was always moving), to capture with his brush the piano, prospect, and atmosphere of that modest, yet momentously important dwelling.

Government concern about manifestations of popular feeling during the Metternich era was concentrated at the political level, a circumstance that undoubtedly favored culture and its pursuit in the private sphere. What Metternich's henchman Gentz and his circle saw as the source of all disintegration was the corrosive, subversive philosophy of critical subjectivism rather than social life as such. It was "spurious scholars, hotheaded fanatical students, and journalists"[19] who spelled danger to the government, principally through their political agitation, and the authorities sought to curb their activites.

Increasingly, as time went on, the government also grew to fear the growing proletarian mass. However, it seems to have been largely oblivious to the signs of the times. Unwilling or possibly unable to see the potential dangers of poverty, rootlessness, and exploitation, the government believed progress lay solely in increased production and rising profits. Social hardship—of the kind, for example, that Archduke John repeatedly denounced—cast a dark shadow over this decade. Yet, as if inspired by some intuitive strength, bracing themselves against the blows of fate, the family and its circle of friends became the scene of increasing gaiety and sheer delight in living. One is reminded of similar postwar periods since then, notably the 1920s and 1950s, which were likewise characterized by an ebullient zest for living that simply turned its back on material difficulties.

In the 1820s a cheerfully confident life-style took possession of the drawing rooms of the middle classes as a booming economy and increasing wealth combined to offer people the most delightful opportunities. Out of these emerged the distinctive style of furniture and interior decoration known as Viennese Biedermeier, characterized by gentle, balanced shapes for seating furniture and simple, almost austere closets, bureaus, writing tables, and secretaries.

The pictures that adorned the walls in Biedermeier homes included some small and medium-sized oil paintings, mainly portraits or landscapes. The great majority, however, were framed watercolors, which found a new function in this kind of setting. In fact, the demand from this source was not the least of the factors that gave watercolor painting such a boost in this decade.

However, the greatest boost to the arts in Vienna's salons continued to come in the field of music with the new fashion for domestic music-making. Music was a constant and ubiquitous presence in Vienna. In 1833, August Ellrich reported to Berlin: "While little is done for the higher sciences in Austria, much is done for the arts. The Viennese are passionate lovers of music and of

48    Moritz Michael Daffinger. *Portrait of Marie Daffinger.* c. 1827.

reer. Daffinger had a violent temper, however, and repeatedly became involved in extremely public rows. (Later—in 1825—he even clashed disastrously with the police.) The couple became increasingly estranged, and in 1822, they finally terminated their liaison.

Daffinger also drank heavily, and throughout his spectacular career he never lost the rough manners and coarse language of his working class origins. He was not afraid to shock even the most exalted clients with some very plain speaking, and it sometimes happened that he turned down quite lucrative commissions if he did not like a face. "You're an ugly wench, though you've got nice eyes," he once told a prince's daughter. Yet despite this kind of "artistic" licence, Daffinger rose rapidly into the highest circles of Viennese society to become the most sought-after and successful portrait painter. There were few names, from the imperial family and the high nobility to the successful bourgeoisie and the world of high finance, that did not figure on Daffinger's list of clients.

One of the most attractive townhouses in Vienna was situated in the narrow Ballgasse. It was the home of the wealthy businessman Nikolaus Smolenitz von Smolk, whose family had emigrated to Hungary from the Epirus in Greece and become very successfully involved in the wool trade in many parts of the monarchy. Nikolaus, who managed the Vienna branch of the family firm, had married and been ennobled in the city. The Smolenitz von Smolk family revolved around their daughter Marie, born in 1808, who before long elicited justified admiration as a "divine beauty."

In a small bachelor apartment across the narrow street lived a friend of Daffinger's, Franz Grillparzer —poet, playwright, civil servant, and later director of the Imperial Archives (Hofkammerarchiv). Grillparzer was a fervent admirer of young Marie, whom he idolized and whose praises he sang in verse:

*Allmacht ist deine Macht, o Schönheit, mächtige Venus.*
*Was dein Szepter berührt, ändert das Wesen, die Art.*
*Als ich am Fenster sie sah, in papiernen Wickeln die*
*Locken.*
*Glaubt' ich die Charis zu sehen, weissliche Blumen im*
*Haar.*

All-powerful is your power, o Beauty, mighty Venus;
What your scepter touches changes its very nature.
Seeing her at the window, her locks in paper curlers,
I thought to see Charis herself with whitish flowers in her hair.[22]

In a letter written in 1827, for example, he states:

To add to all the things that, as you well know, lie so heavy on my heart, I must now believe you unfaithful. The other day as we sat facing each other, cards in hand, looking as if we were playing, and your knee was so slow to return the accustomed greeting, you were drawing a Roman capital S on the slate beside you; simultaneously your lips formed the same letter. I know the name that beings with that S!

Do not scold me for my suspicions. I have a right to be suspicious. You are the loveliest of women; never have I seen a lovelier one! As for me, anyone who does not find me repulsive does me great honor . . . .

I am a fool, Marie! With what good cause do I distrust you, and how often and how greatly have I distrusted you; yet there is not a doubt that could resist the power of your glance, nor do I have any weapons against you! So how is one to account for it? Is it that your smoothly parted hair snakes like a black river of hell around a forehead far too dark for a heaven, a forehead that is possibly too low and that you—deceitful flirt!—divide across the middle with a ribbon, the more surely to ensnare?

None of this, however, deterred Marie from bestowing her impetuous affections upon the poet's considerably more purposeful friend Moritz Michael Daffinger. Her father did what he could to dissuade her, though without success. Once, apparently, he even attempted to drive the painter from the house at knife point. It is said that, after a particularly stormy scene one evening, Daffinger actually abducted Marie from her parental home. Be that as it may, in 1826 she gave birth to their daughter Mathilde. When, on December 30, 1827, she and Daffinger were finally married, the couple lavished enormous devotion on bringing up their child.

It must have been a turbulent marriage though, for they were an ill-matched pair. Marie was well-bred, cultured, spoiled, and much courted. Daffinger was violent and irascible, and while he may well have been extremely fascinating, he was repeatedly driven to fresh outbursts of jealous rage. Scenes in the street, with a crowd looking on, were a common occurrence.

Throughout these years Grillparzer remained bound to the couple in friendship, often seeking to smooth things out between them—unsuccessfully, for the most part, as these extracts from his diary suggest:

*February 19, 1829.* Met Daffinger and his wife. Escorted her home. Lent an ear to martial tiffs and did my best to mediate . . . .
*February 24, 1829.* Afternoon at Daffinger's. His wife is breathtakingly beautiful. Had a boring time nonetheless . . . . He maltreats her in the most literal sense of the word. How far quite unjustly, I do not know. I am inclined to distrust such innocent airs. The woman is a total mystery to me . . . .
*October 3, 1832.* The day before yesterday, just as I was quitting my old apartment, D. [Daffinger] came and fetched me to act as arbiter between himself and his wife, whom he said he was about to leave for good. I went—to her who was once my own delight and who may, at the time, have loved me. However, the cause of the current domestic upsets is—a new lover . . . . I gave the wife a talking to, read the husband a lecture, promised on her behalf that the affair was over (there had never been much to it anyway), reconciled the couple (it won't last, of course), and eventually went off like a

49   Moritz Michael Daffinger. *Portrait of the Dramatist Franz Grillparzer.* 1827

stage uncle—I who years ago was the lover myself and saw the selfsame preparations for parting being made on my account . . . .

*March 14, 1834.* Saw Marie recently with her husband and child. She has aged. She is only twenty-five, but the change is still noticeable. That once truly divine face has received an admixture of humanity. Although I am sure she is now utterly indifferent to me, she still tried a few tricks with her eyes. I was careful not to get involved, though even the memory of what I have to reproach her with had pretty much faded . . . .

Marie, nevertheless, was and remained Daffinger's loveliest model—a young woman whom, in his almost feverish desire for her, he immortalized with his art over and over again. He made her a symbol *par excellence* of the Viennese beauty of the Biedermeier years.

When their beloved only daughter Mathilde, then just fifteen, suddenly contracted a typhus-related fever and died on August 12, 1841, her parents truly found each other for the first time in response to their deep shock and despair. Grillparzer composed the moving inscription for Mathilde's gravestone:

> *Ein Engel flog zum Himmel*
> *Die Hülle blieb zurück*
> *Und nichts ist hier gestorben*
> *Als zweier Eltern Glück.*

> An angel, flying heavenward,
> Left behind an emptiness,
> And all that perished here below
> Was two parents' bliss.

Even more moving, however, was how all superficial conflicts between the two spouses now evaporated to make way for a quiet life of shared withdrawal and a further eight years of supreme artistic achievement, for that was the length of time by which Daffinger survived

his daughter. Those years, however, belong to another chapter.

## PETER FENDI: THE MODESTY OF A GENIUS

They were a familiar sight in Vienna: an elderly woman and her son—a small, squat, crooked figure leaning on her arm, dressed in a frock coat and a top hat and carrying a sketchbook—making their way from suburban Heumarkt into the inner city. That is how they were portrayed in an etching published in 1824 as a supplement to "M. Auen's printed illustrated magazine *Faust*."[23] What an artist hid beneath that unprepossessing exterior! What a master of watercolor painting, unsurpassed in his manner and in his day!

Peter Fendi. *The Artist and his Mother on Their Way from Suburban Heumarkt into Vienna.* 1824. Etching. Graphische Sammlung Albertina, Vienna (Ö. K. XIX "Fendi").

Peter Fendi. *Emperor Francis I and Carolina Augusta with Their Grandchildren.* 1834. Watercolor. Private collection.

50   Peter Fendi. *The Wedding Morning from Schiller's "The Lay of the Bell."* 1832

Peter Fendi, victim of a tragic accident in infancy (he fell off a table, causing irreparable damage to his spine), had developed into a very special kind of artistic personality. Long and glorious though the list of Viennese watercolorists already was, what Fendi achieved could not have come from any of them. He made his colors blend into one another as no watercolorist had ever done before and formed the most delicate nuances. Fendi modeled his figures with a combination of vigorous colors and transparent effects of light that arose from exposed areas of white paper. This perhaps comes out most clearly in his smaller sketches. Although they consist of little more than a few patches of colored washes, they possess a charm and a touching magic that lift them above almost every other kind of painting. Even today Fendi's colors retain the splendor and luminosity of precious stones.

That is only one aspect of Fendi's art. He also adopted a new type of subject matter; later it came to be seen as representing the quintessence of Viennese genre painting.[24]

This generation's rejection of history painting had resulted in artists portraying ordinary, everyday scenes, with either a positively moral or an associatively emotive content. Even when Fendi tackled a subject touching on social criticism—poverty, hardship, loneliness, fear—he made his individual figures charmingly attractive and filled the picture with what Leo Grünstein called "tender concern."[25] A lyrical spiritualization is always the guiding element in Fendi's work. He was tellingly described by a contemporary as "the Schubert of painting."[26]

Fendi's life—with that one tragic exception—was without dramatic incident. Born in 1796, the son of a poor private tutor, he knew desperate hunger and hardship in his youth and lost his father (who died on March 24, 1814) at an early age. The sickly but exceptionally talented boy was accepted at the Academy in 1810, where he trained under J.M. Fischer, H. Maurer, and J.B. Lampi. A neighbor, Professor Joseph Barth, a doctor and art collector, employed Fendi to draw the archeological specimens in his collection, which brought the artist to the attention of the president of the Academy, Count Anton Lamberg-Sprintzenstein.

The count commissioned Fendi to draw the classical vases in the same collection and eventually recommended him to the Imperial Coins and Antiques Cabinet, where the artist earned his living as a draftsman from 1816–17 onward. There he produced incredibly accurate drawings of coins, reliefs, vases, and sarcophagi; the Kunsthistorisches Museum still has some two thousand examples. The work must have been almost unbearably tedious, however, and one can appreciate that Fendi's two official trips—to Salzburg from July 4 to September 23, 1817 (to draw a mosaic floor that had been discovered there) and to Venice in the spring of 1821 (accompanying his employer to collect specimens)—were high points in his life. The Cabinet's director Anton von Steinbüchel aptly characterized Fendi in a petition to the emperor as being "almost indispensable for the job, loyal, honest, of good conduct, quick to learn"[27]—whereby he doubtless also had in mind this young employee's quite exceptional amiability, modesty, and tact.

Peter Fendi never married; he continued to live with his mother until his death in 1842. In this context, it has been said that, handicapped by nature and denied a family of his own, Fendi was driven by personal affliction to portray the blessing of children so often.[28]

Peter Fendi. *Sketch for "Returning from the Fields."* Before 1834. Watercolor over pencil. Sammlungen des Regierenden Fürsten von Liechtenstein, Vaduz Castle, Vaduz (295).

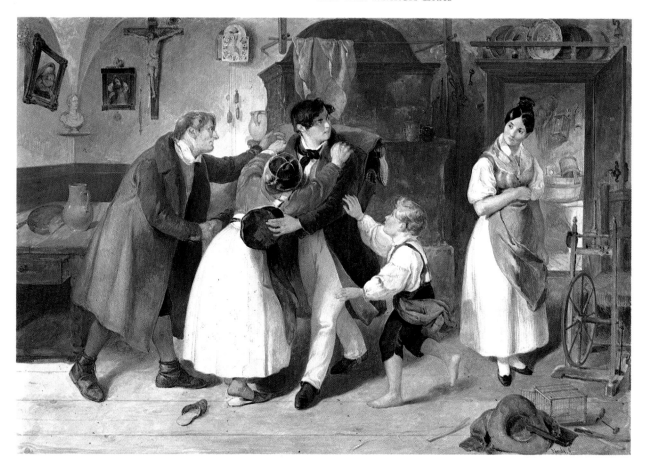

51   Peter Fendi. *The Son's Homecoming from Schiller's "The Lay of the Bell."* 1833
52   Peter Fendi. *Returning from the Fields (Ave Maria) from Schiller's "The Lay of the Bell."* 1833

Peter Fendi. *Mother and Child.* c. 1835. Watercolor over pencil. Sammlungen des Regierenden Fürsten von Liechtenstein, Vaduz Castle, Vaduz (228).

Peter Fendi. *Two Peasants Resting Beside a Shrine.* 1840. Watercolor. Graphische Sammlung Albertina, Vienna (25.469).

Undoubtedly, however, his strong relationship with his mother also influenced his choice of subject matter, and in particular, the family atmosphere of his genre work. (Besides caring for her son, Fendi's mother looked after a whole group of young artists who gathered round their exemplar and teacher.)

Fendi probably tapped the sources of his art largely on his own; his teachers at the Academy appear to have had no influence on him. He learned much more from copying the works of seventeenth-century Dutch artists represented in the Academy gallery. Genre painting had enjoyed an extremely lively prelude in Vienna with Johann Peter Krafft's Realism and new choice of subject matter, and Fendi certainly began by coming to terms with Krafft's example. Indeed, in many respects he followed it.

Nevertheless, Fendi was the true creator of the new genre painting, because his subjects (the more so for being painted in watercolor) possessed a new kind of poetry. Invariably they pursued a delightful poetic idea and no longer degenerated into a pathos that was still overly historical in flavor.

Fendi's greatest contribution to genre painting, however, was in technique and expressiveness. He nearly always used very small formats, beginning with a delicate pencil drawing before applying his brush with the most extraordinary precision. He laid on his color sketchily and swiftly, which made it possible to achieve the lightest of washes and produced a supremely relaxed effect. In the words of Hubert Adolph, "[Fendi's] watercolors combine the tingling freshness of a sketch with the delicate beauty of a finished miniature."[29]

In 1833 the Imperial Coins and Antiques Cabinet received a new director in the person of Count Moritz Dietrichstein. He drew the attention of certain members of the imperial family to his official draftsman, though Fendi was not by any means unknown at court at this time. Both Empress Carolina Augusta and her daughter-in-law Archduchess Sophie (1805–72) were enchanted with Fendi's work. (Sophie, the Bavarian princess, was beginning to play an increasingly prominent role at court, having given birth to the future Emperor Francis Joseph I in 1830.) Fendi's pictures of children especially pleased them, and the two women became his most determined patronesses.

Initially Fendi was commissioned to paint Sophie's three children. She was delighted with the result. The archduchess herself, as Leo Grünstein was able to report on the basis of original letters of Fendi's in his possession, "encouraged and enabled the artist to execute the well-known cycle of thirty illustrations for poems by Johann Christoph Friedrich von Schiller."[30] This series probably represents the pinnacle of Fendi's achievement.

53   Peter Fendi. *The Thunderstorm.* 1836

54   Peter Fendi. *A Peasant Woman and Child Beside a Statue of the Virgin Mary*, c. 1840

55   Peter Fendi. *Young Woman and Child Beside a Hen Coop.* 1836
56   Peter Fendi. *Two Princesses of Liechtenstein with Their Governess.* 1838

59   Peter Fendi. *Illustration for Schiller's "The Cranes of Ibycus."* 1834

57   Peter Fendi. *Illustration for Schiller's "The Fight with the Dragon."* 1835
58   Peter Fendi. *Illustration for Schiller's "The Fight with the Dragon."* 1835

60   Peter Fendi. *A Visit to the Nun.* 1839

61   Peter Fendi. *Pilgrims' Halt.* 1842
62   Peter Fendi. *Gypsy Encampment.* 1840

115

Fendi had obviously begun to look at Schiller's poem *The Lay of the Bell* in the 1820s.[31] Completed in 1799, this was an elaborate "frame" poem, based on the forging of a bell. The great contemporary critic Wilhelm von Humboldt said of the poem: "I know of no work in any language that spreads so generous a poetical circle within so small a compass, that runs through the whole gamut of human emotions, and that in an entirely lyrical way shows life with its principal events and ages in the manner of an epic bounded by natural frontiers."[32]

These aspects must have made it an ideal subject for Fendi's genre art. He set all the scenes in his own day and in his own environment, involving his mother, his foster-sisters, his neighbors, and his friends. As a result, he achieved an entirely natural liveliness that provided a matchless foil for the poet's words. The pictures made an understandable impression, and Empress Carolina Augusta made a gift of the first of them—*The Wedding Morning*—to her daughter-in-law Sophie on June 15, 1828, adding a dedication (this is not the same painting as our Pl. 50). This series soon became Fendi's best-known work, appearing in a wide variety of copies and lithographic reproductions.

The upshot of all this, in 1832, was Sophie's request to the artist to continue the cycle. A sequence of masterly and extremely impressive watercolors resulted. (For many years they appeared to have been lost.

Key to the people pictured:
1  Archduke Francis Charles
2  Archduke Anthony Victor
3  Crown Prince Ferdinand
4  Marianne, wife of the crown prince
5  Archduke Joseph Palatine
6  Archduke Reginald
7  Archduke Charles
8  H.M. Emperor Francis I
9  H.M. Empress Carolina Augusta
10  Maria, wife of Archduke Joseph
11  Archduke Stephan, son of Archduke Joseph
12  Archduke Albert
13  Archduke Maximilian of Este
14  Archduke John
15  Archduke Louis
16  Elizabeth, wife of Archduke Reginald
17  Sophie, wife of Archduke Francis Charles
18  Archduke Henry, son of Archduke Reginald
19  Archduke Reginald, son of Archduke Reginald
20  Archduchess Theresa, daughter of Archduke Charles
21  Archduchess Adelheid, daughter of Archduke Reginald
22  Archduchess Hermine, daughter of Archduke Joseph
23  Archduke Charles Ferdinand, son of Archduke Charles
24  Archduke Alexander, son of Archduke Joseph
25  Archduke Friedrich, son of Archduke Charles
26  Archduke Ernest, son of Archduke Reginald
27  Archduke Leopold, son of Archduke Reginald
28  Archduchess Maria, daughter of Archduke Reginald
29  Archduke Francis Joseph, son of Archduke Francis Charles
30  Archduchess Maria, daughter of Archduke Charles
31  Archduke Ferdinand Maximilian, son of Archduke Francis Charles
32  Archduke Joseph, son of Archduke Joseph
33  Archduke Charles, son of Archduke Joseph
34  Archduchess Elizabeth, daughter of Archduke Joseph
35  Archduke William, son of Archduke Charles
36  Archduke Sigismond, son of Archduke Reginald
37  Archduke Maximilian, son of Archduke Reginald

63   Peter Fendi. *Family Reunion of the Imperial House of Austria.* 1834

64   Peter Fendi. *Album Flyleaf for Prince Clemens Metternich.* 1837

65   Peter Fendi. *Evening Prayers.* 1839

Recently, however, they appeared on the market, and after changing hands several times, they are now fortunately united in one large private collection.)

In 1834 Fendi received his most important commission from the imperial family: invited to the Hofburg on October 21 of that year, the artist found the immediate imperial family foregathered in its entirety after dinner around Emperor Francis and Empress Carolina Augusta. He was required to capture this *Family Reunion* in a large watercolor.

Grouping thirty-seven people in detailed individual portraits must have been a horrendously difficult task, even if Fendi did take prompt advantage of this unique opportunity. The second stage—working up individual sketches of each person—likewise presented many problems. The precise execution of the finished watercolor painting constituted a truly epic feat. No doubt one of the greatest problems was portraying the children. "Luckily," Archduchess Sophie wrote to her mother in Bavaria, "they were all in the mood for quiet games that day, because when they are all rushing about it's enough to drive you out of your mind."[33] In fact, the artist had to return the next day (October 22) to draw the children again, seeing each of them individually.

Painting the actual picture took Fendi all winter. On December 2, Sophie informed her mother, "The drawing of our twenty-two children and the rest of us (there will be thirty-seven people in the picture) by Fendi is coming on beautifully. So far he has only painted most of the children and their toys. There really is a kind of movement and grace in all the different groups that only Fendi's genius could give them . . . ."[34]

Such is the almost unimaginable breadth and variety of Fendi's oeuvre that I can single out only a few works here: for example, the collection of 104 watercolor sketches and drawings that Fendi assembled for his special patron Prince Alois II of Liechtenstein (subsequently in the Rudolf Gutmann Collection, acquired by the Albertina in 1969).[35] A similar collection had probably been made for Prince Metternich, but only the title page of this survives with miniature reproductions of Fendi's major works in almost inconceivable detail. Finally, mention must be made of the watercolor that Archduchess Sophie had Fendi paint as a Christmas gift for her husband Francis Charles in 1839.[36] It portrays Sophie and her children (Francis Joseph, Ferdinand Maximilian, Charles Louis, and Maria Anna) at their evening prayers—as indicated by the toys left lying about (in the morning these would long since have been tidied away).[37] The unprecedented aspect of this watercolor is that the artist has executed a family portrait in which there is not a face to be seen. The overall impression of unity that creates a work of art is produced purely by the genre atmosphere, the almost bourgeois, wholly unpretentious intimacy of a mother summoning her children from play to say their prayers.

Peter Fendi had a great influence not merely on the circle of his pupils, to whom he particularly dedicated his final years, but also throughout the painting community in Biedermeier Vienna.[38] From Ferdinand Georg Waldmüller to August von Pettenkofen, Viennese artists picked up crucial impulses from Fendi and took them further. Eventually Fendi's severe physical handicap brought on the heart condition of which he died when he was only forty-six.

## LANDSCAPES THAT MIRROR EXPERIENCE

The younger generation of artists working about 1830 had grown up with a quite different attitude toward nature and art than its fathers had had. Jakob Gauermann's two sons, for example, had grown up in the country, on their father's farm at Miesenbach in the Piesting Valley, near the Schneeberg. Both Carl (b. 1804) and Friedrich (b. 1807) showed exceptional talent at an early age, which their father did his best to foster through diligent practice and instruction. Carl died at the age of twenty-five before he developed as far as he might have done artistically. But Friedrich was to fulfill all his father's hopes for him, and a great deal more besides.

In terms of technique and theory, Friedrich followed his father in many respects. Artistically, however, he followed a very different path. The difference between father and son can be summed up by quoting from something each of them wrote.

Jakob, clearly thinking in terms of the theory of composition of Ideal art, once wrote in his diary: "The artist must make a sketch in accordance with his idea and proceed to alter and improve it until such time as he is satisfied with it. To this end he looks to nature for studies that may assist him in his design. However, he needs to be very much on his guard here, lest in the process of gathering assistance he is substantially diverted from his basic idea. For such aids [materials] are drawn upon for the sake of the Idea rather than just being something wretched thrown together, using the materials assembled."[39] As Archduke John's painter by appointment, Jakob Gauermann had, of course, had another task, namely to make topographical and other records in paint for his employer's survey of Styria.

Both functions were decisively rejected by Jakob's son. Having grown up with the realist tradition, Friedrich no longer saw either the elementary recording of topography or an antiquated Mengs style of Ideal art as a valid objective. Art should be experienced as a whole, according to Friedrich, "Nature knows only birches, pines, oaks, and so on; but painting is concerned only with trees as such."[40] In other words, nature provided the opportunity for an artist to make of it a work of art.

Consequently, Friedrich Gauermann and his friends set out on their walking tours with new eyes, eyes open for the whole experience, for adventurous atmosphere, for exhilarating scenery—in short, for the genre aspect of nature as they found it in the Alpine regions.

R. Feuchtmüller stresses this, "Real life was thus considered as given, both as to details and as to the

Friedrich Gauermann. *With Friends in the Snow near Miesenbach*. 1829. Pencil with watercolor. Sammlungen des Regierenden Fürsten von Liechtenstein, Vaduz Castle, Vaduz (300).

whole; but only for its content, not for the exactness of the actual visual event."[41] As a result of such thinking, Friedrich Gauermann became the first man to portray, freely and dynamically, the poetry of the actual lives of the Alpine people—peasant farmers and huntsmen. He rendered it as a genre picture—and provoked bitter criticism from his contemporaries, who dubbed him a *Waldmensch*, a wild man of the woods. Yet Friedrich's approach influenced a generation of artists.

Friedrich Gauermann concentrated almost entirely on large-format, finished oil paintings, though along the way he also produced some truly masterly oil sketches,[42] as well as a large number of pen-and-wash drawings very much in the style of his father. He did hardly any work in watercolor.

Not so his friend Josef Höger, who was to become one of the most remarkable phenomena in Austrian art in the field of watercolor landscape painting. Technically, Höger owed a great deal to his teacher Joseph Rebell—the glowing backlighting for example—and much of his approach probably stemmed from Mössmer, who insisted so particularly on artists working directly in the open air. Like Gauermann, however, Höger saw as his objective capturing an atmosphere, a sense of the event.

Höger was also—like few other artists (Gurk and Ferdinand Runk are possible exceptions)—enormously successful with a single patron. The vast majority of his works have remained in the collections of the prince of Liechtenstein. As a result, very few people have seen them or know of their existence. Since nothing was ever published about the artist, Höger did not even become famous posthumously. In his later years, following his appointment as a professor at the Academy in 1849 and after he had published a number of lithographic textbooks for the Academy's landscape and tree-drawing department, Höger did gain a reputation as an outstanding teacher—"a tree painter second only to Waldmüller," as a posthumous catalogue of 1878 put it.[43] But Höger's watercolor oeuvre has remained virtually unknown to this day.

Soon after 1825, Höger and Friedrich Gauermann began their walking tours together through the loveliest of the Alpine regions. The experience left its mark on both of them. At first they kept to the country around Miesenbach and to the Schneeberg region, but in 1828 they walked as far as Salzburg and the town of Gastein. They returned to the Salzburg region in the following year to paint near Ischl and Hallstatt, making their way home via Aussee, Admont, and the Enns Valley. In 1831 they again visited Salzburg and Berchtesgaden and spent several weeks near the Lake of König, where they "enjoyed the pleasant company of Court Painter Joseph Karl Stieler from Munich and of Julius Hermann Kummer and Anton Castell from Dresden."[44] On Febru-

Matthäus Loder und Thomas Ender. *View of Bad Gastein.* 1828–9. Pencil with watercolor. Private collection (E. J. 325).

ary 19, 1832, Höger married Friedrich's sister Elizabeth (b. 1810). The summer of the following year saw another joint excursion in northern Tyrol, from which they returned home on August 17. (Also in 1833 Friedrich's other sister Maria, who was a year older than Elizabeth, married another of his painter friends, Wilhelm Pollak.) Shortly afterward Friedrich recorded in his notebook, "Up the Schneeberg at the end of August with Höger, Lisi, Marie von Rosthorn."[45] He "roamed around the Salzkammergut Alps with Höger again"[46] in 1835, and later years saw further walking tours in the mountains.

In 1836, Friedrich Gauermann noted in his diary a fact of enormous importance for the two friends, "Höger has some watercolor commissions for [the prince of] Liechtenstein."[47] In 1842 the two friends took the waters together in Karlsbad (Karlovy Vary), and on the way home they stopped at Zell am See, a lakeside town in the region known as the Pinzgau, a peaceful setting "in which some diligent watercolor painting from nature was done."[48]

R. Baumstark wrote some very pertinent words about Höger's "admirable achievement: giant trees and young saplings are portrayed according to character as individual creatures."[49] Höger's contemporaries were not far wrong when they jokingly dubbed him *Bäume-Raffael* (the Raphael of trees). What found supremely

beautiful expression in this artist's watercolors was the new sense of reality, the freedom of life in nature, the variety of experience, rather than mere details.

## SOME OF THOMAS ENDER'S COMMISSIONS

In the early summer of 1828 Matthäus Loder added a quite astonishing final flourish to his oeuvre. Having accompanied Archduke John and his wife to Gastein, as he did every year, he painted a series of watercolors there that are among his finest works.[50] Some of them, however, were barely begun—sketched in pencil, or carried a few notes, or had had a little color applied[51]—before an attack of his old lung trouble completely incapacitated him. The attack may have been triggered by overexertion, or possibly by the altitude. Be that as it may, Loder was rushed back to Vordernberg, terminally ill, and died there on September 16.

In a will drawn up two days before his death, Loder bade a moving farewell to his wife Louise, to whom he left all his meager belongings with the exception of the *Kunstgemählde* (paintings). He begged that Archduke John should "graciously deign to accept [them] as a poor sign of my deepest respect . . . ."[52]

Undoubtedly there had been some who had looked with envy on the archduke's special liking for Loder. Jakob Gauermann was one who had felt passed over; he confided his most secret thoughts to his diary, noting that "my Archduke John gave me to hope that, when he now undertakes a trip into the mountains, he will have me summoned."[53]

66   Thomas Ender. *The Passage Through the Urtelstein in the Helenen Valley, near Baden.* c. 1830

67   Josef Höger. *Hallstadt,* from an album with views of Ischl commune. 1836

68   Josef Höger. *The Road to the Lake of Gosau*, from an album with views of Ischl commune. 1836

That was not the way it turned out, however; John decided in favor of Thomas Ender, who had returned from Italy in 1822. Ender had already exhibited successfully in Vienna and had received a certain amount of recognition. His most prestigious commission had come from the emperor: to continue the decoration of Persenbeug Palace begun by Joseph Rebell. Rebell had succumbed to tuberculosis in the middle of his great task and had died on a trip to Dresden. Ender became John's painter by appointment under circumstances that were not dissimilar.

On November 6, 1828, the archduke took the extraordinary step of sending to Vordernberg for the works Loder had left him, and handing them over to Loder's successor for completion. As a result, there are now a number of watercolors that feature the hands of both artists. Even more disturbing is the clash of two fundamentally different generations that is plain to see in these works. The lovingly sensitive portrayals of the Biedermeier artist clearly fell into the hands of a seasoned realist. In fact, there are few more vivid illustrations of the changing times, few more graphic characterizations of the new generation of artists.

The year 1829 marked the beginning of a new chapter in Thomas Ender's life, and for the next twenty years he enjoyed a wealth of opportunities and commissions. Archduke John wanted to create, in a manner that had never been envisaged before, a pictorial record of Alpine landscape. The artist began by visiting John's estates, starting with the Brandhof, before setting out on his first major walking tour in the mountains.

In 1828, John had made a famous and quite extraordinarily dramatic attempt to climb the Grossvenediger (one of Austria's highest mountains, 3,674 m.). Ender's first task in the following year, therefore, was to capture the finest views of this massif.

Whereas Loder had always accompanied his master, staying very close to him, Ender soon adopted a different pattern of working, due in part perhaps to his appointment to a chair at the Academy in 1836. Before each trip, Ender was given a clearly defined task for the next journey, which he duly undertook in the summer months. Then he spent the following autumn and winter executing the works and eventually delivered them to the archduke.

Ender's detailed reports make it possible to follow his routes precisely (which is important in so far as Ender never dated his work). Very briefly, his principal destinations in the early years were as follows: (1829): the Venediger massif, Schareck, Gastein; (1830): Hochschwab, Salzburg, Gastein, Rauris, Kaprun; (1832): Gastein, Mallnitz, the Grossglockner; (1833): the Felber Valley, the Pinzgau, and the Grossvenediger; (1834): Rauris and the Glockner massif.[54]

At this point a new situation emerged. In 1813, exactly twenty years after imposing it, the emperor removed the ban on Archduke John that had prevented him from ever again setting foot in the Tyrol (there had been some question of a "conspiracy" in connection with the treason of the Alpine League). John promptly dispatched Ender to the province to record further views, and in 1835 and 1836 the artist visited only Tyrolese regions.

In 1837, Ender was in the middle of preparing working drawings for the Viennese publisher C. A. Hartleben for a work to be entitled *Danube Journey*. In July he had taken some pupils to walk the stretch of the river that ran through the Wachau, when an urgent message reached him from the archduke: he was to return to Vienna immediately and take ship down the Danube to Odessa with the archduke's party (John had been asked to visit the czar of Russia on the emperor's behalf, as his representative.) The archduke needed Ender to make a pictorial record of this important trip. It was to prove a fascinating commission; it became one of the most important in Ender's whole life, as we shall see in the next chapter.

## BUILDING TO A CLIMAX—RUDOLF ALT'S JOURNEYS FROM 1831 TO 1845

In 1829 the sixteen-year-old Rudolf Alt completed the elementary art course at the Academy and was allowed to join the landscape class. His teacher there was Josef Mössmer, though Mössmer's methods gained little influence over him. Apart from the instruction he received from his father, the way Rudolf Alt learned was by working with open eyes, when confronted with the multifarious spectacle of reality. Very quickly (from 1830 on) what was maturing inside him became evident: complete emancipation from the *veduta*, coupled with rejection of painting the kinds of moods that attracted genre painters. In the process Rudolf Alt became the greatest Austrian master of the watercolor. I agree totally with Otto Benesch's statement made on

Rudolf Alt. *The "High Market" (Hohe Markt) in Vienna.* 1835. Watercolor and pencil. Sammlungen des Regierenden Fürsten von Liechtenstein, Vaduz Castle, Vaduz (2.246).

73   Jakob Alt. *View from the Artist's Studio.* 1836

74   Rudolf Alt. *Self Portrait*. 1835

the occasion of the Alt exhibition held at the Albertina in 1955, "[The] mastery of light and atmosphere, revealed particularly in the watercolors painted in Italy, places these works of art on a par with the best [works by] Turner and [Richard Parkes] Bonington. Indeed, in terms of virtuosity of draftsmanship they are superior."[55]

This book is limited in scope; therefore, I cannot go into Alt's wonderfully rich and varied life and work in anything like the detail they both deserve. I can only refer the reader to the very adequate literature on the subject.[56] I shall, however, very briefly pass in review the main stages of his development.

In 1830 Jakob and Rudolf Alt made their first major trip to Gastein. Whether they were drawn thither partly by the hope of finding a place among the painters on the archduke's staff now that Loder was dead has never been quite clear. The fine picture by them of Archduke John's house might suggest such an ambition.[57] In the following year, the work of the father-and-son team was completely dominated by the lithographic series, *Scenes from the Alps*[58] (which Jakob Alt dedicated to Archduke John!). The laborious hand-coloring was Rudolf's contribution and formed the basis, as I have stressed, of his later mastery with the brush, which was truly superb and came close to technical perfection.

In 1832 Rudolf Alt quit the Academy entirely in order to make an immediate start on another lithographic series, *Vienna's Squares and Environs*.[59] This time he did the working drawings himself, and Jakob transferred them to the stone.

Another journey in 1833 took the two artists to Italy for the first time: here Rudolf gained a new feeling for color. How much this tour of the towns of Upper Italy meant to him is known from his own account. In the work from this tour, Rudolf achieved a unique blend of contrasts, combining the permanent with the ephemeral

to the most beautiful artistic effect, depicting the peace and harmony represented by the perfection of classical architecture. He captured the last with crystaline clarity in a nobly proportioned fabric of light and shade, teeming with life and with lasting impressions.[60]

Immediately following their return, the emperor's commission for peep-show pictures appears to have become a full-time job. This was to constitute the Alt family's chief source of income for many years to come, despite the fact that the fees involved were shockingly low. Initially the Alts received 20 florins per watercolor (at a time when Archduke John, by comparison, was paying his painters 100 florins per painting on top of a monthly stipend). However, this "family firm" was so industrious that it still managed to make an average of 700 florins per year out of the commission—roughly the income of a professor at the Academy.

The next big step in the Alts' life was another trip to Italy in 1835, a carefully prepared and preplanned journey that took them mainly to Rome and Naples. Prince Metternich had to obtain permission for the trip through official channels, with due reference being made to the merits of the two artists. When everything was settled, a very special year began for father and son, crammed with excitement and enthusiasm, a great deal of hard work, and some enthralling studies and artistic discoveries.

Even today it is a stirring experience to retrace this journey in Rudolf Alt's watercolors, seeing it through the eyes of the twenty-three-year-old artist. His use of color lost its glare and cultivated a glow in the light that appeared to come from within; this was achieved by

Jakob Alt. *View of The Castel dell'Ovo from the Riviera di Chiaia*. 1835. Watercolor over pencil. Sammlungen des Regierenden Fürsten von Liechtenstein, Vaduz Castle, Vaduz (11).

75   Jakob Alt. *Italian Port.* 1835
76   Jakob Alt. *View of the Church of San Giovanni in Laterano, Rome.* 1835

77   Rudolf Alt. *Eisgrub Palace before its Reconstruction.* Before 1845

78   Rudolf Alt. *The Bay of Cattaro in Dalmatia.* 1840

Rudolf Alt. *The Princesses Fanny and Marie of Liechtenstein at Their Prayers in the Oratory of the Chapel of Feldsberg Palace.*
c. 1840. Watercolor. Sammlungen des Regierenden Fürsten von Liechtenstein, Vaduz Castle, Vaduz (62).

Rudolf Alt. *The Artist's Wife Hermine.* c. 1841. Watercolor and pencil. Graphische Sammlung Albertina, Vienna (35.469).

81   Rudolf Alt. *View of Vienna from the Spinner-at-the-Cross Shrine.* 1841

79   Rudolf Alt. *The Solar Eclipse over Vienna on July 8, 1842.* 1842
80   Leander Russ. *The Solar Eclipse over the Marchfeld Plain on July 8, 1842.* 1842

82   Rudolf Alt. *The Prince of Liechtenstein's Study in Vienna.* 1842

83   Rudolf Alt. *The Garden Room in Rasumovsky Palace in Vienna*. 1845

84   Rudolf Alt. *View of Dürnstein in the Wachau.* 1843

85   Jakob Alt. *View of the Dachstein Mountains in the Salzkammergut.* 1840
86   Rudolf Alt. *View from the Lake of Aussee Looking Toward the Trisselwand.* 1859

lightening the penumbras using the technique known as "glazing." Eventually Rudolf acquired an almost inconceivable command over the play of light, shade, architecture, proportions, and perspective.

The two men also spent unforgettable hours in the company of fellow artists in Rome, on Capri, and in Amalfi—hours that they recalled and recounted repeatedly, long after their return to the more confined atmosphere of Vienna and to the deteriorating political conditions that followed the death of Emperor Francis I.

Rudolf continued to travel regularly, accompanying friends on trips up the Danube and to Lake Como in 1837. On his return he became engaged to the pretty Hermine Oswald, then aged seventeen. Rudolf promptly set to work with redoubled courage and industry in order to make enough money to set up house on his own. It took him several years however, and he had to complete an overwhelming number of commissions before he managed it: trips to Galicia and Poland first (in 1839); then, in 1840, the trip to Dalmatia which, from the artistic point of view, was to prove the most crucial of his life. The work Rudolf Alt produced on this journey from Trogir to Kotor bears

Rudolf Alt. *The Imperial Palace (Hofburg) in Vienna Seen from the Bellaria.* 1842. Watercolor and Chinese white. Graphische Sammlung Albertina, Vienna (34.681).

comparison with any in the world. In fact, the eight years from 1840 to 1848 constitute both the zenith of Rudolf Alt's achievement and a heyday of watercolor painting.

Alt's personal happiness at this time shines through his work. On August 9, 1841, he was at last able to marry his Hermine. Rudolf was now in great demand as an artist; publishers kept him busy with commissions for fresh series. The pressure became almost intolerable in fact, impairing his concentration and driving him close to despair; "Felt absolutely rotten today," he wrote to Hermine on August 19, 1842, "and got almost nothing done. Pitied you hugely for having a husband who is nothing but a wretched bungler. Determined to do everything in my power not to go under."[61] This was written at a time when Rudolf Alt was producing the most beautiful, most brilliant paintings in his entire oeuvre. It is sufficient to compare a masterpiece such as Alt's *Solar Eclipse* with another equally distinguished rendition of the same event to understand how far above everyone else Rudolf Alt already stood.

Life, however, is full of pitfalls: on November 23, 1843, Hermine died in childbed. Rudolf Alt was a broken man. Nonetheless, it is fascinating to note how his escape into painting actually strengthened, deepened, and enriched his work. When the Russian diplomat Count Barjatinsky commissioned a set of views of Vienna in 1844, to be painted in a size hardly larger than a visiting card, Alt produced one of his most astonishing masterpieces.[62]

Then the events of the Revolution of 1848—that great invasion of external circumstances into all spheres of life—brought Rudolf Alt up short. In the 1850s, artistically as well as in terms of subject matter and technique, he failed to lift himself out of a painful state of depression. All his struggles to succeed only seemed to make things worse. When he finally emerged from this depression, another, quite different age had long since dawned.

Rudolf Alt. *Aboard the Danube Steamer "Maria Anna."* 1837. Watercolor and pencil. Staatliche Graphische Sammlung, Munich (45.139).

# V  A World Still Intact, and the New Pre-March Spirit

## A Pilgrimage to Mariazell

The year 1835 was a momentous one for the painter Eduard Gurk, too. Prince Metternich, in a letter written from Marienbad (Mariánské Lázně, Czechoslovakia) on September 12, 1825,[1] actually referred to Gurk as *dessinateur de l'Empéreur*. Metternich was mistaken: Gurk was not and never became an imperial court painter, though that would always be his aim.

From earliest childhood Gurk, whose family was independently wealthy, had received a broad and varied education. His father, a librarian on the staff of Prince Nikolaus Esterházy, was also a remarkable inventor who built an assortment of devices including musical clocks and automatic musical instruments. The greatest achievement of Eduard's father was an organ, with which he toured Europe at Esterházy's request. In the process he not only amassed a fortune but also took advantage of every opportunity to pursue his own artistic inclinations. In particular Eduard's father studied watercolor painting in England, which in turn enabled him to provide his son with an excellent technical grounding.

Returning to Vienna in 1819, the eighteen-year-old Eduard Gurk struck up a crucially important friendship with two court painters, Johann Baptist Hoechle and his son Johann Nepomuk. Until then the Hoechles had virtually sole responsibility for making a pictorial record of events at court. By 1825, however, when the coronation of Queen Carolina Augusta in Bratislava was being portrayed, that responsibility was being shared by Gurk. The emperor and the crown prince noticed Gurk's work and started to give him direct commissions, which forced him into a rather different situation. As he put it later (in an application for the position of imperial court painter in 1836), "The commissions received continuously from that time on led [me] from the initial natural-history drawings to landscape and architecture, and eventually to small-scale historical compositions."[2]

Gurk now spent much of his time producing sets of lithographs on a wide variety of subjects. He depicted current events, such as the arrival of the first giraffe acquired by the Schönbrunn menagerie (this led to a new craze that swept through the ballrooms of Vienna: a dance *à la giraffe*, likewise portrayed by Gurk). He completed an extensive series of pictures of Turkish uniforms, and finally he produced a series illustrating Ferdinand's coronation (as King Ferdinand V of Hungary) in Bratislava on September 28, 1830. It was doubtless this last work that prompted Ferdinand, in 1833, to turn to Gurk first when he wanted pictures for his peep show.

Be that as it may, Ferdinand's decision inspired what is possibly Gurk's finest body of work. In that year the crown prince undertook a three-day pilgrimage from Vienna to Mariazell, accompanied only by a small retinue on horseback; among that retinue was Eduard Gurk.

On the first day the party set off at dawn from the Spinner at the Cross, a famous landmark on the outskirts of Vienna. Proceeding by way of Mödling and the Hermitage, they followed the Brühl road to Gaaden and their second waystation, the monastery of Heiligenkreuz. Continuing via Alland and Hafnerberg, the pilgrims reached Hainfeld and eventually St. Veit on the River Gölsen, where they spent the first night.

The second day's journey took them to the monastery of Lilienfeld, to Türnitz, and on to Annaberg, where they had their first magnificent view of the Ötscher (1,893 m). Crossing the Joachimsberg, their tenth waystation, they ended the second day in Wienerbruck.

The third day brought a wealth of natural splendors: the Ötscher Valley, Lassing Falls, and the Josefsberg made a tremendous impression on the party. At last they caught their first glimpse—from the so-called *Urlauberkreuz* (the Vacationists' Cross) in Weissenbach—of the tall Gothic tower of Mariazell. Soon afterward this picturesque pilgrimage reached its climactic conclusion as the pilgrims gathered to pray beneath the soaring domes of the pilgrimage church.

Working from initial quick sketches and more detailed studies (no doubt made on a more leisurely return journey), Gurk spent the whole of the following winter (1833–4) producing a complete portfolio of forty watercolor paintings. This important series—an exceptional document of Austrian watercolor painting that

87   Eduard Gurk. *Markt Mölding on the Pilgrimage to Mariazell.* 1833-4
88   Eduard Gurk. *Glassworks near Türnitz on the Pilgrimage to Mariazell.* 1833–4

89   Eduard Gurk. *View from Annaberg Looking Toward the Ötscher on the Pilgrimage to Mariazell.* 1833–4
90   Eduard Gurk. *View of Mariazell on the Pilgrimage to Mariazell.* 1833–4

91    Joseph Gerstmeyer. *Emperor Francis I and the Empress Entering Mariazell.* Before 1835

92   Eduard Gurk. *The Royal Castle and Archbishop's Palace in Prague.* c. 1836

the Niederösterreichisches Landesmuseum, Vienna, was able to acquire from the imperial collection—has received a thorough evaluation from Rupert Feuchtmüller.[3] After pointing out both its historical value and its artistic significance, Feuchtmüller concludes, "In terms of subject matter, Gurk is a true Biedermeier artist in this series. This comes out in the colorfulness of the folk scenes, in the narrative variety, in the gift of firsthand observation apparent in the genre scenes, and above all in the artist's love of the picturesquely romantic motives from nature. For Gurk was no mere topographer; he was capable of being thrilled by the beauties of nature."[4]

This series rapidly consolidated Gurk's position. His financial circumstances were such that he was able to purchase and live in a particularly fine house in the Penzing district of Vienna. 1835 was a momentous year for Gurk. His father died on May 5, and Eduard inherited a considerable fortune. Meanwhile the old Emperor Francis had died on March 2 and been succeeded by Ferdinand, who had such a predilection for Gurk's work. Finally, when the imperial court painter Johann Nepomuk Hoechle also died (his father had passed away three years before), Gurk not unreasonably hoped to be appointed to fill the vacant post. He had reckoned, however, without the ins and outs of bureaucracy.

Tracing the case in the state archives is as baffling as trying to make sense of one of those distorting pictures.[5] Inquiries, reports, and memoranda followed one another in endless, wearying succession, and when after seven years those responsible felt bound to take up the matter of Gurk's application once again, they were able to note with satisfaction that the petitioner was no more (Gurk had died on a visit to Palestine in 1841), so the file was closed.

Though the years 1835–40 saw him produce his finest works for the emperor, Gurk undoubtedly experienced great frustration and disappointment during this period. So it must have been with especial delight that he accepted the invitation of a patron, Baron Johann Karl von Moll, currently chamberlain to the emperor and a member of a distinguished Upper Italian family, to paint the baron's Villa Lagarina, near Rovereto. The detailed letters that Gurk wrote on the journey appeared regularly in the Viennese press, where they aroused widespread interest. They constitute a quite exceptional historical source.[6]

Richly informative and containing some beautiful descriptive writing, they reveal much of Gurk's mind and personality. They are not short of lighter moments, either, as when he criticizes the visitors to the health resort of Ischl for having more to say about the excellence of the trout than about the beauty of the lakes and mountains! Gurk gives an impressive description of climbing the Gaisberg (1,288 m) near Salzburg at night, in order to experience the famous view of the sunrise. The journey also took him, via Bolzano and Merano, to the Passo dello Stelvio, or Stilfser Joch (where blizzards held him up), then down past the Ortler (3,899 m) to Lake Como and Milan, and finally back east to Rove-

reto, where he arrived in early November to spend several thoroughly pleasant weeks.

Working on his commission there, Gurk was increasingly possessed by one idea: from Venice he could reach the Near East, where an Austrian fleet had recently fought so gloriously off Beirut. There he could paint a panorama and bring it home to exhibit in Vienna, possibly even building a warship in the Prater. Gurk approached Prince Metternich and even the emperor himself, received permission immediately, and set out on what was to be his last journey.

His appalling experiences on that stormy sea voyage would fill a chapter of their own. Eventually he reached Beirut and began painting busily; he went on to Sidon and the country around it, and finally seized an opportunity to go down to Jerusalem to visit the Holy Places.

There Gurk fell ill, and after three weeks of being nursed in the Terra Santa Monastery, he died. In his will, which he had deposited in Vienna and which was faithfully executed, Gurk left all his money to help the indigent sick. Yet despite this generosity and a moving obituary, Eduard Gurk was soon forgotten; he was forgotten as an artist too, and has—quite unjustifiably—remained so to this day.

## Journey to the Crimea, 1837

When, in a letter of June 19, 1837, Emperor Ferdinand instructed his uncle Archduke John to accept the invitation of the czar of Russia on his behalf and to attend the military maneuvers in Voznesensk as his representative, he paved the way for events of enormous political importance: preparations for an alliance with Russia and assurances of political aid in Greece. The return journey was to be effected by ship from the Crimea to Constantinople and then via Greece to Trieste. Elaborate preparations were put in hand. Twenty-seven officers were chosen from the different branches of the armed forces and from its most famous regiments for the military delegation. They included, with the rank of captain, Baron Bianchi and Baron Jellačič, Count Leiningen, Count Draskovich, Count Neipperg, Count Pongràtz, Count Colloredo, Count Festetics, and Count Wrbna, as well as the prince of Liechtenstein, who was a colonel. The military delegation was headed by Lieutenant General Prince Windischgrätz and a balanced selection of the elite of the monarchy and, above all, of the different nations that composed it.

For the overland journey via Galicia, a plan of march, a cavalcade commensurate with the size and power of the empire, was organized down to the last detail. A hundred fresh horses were waiting at each staging point, together with local guides, escorts, and billeting officers to ensure that the emperor's representative received all the honors due to the emperor himself and that proper respect was generated among his politically indispensable allies.

101   Carl Schindler. *On the Dance Floor.* 1840

Carl Schindler. *Man in Frock Coat and Top Hat.* c. 1840. Watercolor over pencil. Sammlungen des Regierenden Fürsten von Liechtenstein, Vaduz Castle, Vaduz (6477).

military subjects: for example, from the lives of craftsmen, or of country folk, or studies of curious types of people encountered in the city.

Two works in particular come to mind: the effervescent watercolor of a boisterous wedding party bowling along in a cart,[26] and the one depicting a Styrian dance,[27] a picture that superbly exploits all the advantages of free, spontaneous watercolor painting. The latter, Schindler's *On the Dance Floor,* invariably reminds one of the letter that Peter Fendi wrote on his trip to Salzburg in 1821:

> And when there is a church festival in the valley or some other occasion for music-making, dozens of girls and boys make the two or three-hour journey down from the highest Alps, leaning on their tall sticks; several times I saw them dance the famous Styrian dance; it is a real pleasure to see these strong, healthy people and the delight and merriment with which they spend their days.... I was quite alarmed when she [a powerful peasant lass whom he has just described at length] started to dance the whirling Styrian dance in her short skirts, a dance that lasts for at least an hour. Skirts flew up above the knee and frequently even higher as the dance pursued its alarming course, performed with such frenzy as to make me fear at every moment that the building would collapse about our ears....[28]

When Carl Schindler died on August 22, 1842, at the age of only twenty, he was universally mourned. Obituaries, tributes, and funerary odes all swore that Viennese art had lost—but would never forget—one of its most valued figures, a man who had been distinguished by so many qualities, "by talent, trustworthiness, a passionate love of art, and a modesty rare in our day, a jewel among our young artists."[29]

What they could not know was that, with Carl Schindler's death and with that of Fendi shortly afterward, a whole glorious era of Austrian art had come to an end. Symptomatic of this was the fact that, from the day of his teacher's death, Albert, the other Schindler in the group, completely abandoned the Old Viennese style of genre painting.

DAFFINGER'S WATERCOLORS OF FLOWERS

On November 7, 1850, the Ministry of Education and Religious Affairs approved a special purchase:[30] 6,000 gulden were set aside to buy a portfolio of 415 watercolors from the estate of Moritz Michael Daffinger. The move was in response to a request from the Academy, which had said it was concerned "to acquire this intellectually and artistically edifying creation of Daffinger's in its entirety for the Academy library, the sooner the better...."[31] The ministry's action duly ensured that one of the greatest treasures of Austrian watercolor art was preserved for posterity, complete and in excellent condition.

aration for this commission. It is interesting to note how a generation that had grown up in peacetime suddenly began to idealize the events of the war.

In 1837, as we have seen, Schindler and Treml went to study with Fendi.[25] Their new teacher lost no time in parading the achievements of his young pupils before his own patrons, both in the imperial family and among the high nobility. Academy exhibitions, too—notably that of 1839—positively catapulted Carl Schindler to fame. The result was an astonishing quantity of drawings, sketches, watercolors, and oil paintings by his hand—for the most part works of supreme artistic mastery. Carl Schindler also produced major works on non-

102   Moritz Michael Daffinger. *Orchid.* c. 1840

Moritz Michael Daffinger. *European Cyclamen.* c. 1840. Watercolor. Akademie der bildenden Künste: Kupferstich-kabinett, Vienna (7.628).

A few weeks before that action was taken, the Academy had been informed by Education Minister Count Leo Thun-Hohenstein that the artist's widow Marie Daffinger was "probably prepared to sell the collection of flower portraits, consisting of 415 matchless portrayals of plants from the Austrian (mostly Lower Austrian) flora, for 6,000 gulden."[32]

Two distinguished professors and artists (Leopold Kupelwieser and J. von Führich) were immediately asked to give an opinion. Their verdict was extremely positive. In fact, Führich's telling words have been preserved: "Daffinger's flowers seem, in their perfection, to lie somewhere beyond the sphere of mere art. It is through that mysterious rapport with which the created world, both in its individual manifestations and as a whole, calls to mankind and to the human heart that these reconstructions of nature are raised to a pitch of perfection to be sought, surely, no longer in the sphere of artistic skill but in a mystical relationship—of which the artist may be unaware—between himself and the area of nature that he portrays."[33]

Once acquired by the Academy, Daffinger's watercolors of flowers were never exposed to wear as teaching aids but were carefully preserved as a special treasure and held in the highest esteem.[34]

When the Austrian novelist Adalbert Stifter had his portrait painted by Daffinger in 1846,[35] he wrote to his publisher, "Daffinger is an astonishing master of watercolor, and his botanical paintings, which he was keen to show me, are quite possibly without equal anywhere in the world."[36] An accomplished artist himself, Stifter knew what he was talking about.

Later sources, too, are unanimous in their praise of these watercolors. When it comes to interpreting them, however, opinions differ. Fritz Novotny saw them as "an extreme form of the artistic-naturalist representation of nature,... a hybrid from a fringe area of art—half naive, half scientific illustration of supreme perfection."[37] His view was categorically rejected by Barbara Dossi in her dissertation, where she consigned Daffinger's watercolors of flowers to the sensitive imitation-of-nature school, stressing the "sensuality and deeply felt personal relationship with nature that went far beyond all rational considerations."[38] More recently, Ulrike Jenni found this interpetation as impossible to accept as Novotny's view.[39] For Jenni, the artist's scientific interest is what prevailed; his aim, she asserts, was absolute fidelity to nature, which he achieved through precise observation, technical mastery, and by treating each flower as an individual.

All these opinions may have their relevance, yet they do not go far enough. Jenni ends with a quotation from Goethe;[40] I should like to add what I consider a more pertinent quotation from the great thinker's *Some Thoughts on Drawing* (here on the subject of "Diderot's Essay on Painting"): "Art does not set out to emulate nature in its breadth and depth; it confines itself to the surface of natural phenomena; but it has its own depth and its own authority."[41] That is precisely what I miss in critical studies of this kind. Granted, Daffinger's watercolors of flowers are delicately executed reproductions of natural phenomena; they may even have been painted in pursuance of scientific goals. Their true importance, however, lies in the fact that, beyond that—a long way beyond it—they possess their own strength and carry their own message as works of art. Once again one thinks of Goethe urging, in a dedication to Johann Heinrich Merck, that attention be paid to even the least little object ("God grant you love of your slipper, respect for every gnarled potato . . . ."[42]), because a single meaning underlay everything; "Know the guise of each thing and sense how the mighty firmament holds the whole earth together . . . ."[43]

This is the level at which Daffinger's flowers constitute a climax (and mark the culmination of a very special relationship with nature, which can be said to have characterized this whole period). This approach was marked by humility in the face of the diversity and perfection of the created world, which the men of this period contrived to approach with all their skills, both cognitive and intuitive—that is to say, with science as well as with art, with knowledge (use of the tools of classification) and also with feeling (sensitivity to beauty). In other words, these artists brought their whole being to bear on their work. Therein lies the true fulfillment of this era and its creations.[44] Only by recognizing just how far and how fully Daffinger's watercolors of flowers met and complied with these demands can we do justice to their mastery.

103   Moritz Michael Daffinger. *Stemless Primrose.* c. 1840

Moritz Michael Daffinger. *Pasque, or Easter Flower.* c. 1840. Watercolor. Akademie der bildenden Künste: Kupferstich-kabinett, Vienna (7.677).

However, academic controversy has concentrated far less on this aspect of Daffinger's achievement than on the problem of dating his paintings of flowers. Here too there is a clear need for some demythologizing. Let me recapitulate.

In 1858 Constant von Wurzbach stated that Daffinger had completely given up portrait painting after his daughter's death and painted only flowers, for his own satisfaction.[45] He no longer attempted to get commissions or to earn money; he had enough to live on and what was the point of amassing a fortune now? Henceforth all Daffinger's "portraits" were of flowers.

This sentimental picture of an emotionally shattered artist rejecting his fellow men and turning to nature permeates the subsequent literature, culminating in Emil Pirchan's 1943 version: "To deaden the searing anguish and ease the crushing, leaden burden of his grief, the stricken father fled the haunts of memory and the painful past and went out into the fields and forests around Vienna. He climbed the nearby hills; from them the emperor's capital—reclining against the vine-clad breasts of the hills, embraced by the silver ribbon of the Danube—was no more than a far-off dream, borne out of the shimmering distance on the wings of a blue haze . . . ."[46]

One can understand that a younger generation of art historians adopted a different approach. Ulrike Jenni revised the traditional view with some cool reasoning.[47] Obviously, she argues, the dates that actually appear on the paintings—the earliest is 1841, the latest 1846—had caused Novotny to place all the flower pictures within that five-year period. However, Novotny's thesis is untenable for various reasons. Firstly, only 5 of the 415 paintings are marked with a year. Secondly, several criteria are incompatible with Novotny's *terminus post quem*—the death of Mathilde in August, 1841. For example, there are spring-flowering plants dated 1841—that is, before the girl died—and there are watermarks on the paper that point to very much earlier dates of execution. According to Jenni, Daffinger was already painting flowers in the 1830s; and his successively increasing levels of technical and artistic expertise also appear to confirm this.

Though that may be true, it is not particularly relevant. The artist is known to have been a keen botanist, to have studied botany intensively over a long period (as intensively as he later studied Rembrandt's etchings), and to have cultivated the acquaintance of the most eminent scholars of the subject (Heinrich Reichardt, August Neilreich, Count Johann Zichy). It seems thoroughly likely that he also painted flowers over an extended period, just as he collected them.

What is beyond doubt, however, is that in the immediate aftermath of the death of his beloved child, Daffinger behaved as if he had gone out of his mind.[48] In the years following their tragic loss, he and his wife adopted a very different life-style. They began to take long, rambling walks in search of rare and beautiful flowers. They fell into a very withdrawn, steady, contemplative pattern of existence. A well-known etching, *Woman Seated Beneath a Tree*,[49] apparently depicts Daffinger's wife Marie and illustrates this new situation. This naturally also gave the artist the opportunity to have fur-lined clothes and boots made to his specifications for his wife to keep her warm during the long hours she spent out in the open while he was working.[50]

Just how much Mathilde's death had tempered Daffinger's hitherto coarse and violent nature became clear when the dramatic events of the Revolution of 1848 left him quite unmoved, in spite of the fact that, from his former clashes with the Austrian police state, one might well have expected some sort of revolutionary outburst. Nor was Daffinger moved by anything until June, 1849, when—heralded by veritable prophecies of doom—a dangerous epidemic of Asian cholera reached Vienna. The court barricaded itself inside Schönbrunn Palace, and anyone who could left the city in a hurry. Daffinger, panicking, took refuge in the country house of a friendly Hungarian magnate. Not until the beginning of August, when news reached him that the plague was over in Vienna, did the timorous artist return. As he was celebrating his homecoming in Lichtental (the suburb

Moritz Michael Daffinger. *Woman Seated Beneath a Tree* (Marie Daffinger?). c. 1845. Etching. Graphische Sammlung Albertina, Vienna (Ö.K. XIX, fol. 7, no. b).

of his birth), carousing with friends until the early hours, the dreaded disease struck Daffinger down. He collapsed in great pain on his way home and was carried unconscious from St. Stephan's Square to his apartment in the Rauhensteingasse, where after three days of agony, he died on August 22, 1849.

With Daffinger's passing, recorded in immortal words by his friend Franz Grillparzer, Viennese art lost one of its greatest geniuses. Since Daffinger's death coincided with a time of unparalleled political, social, and economic upheaval, a whole era can be said to have passed away with him.

With touching loyalty Marie Daffinger administered her late husband's valuable estate, arranging immediately for his chief work—the watercolors of flowers—to pass safely into the possession of the state, thus insuring that this important body of paintings stayed together. (The remainder of the artist's estate was disposed of by later heirs, after the First World War. It was sold by auction,[51] and was scattered all over the world.)

Marie remarried after six years, and her union with the retired Colonel Josef von Turszky provided a harmonious and happy conclusion to her life. She died in 1880 at the age of seventy-two, having survived Daffinger by thirty-two years.

## THE GOLDEN 1840S

In the 1840s, Austrian watercolor painting had reached its zenith. This was an astonishing period in which a host of artists in a wide variety of fields all played their part. Unfortunately it was brought to an abrupt and premature end by the events of the Revolution of 1848. In this period the variety of watercolors is the most astonishing aspect.

The arts are rightly said to constitute a mirror of their time, giving expression through their content and through the forms they adopt to the totality of the period in which they were created. The perceptions encoded in paintings, for example, undoubtedly reflect the joys and fears, the self-awareness and general outlook of a particular moment in history. Each work represents the distilled experience of an individual who is, at the same time, an integral part of an environment. A work of art does not exist in a vacuum, and the Spanish philosopher José Ortega y Gasset (1883–1955) warned that "the foolish tradition that lifts art into some kind of… extravital sphere must be demolished resolutely."[52] Perhaps the Austrian art of the 1840s can issue a caveat here, suggesting that one should beware of adopting such a view too lightly or simplistically.

There can be no doubt; this was an unhappy period. Politically it was unhappy because of the weakness of the government, due to the sick emperor's incapacity and to Metternich's age and isolation. Economically, the structural problems arising out of the spread of mechanization and industrialization were aggravated by poor harvests and by soaring prices. Socially, poverty and unemployment went hand in hand with a wild, unscrupulous search for profit. To make matters worse, there were ethnic and national problems throughout the multinational Austrian Empire, lingering effects of the later Enlightenment and Josephinism, religious and interdenominational tensions, a growing "Greater Germany" movement, seething student unrest, and rigid class barriers surrounding the nobility and the bourgeoisie. This all added up to a period of appalling stresses and gloomy prospects. Yet in spite of all external events and circumstances, artists in Vienna created works of beauty, perfection, and deep inner harmony unequaled either before or since.

This shows that the real truth about a period does not stem chiefly from the sorts of thing people usually look at—political circumstances, economic conditions, nationalist agitation, social discontent. It stems from far deeper processes, such as the way a particular generation looks at nature, the way it sees itself as a part of creation, what it takes to be the point of human life, individually and communally, what shapes its basic ethical and moral stance, and what dictates its need for beauty. Art tells us about all these things, and that most sensitive branch of art—watercolor painting—tells us most of all.

Precisely in watercolor painting a climax was now reached, for this spontaneous means of capturing and

169

preserving fugitive existence had become a means of discovery: the discovery of the moment (*Augenblick* in German, literally, "eye-glance"), the recognition that true reality is an entity that cannot be apprehended simply as a juxtaposition of tangible details. Perception of the intangible element in the real world had now become a goal. Watercolor painting was no longer used for producing mere sketches or preliminary studies for another work of art; it produced works of art in its own right, having attained its special status as a "climax in the ideal that encompasses the categories of life and art, material and form...," so convincingly spoken of by Bruno Grimschitz.[53] The postwar generation of the aspiring middle class, which had begun by mastering reality, was now at the stage of spiritualizing it.

An enormous number of watercolorists were at work in a bewildering variety of fields. A brief summary of the seven main fields must suffice here:

1) The most important field for watercolor was *landscape painting*. Two distinct tendencies apparently coincided with the split between Naturalism and Ideal art in Biedermeier painting. The first tendency was interested simply in nature, in examining and experiencing the sheer variety of the created world from wooded landscapes with animals to romantically conceived buildings such as mills and mountain huts. The second tendency sought out the special beauties of quite specific outstanding locations: Salzburg, the Lake of Traun, the Grossglockner massif, Hallstatt, and so on. Initially such beauties were found in the domestic Alpine landscape, but soon artists turned increasingly to Italy, the sea, picturesque harbors, classical sites such as Rome and Paestum, cathedrals and colorful marketplaces. Around 1840 Dalmatia was added to the list, and such places as Dubrovnik and Kotor inspired some particularly fine works.

2) To be distinguished from landscape painting, despite a certain amount of overlap, is the *watercolor "veduta"*. Here the subject is neither open country nor an outstanding view—a panorama of Vienna, for example—but a particular piece of architecture, be it St. Peter's in Rome or, in Vienna, St. Stephen's Cathedral, the Belvedere Palace, or the Hofburg. Views of lesser palaces, country houses, and middle-class town houses were increasingly added to these; they were privately commissioned by their proud owners. As a result, this group reflects the vital consciousness of the age in a very special way.

3) So, to an even greater extent, does the next group: *watercolors of interiors*. This was a generation that believed in cultivated living, and the many portrayals of its fine furniture, display cabinets, chandeliers, and decorative art provide an incomparable picture of Viennese life during the period.

4) The vigorous directness of watercolor painting in terms of both color and drawing made it a favorite medium for *pictorial reports* of special events, as well as of everyday life: coronations, state visits, parades, church festivals, special occurrences in nature, markets, street scenes, and regional costumes. Such paintings often served as working drawings for the lithographic reproductions that were so popular at the time.

5) One of the chief functions of art in almost every age has been *portraiture*. Men have always sought to capture and preserve the fleeting image of a member of the family, a woman they admired—using art to combat the inexorable process of decay. Watercolor could do this both on folio paper (to which its free technique particularly lent itself) and in small-format miniatures painted on ivory. The latter, especially, came to typify the Biedermeier years. It was also obvious that, given the merry, often exuberant mood of the era (and the many odd types of people encountered in a large city), watercolor painting would find an additional outlet in caricature.

However, in 1839, something had happened that, without exaggeration, changed the world. An invention was made public in Paris, whereby pictures could be recorded mechanically by means of a lens playing on a light-sensitive plate in something called a *camera obscura*. "Daguerreotypy" was taken up everywhere (particularly in Vienna, as a result of the personal intervention of Prince Metternich[54]) and developed further.

Portraiture was the first field of art to feel the effects. From this historic moment on, reality and art began to part company. Those whose aim was to apprehend the visible world believed that, with the aid of an "objective"—as the lens significantly came to be called (French *objectif*, German *Objektiv*)— they could now do this perfectly, without any distortion. Others attributed to the subjective artist, who now increasingly distanced himself from mere representation, a capacity for revealing pure truth.

Hitherto a relative unity had prevailed. People had felt that the artist's task was to represent and, at the same time, interpret the visible world—to represent it as it appeared to his eye, to interpret it as his perception of the real world presented itself to his inner eye—as his total experience moved him to blend knowledge and emotion into a whole. That was held to be how artists were able to open other people's eyes for them, revealing deeper meanings. Artists felt they had the ability to portray nature in such a way that it could be experienced through them—they felt they had a particular flair for expressing it. Now, however, a parting of the ways was to occur.

The shock provoked by the invention of "light-drawing" (photography) may never have found clearer expression than in the jubilant outburst that appeared in the columns of the *Wiener Zeitung* on September 30, 1839, under the title "The Austrian Spectator." The writer crowed, "At this point the draftsman must lay down his stylus and the engraver his burin, frankly admitting that he cannot do, nor will he ever be able to do as well...."[55] Fortunately, that was not at all the way things turned out.

6) Even scientific tasks continued to be assigned to painting, as witness the comprehensive body of work that Leopold Stoll, a flower painter of Dutch extraction,

104   Josef Höger. *The Radhausberg, near Gastein.* 1831
105   Thomas Ender. *View of Clam Castle.* c. 1835

Franz Xaver Petter. *Leaves of a Thistle.* c. 1835. Watercolor and gouache. Graphische Sammlung Albertina, Vienna (34.900).

produced in response to an imperial commission between 1834 and 1869.[56] Most *flower painting* in Vienna was done in connection with the famous Royal-Imperial Porcelain Factory, with the Academy providing the training and indeed turning out some splendid artists. But the finest flower paintings in watercolor—the work of Jakob Alt, for example, or of Moritz Michael Daffinger—went far beyond this. Few pursuits held a greater appeal for Biedermeier Vienna than this kind of immersion in the quiet beauty of nature.

7) One of the principal fields in which watercolor painting enjoyed a heyday in the 1840s was *genre painting*, the bourgeois portrayal of customs and manners. Realistic representation left limited scope for the exercise of artistic imagination; here it was able to unfold itself lavishly. A broad range of subject matter was tapped. Military scenes and scenes from the lives of ordinary people sought—sometimes entertainingly, sometimes in a thought-provoking manner—to bring out virtues or to elicit sympathy. Artists found material for all this. Two areas were avoided, however: the pathetic and the banal. Heroism, too, was kept in proportion—even in Carl Schindler's portrayals of past battles—and "history" was purely a peg on which to hang an incident, never an end in itself.

As long as this was so, the "genre piece" retained its artistic status. Precisely in this area, however, decline set in rapidly. According to Bruno Grimschitz, the "bank-ruptcy of bourgeois realism" became most obvious in the field of genre painting, and this happened when "a shallow, vacuous naivety, making use of unproblematical superficiality, contented itself with [portraying] the most trivial everyday sensations."[57]

We have seen something of how many and varied were the processes that presided over the passing of this complex era, an era as peaceful as it was full of tension, as fertile as it was constrained—in short, a fascinating era that produced some of the loveliest art in the world. Ultimately, what was involved in its dramatic end was a mysterious conjunction of historical and artistic events. The year 1848 had arrived for one and all.

Let us turn our attention to the principal artists active during the 1840s. Not all of them were blessed with success, neither did they all have access to wealthy patrons and generous clients. Many of them, in fact, experienced shocking poverty and hardship. Nevertheless, the number of collectors had certainly increased, and watercolors had become collectable.

They were much in demand at the imperial court, where Emperor Ferdinand went on expanding his peep-show series, Archduchess Sophie patronized Fendi and his circle, and Archduke John continued to keep his staff of painters busy. Watercolors were sought after by other royal families (one thinks immediately of Alois II of Liechtenstein, who employed Höger, above all), and they were now being bought by a new clientele, the wealthy bourgeoisie. The collections of such middle-class patrons as the textile manufacturer Rudolf Arthaber, the glass manufacturer Ludwig Lobmeyr, the art dealer Georg Plach, or Friedrich Jakob Gsell, a man of independent means, must have been among the finest in Vienna.

Perhaps this survey should begin with an artist who was something of an outsider, though one who deserves rather special attention. Friedrich Loos was born in Graz and trained in the landscape class at the Vienna Academy under Rebell and Mössmer. He also studied with the Viennese artist Josef Fischer (1769–1822) before moving to Salzburg in 1826. Back in Vienna between 1835 and 1840, Loos painted watercolors that occupy a unique place in the history of the medium. Loos took his free, relaxed technique considerably further than many of his contemporaries; it has even been said that his vision anticipated that of the Impressionists. The remark is of no more than superficial relevance, however, for the optical desubstantiation that took place in the visual arts in these years was based on quite different premises than the intellectual theorizing of the later French school.

Friedrich Loos. *A Corner of the Prater.* 1846. Watercolor. Graphische Sammlung Albertina, Vienna (28.432).

Josef Höger. *Calvary near Zell am See.* 1835. Watercolor over pencil. Private collection, Munich.

106   Johann Fischbach. *View of Salzburg with the Kapuzinerberg.* 1840

107  Franz Barbarini. *View of Salzburg from the Kapuzinerberg.* c. 1840

Andreas Staub. *Portrait of a Lady.* c. 1835. Watercolor. Private collection.

Marie Krafft. *Portrait of Lotte Krafft, née Müller.* 1834. Watercolor. Graphische Sammlung Albertina, Vienna (35.403).

out an income by teaching drawing at the Theresianum. After many adversities, Kriehuber, one of the most successful artists of the Pre-March period, eventually died a pauper in 1876.

In addition to Kriehuber, a number of other highly qualified portraitists deserve mention here. Two who were very active in the 1840s were Friedrich Lieder (1780–1859) and Franz Eybl (1806–80). The latter became curator of the Imperial Art Gallery in 1853. Others were Leopold Fischer, whose watercolors and miniatures were widely imitated, and Marie Krafft, daughter of the artist Johann Peter Krafft. She was a pupil of Thomas Ender but abandoned her artistic career in 1840 when she married a bank officer named Franz Troll, who was the founder of a dynasty of public servants.

Other artists did not survive into the 1840s. Andreas Staub, who like Kriehuber devoted himself largely to portrait lithography and also painted some brilliant watercolors, committed suicide at the age of thirty-two. Josef Eduard Teltscher met with a fatal accident on a visit to Greece. The accident happened on July 7, 1837. On November 1 of the same year, Archduke John described in his diary, "[We were driving out near Athens] through a cheerless region, leaving on our right the high ground of the Phalerius, on a ledge of which the painter Teltscher lies buried. He had long resided in Gratz [the old spelling for Graz], where he was univer-

Joseph Eduard Teltscher. *Dr. Bachler, Colonel of the Graz Civic Guard, in Front of the Old City Hall.* 1835. Watercolor and pencil. Historisches Museum der Stadt Wien, Vienna (133.942/12).

Josef Danhauser. *Portrait of a Young Woman in a Yellow Poke Bonnet.* c. 1830. Watercolor with traces of pencil. Graphische Sammlung Albertina, Vienna (26.704).

Josef Danhauser. *Study for the Painting "Poetic Love."* Before 1838. Pencil with watercolor. Graphische Sammlung Albertina, Vienna (25.120).

sally liked and where I made his acquaintance. He and some fellow countrymen were on a visit to his friend [Count] Prokesch[-Osten]. While they were all swimming here one day, he was overcome by cramp and drowned."[72] Teltscher, a native of Prague, had come to Vienna at an early age. There his wit and sensitivity had soon made him one of the best-loved painters in the circle of friends that formed round Franz Schubert. From 1829 to 1832, Teltscher had been based in Graz, where he painted many delightful pictures.[73]

Apart from the circle of Peter Fendi and his pupils and Ferdinand Georg Waldmüller, the most important artist to find his artistic vocation in genre painting was Josef Danhauser.[74] (His style of genre painting was also derived from Johann Peter Krafft.) As with Waldmüller, watercolor occupied only a small place in Danhauser's oeuvre. Yet he did produce watercolor paintings that were delightfully expressive of his day, not only in his early, Biedermeier period but also in his second creative period after 1836. That year Danhauser took up painting again after an interruption caused by his father's death (1830; he had had to take over the running of the family furniture business. In the process, he became one of the principal authors of the Viennese style of furniture.)

Danhauser's 1838 painting *Poetic Love,*[75] the first genre picture to be given neither a contemporary bourgeois setting nor a military setting (which Danhauser never employed), was set as a historical scene, a moving "costume" drama of destiny; the painting was first conceived in watercolor. This procedure was the exception with Danhauser, however, who painted only a few watercolor studies; he was a draftsman. As Veronika Birke noted, "Line, from the outset, was more important to him than color."[76]

Mathias Ranftl was a friend of Josef Danhauser (they were exactly the same age), and like the latter he specialized in genre painting. However, Ranftl painted very different subjects from Danhauser's and used an entirely different technique. Ranftl sought to capture his subjects lightly and freely in studies executed in swift brushstrokes, at which few painters were more skilled. His earthy portrayals repeatedly featured his own milieu—a saloonkeeper's family in the Favoriten district of Vienna—despite the fact that Ranftl was widely traveled and had visited Moscow and St. Petersburg in 1826–7, and London and Paris in 1836.

The contemporary derision of his work was inappropriate—a well-known jibe termed him the "Raphael of dogs" *(Hunde-Raffael),* and dogs do indeed play a prominent part in his work—but Mathias Ranftl's contribution to Viennese genre painting in the 1840s was actually of enormous importance.

In conclusion, if this vibrant decade is passed in review once again, with all its enormous variety of styles and personalities, there is really only one thing to be said. Only the work of a single artist—the young Rudolf Alt—managed to surpass, in every respect, all that was created during the 1840s in terms of watercolor

117   Leander Russ. *Allegory of Emperor Ferdinand I's Reign.* 1843

118   Leander Russ. *Emperor Ferdinand I Opening the Road over the Semmering Pass.* 1842

119   Leander Russ. *The Unveiling of the Emperor Francis Monument in Graz.* 1842
120   Leander Russ. *Emperor Ferdinand I Visiting the Schlossberg in Graz.* 1842

art. Beset by appalling adversities, a constant prey to depression and anxiety, Alt had pushed on alone, painting incessantly; he was always searching for an ideal, desperately hoping, and then rejecting everything again because he considered it inadequate. At this point, however, Rudolf Alt was not even known, let alone recognized. Complex and varied though the rest of this story is, as I trace the further development of watercolor painting in Austria, it is virtually, in its entirety, the story of Rudolf Alt.

## THE PRE-MARCH PHENOMENON

While painting at the Villa Lagarina, Eduard Gurk had been overjoyed to receive the emperor's blessing for his projected journey to Syria. "In the interest of art" were the actual words used in the permit—and reportedly they were the emperor's own. Gurk's letter of December 8, 1840, communicates his enthusiasm: "What I dared dream of only as a modest idea is now fulfilling all my desires in becoming the most beautiful reality. I see in my mind's eye so many advantages from its inherent interest, that I can only pray to God to strengthen my talent that my efforts may be worthy of my exalted task."[77]

Gurk's last letter, written from Beirut on March 16, 1841, ends with the last of the artist's words that have come down to us: "I take the liberty of laying at the feet of His Majesty, my most gracious Lord and Emperor, Her Majesty the Empress, and all the members of the imperial family, this expression of my most humble reverence and gratitude; and I further permit myself to beg my exalted patron, to whom my letters are addressed, to continue his gracious benevolence . . . ."[78] Under the circumstances, this patron can only have been Prince Metternich himself.

However, the era that came to bear Metternich's name was drawing to a close. Ineluctably, the times were changing. The prince was now an old man and politically impotent. The reins of power had long since slipped from his grasp. Franz Grillparzer had said of him back in 1839, "If not dead, he is certainly no longer alive."[79] And, in 1842, the same writer referred to the present "that would do much and can accomplish little."[80] Nor was Grillparzer alone in his view. In *Ein Jahr meines Lebens (A Year of my Life)*, Count Alexander von Hübner recalls:[81]

It was a sorry time. A sick man on the throne with, beside him, two old men—one of them, albeit in full possession of his faculties, now wholly devoid of influence; the new spirit that Francis I had fought with every weapon starting to infiltrate the higher levels of the administration; power increasingly falling into the hands of small men—into the hands, that is to say, of a bureaucracy that, while still honorable and upright, was without prestige, judgment, or direction and was already more or less converted to the ideas it behoved it to combat. Though distant thunder heralded the approach of the storm, there was no one who might have guided the perplexed along the right track, or calmed and given encouragement to the dejected. No word that spoke to the heart, that addressed the nation's nobler instincts, its more exalted feelings. Nothing but silence and immobility.[82]

Karl Gutzkow, a traveler from Berlin who visited Vienna in 1845, began his *Wiener Eindrücke (Viennese Impressions)* in a poetic vein– "The city is beautiful, delightful, picturesquely embraced by an arm of the Danube..."; he concluded them with the terse observation, "Times have changed and so have people."[83]

The change was by no means peculiar to Vienna; it was affecting the whole of Europe. The Machine Age had set in train the Industrial Revolution, but Vienna had done little about the consequences.

As early as 1810 it was reckoned that no fewer than 27,000 of the city's inhabitants belonged to the rootless proletariat. From then on things went rapidly from bad to worse. As textile and paper mills, tanneries, and glassworks grew up around Vienna, so did the attendant social problems. Aggravated by the arrival of the chemical industry and sugar and machine-tool factories, those problems began to spiral out of control—the more so since, during the 1840s, a growing sense of insecurity was spreading remorselessly behind the still brilliant facade of public life.

Caught in the vicious circle of entrepreneurial paralysis, stagnant markets, and falling capital investment (as convincingly portrayed by the historian Heinrich Srbik[84]), the economy slid inexorably into crisis. This, in turn, led to poverty and eventually to a mindless despair that one day, inevitably, broke out in social unrest.

Serious consequences started to become apparent in the early 1840s, aggravated by a disastrous harvest in 1842. Food shortages, unemployment, and inflation nourished the growing hatred of entrepreneurs and machines. And so things went on until 1848. Even the circumspect Archduke John noted in his diary: "While the world rushes on, we maintain our old, ponderous pace, displaying a doggedness that is leading us to ruin. I tell everyone so, until I am exhausted, but to no avail. I cannot get them out of their rut. I am at my wits' end. I shall go on shouting, begging, grousing, and bullying as long as I can still move. Things are bad. Poor Austria."[85] Those words were written on February 6, 1848, when the explosive Revolution of 1848 was only weeks away.

# VI  CHANGE AND REORGANIZATION

THE YEAR 1848

The population was in the grip of unrest and needed only a nudge to push it into actual violence. Events in France in February, 1848, acted like a spark to a powder keg. "The revolution in Paris has lightened the darkness of our situation like a thunderflash,"[1] Count Carl von Vitzthum wrote in his journal on March 5. "The petty bourgeoisie is in a state of open ferment. The most sinister rumors are circulating. There is widespread ill feeling, and my fear is that those in authority will fail to give it due recognition. The day before yesterday a mob gathered in the Graben under the windows of a Jewish banker who was giving a ball. The message was: there should be no dancing as long as the people have no meat. We can now expect with certainty to find ourselves wading through rivers of blood."

Students presented a petition making five demands: abolition of press censorship, academic freedom, religious equality, a voice in government for all classes, and public court proceedings, including trial by jury. In other words, the students took the lead politically.

It is a mistake to try to account for the events of March, 1848, purely in terms of social motivation. The revolution had many motives: political, cultural, and national as well as social. Underlying them all, however, was a far deeper question. Could Austria, as it was constituted at present, continue to justify its existence? Did Vienna have any right to go on seeing itself as the imperial capital, the hub of the Austrian Empire? The importance of the German-nationalist element must not be underestimated either, the body of opinion that aspired to unite all German peoples in a Greater Germany. The Revolution of 1848 in Vienna was not some kind of putsch by the urban proletariat; it was part of a trial of strength that extended to every corner of the monarchy.

In the summer of 1848, world opinion already thought that this multinational state had little chance to survive. Certain European states positively hoped it would go under. Nevertheless, Austria, Vienna, and the monarchy did survive the Revolution of 1848 by more than two generations. Therein lies the true historical significance of the following half-century of blooming development. The political role played by a multinational Austria at the heart of Europe set an ageless example to the rest of the world.

The German dramatist Friedrich Hebbel (1813–63) gave very clear expression to the intensely hopeful atmosphere of this time of upheaval. "This Austria is a little world in which the greater world rehearses," he wrote in a festival prologue 1862; "if balance reigns among us here, day is sure to break there too."[2] According to R. Kralik and H. Schlitter, writing in 1912, what Hebbel really meant was "that Austria with her many peoples is required, through arduous trials, to resolve the problems that shall one day redound to the benefit of a superior common organization of all the peoples of the earth."[3] Considering the state of the world today, more than two generations after the fall of the monarchy and more than a generation after the founding of the United Nations, Hebbel's euphoric words have a tragic ring.

The actual events of the Revolution of 1848 are quickly described. On March 18, following the submission of the students' petition, the man whom most people blamed for the present state of affairs, namely Metternich, resigned and fled into exile in England. Press freedom, a constitution, and the formation of an armed National Guard were all promised, and a delighted populace believed the revolution was over.

On April 25 the constitution was finally proclaimed. It was in complete conformity with liberal ideas and was given an enthusiastic reception—including a torchlight procession for the emperor. Encouraged, the radicals began to make their presence increasingly felt. They tightened up their organization and staged the first deliberately provocative incidents.

The parliament in Frankfort met on May 18 to elect a *Reichsverweser* (literally, imperial administrator). Archduke John of Austria was chosen by a total of 436 of 548 votes cast, "not because of, but in spite of, his being an imperial prince," as the president of the parliament, Baron Friedrich von Gagern, put it. It was the beginning of a most unhappy period politically and, for the archduke, personally.

Meanwhile, in Vienna ferment had risen to a climax. A radical Mobile Guard was formed from a splinter

Carl Goebel. *The Announcement of the Emperor's Concession to the Insurgents in Michael's Square in Vienna on May 15, 1848.* 1848. Pen and ink over pencil with wash. Historisches Museum der Stadt Wien, Vienna (20.218).

group of the National Guard. The students were too weak to resist the extremists.[4] As a result, on May 15 their so-called Storm Petition, backed by armed pressure, succeeded in forcing compliance with its wide-ranging demands. The emperor and the court fled to Innsbruck. Indeed, many prudent spirits quit Vienna at this point. They included the author Adalbert Stifter who, describing himself as a man of moderation and freedom, noted that "both, unfortunately, are now in jeopardy."[5]

Barricades were thrown up in the suburbs of Vienna (on May 26), street fighting broke out in Prague, and in Italy there were violent armed clashes. Field Marshal Count Joseph Radetzky finally resolved the military situation at Vicenza (his victory moved Johann Strauss the Elder to compose the "Radetzky March," first performed in August, 1848). Franz Grillparzer concluded his own reflections on the events with the quintessentially Austrian couplet: "Nor here nor there versed in extremes, I am a man of sense, it seems."[6]

In the visual arts this turbulent period produced virtually nothing of any quality. The countless lithographed or drawn situation reports are of immense value as historical documents,[7] but very few topical subjects attracted the attention of this period's artists, men such as Pettenkofen, Romako, Schönn, L'Allemand, and Goebel.

Far more typical, it seems to me, was the attitude of Rudolf Alt. Until March, 1848, Alt had never concerned himself with questions of politics,[8] not to mention revolutionary politics. When the revolution broke out, he first packed his wife and children off to his parents-in-law in Opava, some 200 kilometers northeast of Vienna, then he dutifully volunteered for the Civic Guard. His mother fled in the opposite direction—to her family home in Ybbsbach. Her letters from there implored Rudolf to let her know "how things are with our beloved Vienna, whether one can soon come home again, or what is yet in store for us."[9]

Alt's replies complained of having to do guard duty in Vienna, clean weapons, and take part in endless parades and flag dedications: "We fritter away our time with a whole host of such things. Tomorrow (Saturday), worst luck, it's my turn for sentry duty at the Red Tower Gate [Rotenturmtor]. And I should so much have liked to pay a visit to Klosterneuburg, to get out of the political rat race for once and really take my ease in the bosom of nature, which God has made so beautiful."[10]

Rudolf Alt was not born to man barricades. As events came to a head and an armed confrontation loomed, it all became too much for him. He and the young artist Ludwig Passini fled the city abruptly—"leaving the food on the table, untouched."[11] As they settled into temporary accommodation in the Lower Austrian town of Wilhelmsburg, some 50 kilometers west of Vienna, Alt began to paint superb tree studies glowing with the brilliant autumn colors of the nearby hardwood forests.

In October, heavy fighting broke out in Vienna, provoked by an incident at the Danube bridge to Tábor on the sixth of the month: troops marching out to quell the Hungarian uprisings were attacked by units of the National Guard. Further clashes followed all over the city. There was fighting at the barricades, and a furious mob stormed the Imperial Arsenal in the Renngasse. Another mob poured into the War Ministry in Am-Hof Square and brutally manhandled the minister, Count Theodor Baillet-Latour, before hanging him from a street lamp.

The situation had turned critical. Chaos and anarchy reigned, and military intervention began to look inevitable. The most radical agitators now took the lead on the revolutionary side. A writer, the former first lieutenant Wenzel Messenhauser became nominal chief of the revolutionary Mobile Guard units of the National Guard, while a Pole, Josef Bem (who had taken an active part in the Polish Revolution back in 1830), became its political leader. A deputation of Frankfort left-wingers —Robert Blum and Julius Fröbel—arrived in Vienna on October 17 and began actively to influence events.

Meanwhile Field Marshal Prince Alfred Windischgrätz was advancing on Vienna with a large army that had assembled in Bohemia. Count Josip Jellačić, ban (governor) of Croatia, had already arrived in the capital with his loyal troops. Eventually the city was hermetically sealed by imperial forces. The Hungarian relieving army, so anxiously awaited by the revolutionaries, was heavily defeated at Schwechat. Vienna was bombarded and eventually—after the heavily fortified Castle Gate (Burgtor) had been blown up—taken by storm. The revolutionary leaders were arrested, and several of them, including Blum and Messenhauser, were court-martialed and shot.

The political consequences of this dramatic year, which ended with the abdication of the emperor, were unclear at first. Individual destinies were mangled beneath the wheels of the inexorably changing times.

Take the case of Thomas Ender, for example. The Academy had been in a state of great excitement since March. Its curator, Metternich, had disappeared; systematic teaching had virtually gone by the board, and the authority of the staff was clearly on the wane. In June Ender set out with his students on what, since 1830, had been the regulation annual field trip. Given the circumstances, they were not planning to go very far on this occacion. They took the train to Gloggnitz, then continued by horsedrawn wagon over the Semmering Pass, up the Mürz Valley to Mürzsteg, and into what is known as Dead Woman's Gorge.

The students complained that the trip was not spectacular enough for them and that it was too out-of-the-way; they had wanted to visit the Salzkammergut.

August von Pettenkofen. *The Refugees.* 1848. Watercolor and gouache. Kammersänger Anton Dermota Collection, Vienna.

Eventually they rejected any kind of discipline, were downright offensive to their professor (Ender said later in his statement that he "felt ashamed in front of the simple peasant folk"[12]), and demanded to be paid their travel allowance and given leave to continue on their own.

Ender tried to calm the situation by setting an example of diligence: "I woke them every morning and was the first to quit the house with my paintbox, and [I was] almost always the last one left working."[13] But it was no good. Other students passing through further poisoned the atmosphere. They shouted "You Philistines!" at the ones who remained tractable, until eventually these too became aggressive and started demanding their money on the grounds that "in a constitutional state, only the majority counts."[14]

Their behavior became increasingly provocative (Ender noted with dismay that they had even gone to bed in their dirty boots). "It becomes extremely difficult under such circumstances," his formal complaint concluded, "for a professor to maintain the standing of the Academy and of himself."[15] If he expected justice, however, Ender was in for a disappointment. No one dared agree with him, for that would have meant calling the students to account. Neither his patron Prince Metternich, nor Archduke John was currently in any position to help him, nor could Ender expect support from an Academy badly in need of reform. In the end—and his clash with the artist Franz Steinfeld, another professor at the Academy may have been a contributory factor here—Ender was forced to resign from his post at the Academy.

At this crucial juncture in his career Ender not unnaturally hoped to be able to continue his commissions. He promptly dispatched a letter to Archduke John:

It was with the deepest regret that I learned on my arrival in the evening of July 31, that I was once again too late and might no longer have the great pleasure of seeing my kind master. My Academy course detained me in Neuberg and Mürzsteg with my students until last July. The moment I was free I hurried back to Vienna, but I was too late. The first thing I wanted to ask was whether it is Your Imperial Highness's command that the survey of the Tyrol be continued this year or whether Your Imperial Highness could make use of me somewhere else. For I feel my whole life's purpose to lie in fulfilling such commands. In the exalted position, so felicitous for all Germany, that Your Imperial Highness has now assumed [John had been elected *Reichsverweser*], where every minute is so precious, I do most urgently beg forgiveness for taking up valuable time with these lines . . . .[16]

Ender clearly had little idea of just how much the world had changed. The archduke did not have the time to reply immediately—actually it took years; not until July, 1851, did he write back to Ender to thank him and send him money.

The age of artistic commissions designed to capture the beauty of reality was at an end. It was, in fact, just as Count Vitzthum had written in his Viennese journal back in March, 1848, "All is quiet here. People are showing remarkable moderation . . . . The old Austria has perished. *Sic transit gloria mundi* . . . ."[17]

## THE YOUNG EMPEROR

When the revolution came to a head in October, 1848, the emperor and the court took refuge in the Moravian city of Kroměříž. There, the Constituent Diet met at the end of November, in the palace of the prince archbishop. On December 2, Ferdinand I abdicated in favor of his brother Francis Charles. The latter declined, however; so it was Ferdinand's eighteen-year-old nephew Francis Joseph who mounted the throne.

The problems facing the young emperor must have seemed insuperable. The capital was still in ferment, so that there could be no question of lifting the state of siege. The uprisings in Hungary were more violent than ever. The war in Italy was in full swing, with the European powers almost unanimously hostile to Austria. In Frankfort, the initiative was passing into the hands of the Lesser Germany party, which aspired to a Germany under Prussian leadership that would exclude Austria. Finally, when it became rather abruptly apparent that the liberal constitution of April 25, 1848, was quite unworkable, Emperor Francis Joseph was faced with the most difficult problem of all. Should the new path he must choose be federalist—as demanded by many circles, though this was rejected by liberals and German nationalists alike—or centralist, which Vienna welcomed,[18] but which was fiercely opposed by the nationalist circles among the remaining peoples of the monarchy?

The emperor decided in favor of centralization. However, in line with his motto *Viribus unitis* (with united strength) he wanted the government to place itself "at the head of the movement" in order "to unite all the territories and houses of the monarchy in a single great state."[19] There were two prerequisites for this: Hungary and Italy must be defeated on the battlefield, and the imperial capital of Vienna, as the "emperor's city," must become a mighty metropolis.

Emperor Francis Joseph set about his many tasks with a combination of vigor and shrewd good sense. At first he was able to bring little more to them than a sympathetic personality, youthful vitality, and his proven personal courage and soldierly bearing. He was an outstandingly gifted youth (being endowed, moreover, with considerable artistic skills), and he was capable of making clear decisions. Furthermore, the impact of all his qualities was enormously enhanced by contrast with the almost movingly tragic figure of his uncle and predecessor.

The young emperor, however, elevated one quality to the status of a new ethos, and it was his guiding con-

121  Josef Kriehuber. *Emperor Francis Joseph I of Austria*. 1851

cept: "doing one's duty." The individual's obligation to the community, responsibility for others, and unyielding courage in the face of all vicissitudes were made into an ideal to replace the old indifference of the affluent, the Biedermeier lack of involvement. For more than a generation, all that was best about Austria lived and acted in obedience to, and in accordance with, that principle.

But initially things were more than problematical. The military balance in Italy soon tipped in favor of the Austrian army, and the Hungarian uprisings were quickly crushed. Yet even this process met with objections, as did the emperor's decision to make centralized Absolutism the strong foundationstone of the state. Moreover, Catholicism began to assume an increasingly dominant position, conferring on the Hapsburg dynasty legitimate continuity by virtue of its historical mission. This, in turn, guaranteed a similarly unassailable position to the nobility, together with all the privileges of a class apart. National feelings, liberalism, and the secular principles of Josephinism were all offended by this, and *Deutschtum* ("Germanness") felt itself betrayed. Last but not least, in the light of the unchecked economic expansion and pursuit of gain that now gripped Vienna in a way no one had expected or foreseen, the continued poverty and sullen, defenseless intransigeance of the working class began to take on an increasingly hopeless aspect.

The scenes of indescribable rejoicing that accompanied Emperor Francis Joseph I's entry into Vienna in May, 1849, could not conceal the true nature of the situation for long. A man who quickly assumed a key role in that situation was the very capable Prince Felix zu Schwarzenberg (1800–52), a nephew of Prince Karl Philipp Schwarzenburg, the victor of Leipzig (the 1813 Battle of the Nations).

The younger Schwarzenberg's diplomatic career had been interrupted by a lengthy period of retirement in Brazil following an indiscreet love-affair in London. He had then commanded troops in Italy during the Revolution of 1848. Now, promoted to the rank of lieutenant general and decorated with the Order of Maria Theresa, the prince offered to form the young emperor's first government. Some of the fundamental ideas of Absolutism as well as a number of decisive domestic reforms stemmed from initiatives made by Schwarzenberg before death overtook him prematurely on April 5, 1852, in the middle of a meeting. (Kriehuber's portrait must have been painted very shortly before that date.)

Austria still did not seem to be embarked upon a particularly promising course, however. Then, in February, 1853, a young Hungarian fanatic tried to kill the emperor just outside Vienna's Schotten Gate. The assassin was thwarted by the courage and quick thinking of the emperor's escort. Nevertheless, strange as it may seem, the assassination attempt proved a kind of turning point. From that moment on, Emperor Francis Joseph placed even greater faith in the persuasive power of consensus. Retreating from the Neoabsolutist position, he flouted all military advice by lifting the state of siege in Vienna on August 31, 1853. He further ignored the opinion of his generals on the subject of the belt of fortifications surrounding the inner city.

Joseph Kriehuber. *Empress Elizabeth with her Children.* 1858. Watercolor. Graphische Sammlung Albertina, Vienna (34.670).

122   Josef Kriehuber. *Count Günther Stolberg in the Uniform of a Cavalry Captain.* 1850
123   Josef Kriehuber. *Field Marshal Prince Felix zu Schwarzenberg,* 1852

Alexander von Bensa. *The Imperial Family near Ischl.* Before 1870. Watercolor. Graphische Sammlung Albertina, Vienna (5.031).

What made these decisions even more remarkable was the fact that, since the reigns of Francis I and Joseph II, the army had enjoyed a new and very much more exalted status. Moreover, it appeared to have justified that status by its successes in the field. Despite major differences between the services and between individual regiments, the Austrian officer corps occupied a leading position in society and formed the bedrock of the state in every way. Take, for example, the case of Count Günther Stolberg (b. 1820), scion of a famous German family and the son of a man who had distinguished himself as an Austrian general in 1814. Stolberg was permitted to serve in one of the most fashionable of all the cavalry regiments, the Saxon Cuirassiers. He joined them as a lieutenant in 1842, was painted by Kriehuber as a captain in 1850, and retired with the rank of major in 1858. As a result, Stolberg belonged to the cream of Austrian high society.

Francis Joseph decided that Vienna's old walls, gates, bastions, and bridges should be torn down and the glacis and moats leveled to form a magnificent boulevard—the Ringstrasse—that would gird the ancient imperial capital in a broad sweep. His idea was to create a modern city, made safe from within by its own progress and prosperity. The splendor of Vienna's private and public buildings was supposed to reflect the power and greatness of the Austrian Empire.

The emperor gave Baron Alexander von Bach his basic instructions in a handwritten note on December 20, 1857. The note began: "It is my wish that the expansion of the inner city of Vienna and a suitable linking of the same to the suburbs be put in hand as soon as possible, due consideration being paid in the process to the regulation and beautification of my residence and imperial capital."[20]

It goes without saying that the emperor's decision generated a flood of commissions in the field of the visual arts. In fact, it ushered in an unprecedented cultural renaissance. Bruno Grimschitz was quite right to begin his account of Austrian painting in the second half of the nineteenth century by saying that 1857, not 1848, was the crucial year as far as the history of Austrian art is concerned.[21]

This is not the place to list in detail the imposing architectural monuments built at this time nor to go into the way in which the Ringstrasse reflected the glory of a major world power. Nor are we concerned here with the planning concepts that underpinned the whole scheme. Let us not forget, however, the astonishing achievement it represented—planning, financing, and erecting some 800 buildings in fewer than thirty years. Only a period of extraordinary economic and political progress and prosperity could have sustained the effort involved.

Moreover, after a great deal of careful historical research and artistic evaluation, it is now known that the Ringstrasse project was so successful largely due to the emperor himself. The project neither resulted in an undisciplined mishmash of individual ideas, nor did it peter out altogether, as similar projects in other major cities did; nor did it lead to a purely functional piece of stereotyped town planning. In fact, the Ringstrasse project produced a *Gesamtkunstwerk*, a grand synthesis of the fine arts. The emperor took personal charge of approving all layout plans and architects' designs. While respecting the freedom of the individuals concerned, he reserved all the important decisions to himself. This made it possible to blend the creative energies of the many different builders and architects into a coherent whole.

All this work also wrought far-reaching changes in the visual arts. Painting in particular abandoned quiet, contemplative searching, forgot its touching delight in the atmosphere and beauty of nature. The old (self-absorbed) artistic brooding was out. Painting now began to be employed to portray and decorate a fresh dimension: in a new subordination to architecture, it was concerned to enhance palaces and public buildings —the Court Opera House, imperial museums, the city hall, the parliament, the Burg Theater, the Votive Church, and the rest. In short, painting had become "larger and louder."[22] Art was now an integral part of the self-promotion of an essentially bourgeois world that existed within a thriving political system.

This was precisely the sort of art that watercolor was least capable of achieving. Indeed, after 1848 watercolor painting never again achieved prominence in the nineteenth century. It is significant that, of the 124 plates with which Bruno Grimschitz illustrated his account,[23] 116 reproduce oil paintings, 2 gouaches, and only 6 watercolors (three of those being by Rudolf Alt). The selection may have been subjective, but the ratio accurately reflects the situation. The artist's position in society had also changed completely. It would be wrong to generalize from the unique case of Hans Makart (1840–84). In terms of his influence on his time, in the almost regal social standing that he enjoyed, and in the enthusiasm aroused by his enormous history paintings, Makart was an exception. But the new status of artists did lead to an altered sense of their place in the community, and Francis Joseph accordingly set aside land in the Ringstrasse area for the erection of a *Künstlerhaus* (house of artists).

Begun in 1865, the building was inaugurated in 1870 by the emperor in person, with a huge exhibition, containing 1,152 works. The watercolors shown on this occasion were at a hopeless disadvantage from the outset, being completely overshadowed by huge oil paintings in powerful colors and opulent frames.

Watercolorists were still searchers, however; outsiders, perhaps. They were often lonely figures, less in tune with the prevailing taste but undoubtedly equipped with the finer sensitivity. Of course, some were soon sidetracked —the watercolorist jokers and the manufacturers of *vedute.*

The artistic foci of the medium remained landscapes and genre scenes. Here the historical change was most apparent. Contemporary philosophy of art encouraged this and reflected it, too. Hans Aurenhammer cited the great French critic Hippolyte Taine, who had postulated the influence of mood, context, and environmental circumstances in general on artistic form.[24] Artists no longer saw the landscape before their eyes as a complete and perfect creation, to be approached only through the most meticulous apprehension of every detail. They saw it as "absolute truth," as "nature repeatedly renewing itself in everlasting struggles, pointing to nothing beyond itself."[25]

Conflict was inevitable, for this new approach to nature soon found itself running counter to every view of nature cultivated and handed down by the Academy, however embellished with Alpine and genre scenes. What Adalbert Stifter had called "the reality of the real world"[26] was not to the taste of everyone.

August von Pettenkofen. *Gypsy Girl Carrying a Child in her Arms.* 1854. Watercolor. Sammlungen des Regierenden Fürsten von Liechtenstein, Vaduz Castle, Vaduz (1.724).

## THE DISCOVERY OF HUNGARY

The breadth of Hungary's puszta landscape with its shimmering sunlight, the life lived by its simple folk in picturesque farmhouses with heavy thatched roofs, fountains, and horses, presented a picture of peculiar charm and exotic beauty and atmosphere. The journey that August von Pettenkofen made to Hungary in 1851 initiated an artistic discovery. Yet none of the beauties mentioned above were involved, for Hungary and the discovery of Hungary meant something entirely different at first.

Hungary had always exerted a special fascination, of course: its people with their colorful costumes, attractive dances, and beautiful customs, its lovely young women; the elegance of its high society of proud magnates and distinguished ladies; its splendid soldiers. Indeed it must have been a thrilling sight to see the Hussars at the changing of the guard in Vienna or at imperial coronations in Bratislava, parading in their magnificent uniforms, resplendent on their highly trained horses. But none of these things were involved in this discovery of the country either.

The year 1848 had lent Hungary a new significance; in that year the country had rebelled against conservative Austria. The Hungarian people, believing themselves oppressed, had risen up in arms to demand their freedom. Eventually they had been crushed by a draconian army. The Hungarian uprising was a symbol: socially, the outcry of an oppressed people; nationally, a rebellion against a foreign master; ethically, a demand for freedom. Politically, the centralistic constitution of March 4, 1849, had rekindled the revolution. On April 14, a Hungarian Diet held in Debrecen had enthusiastically deposed the Hapsburgs and proclaimed Hungarian independence. The Honved (a volunteer nationalist army under Artúr Görgey) took the fortress of Buda; Lajos Kossuth entered the city, and the Diet reassembled. The Austrian government took these events as a pretext for calling upon Russia for military assistance—a move that was to arouse a great many emotions.

Pettenkofen's art had been through various transformations. He was the son of a Hungarian-born landowner who, having ruined himself by mismanagement, had set out to travel with his wife and child. Pettenkofen first visited Paris as a child. His father then purchased a small property in Austria in the Lavant Valley in eastern Carinthia, allegedly with the proceeds of a gambling win. When Pettenkofen's father died in May, 1834, he left nothing but debts (the property was lost).

In November of that year, Pettenkofen (whose name may formerly have been Pettenkofer or even Bettinghofer) entered the Vienna Academy. There he became a pupil of Kupelwieser, drawing from classical models and studying history painting. Later Pettenkofen was to sum up the conviction he acquired during this period as follows, "Academic instruction is the ruin of art."[27] Indeed, his true influences came from other sources. Chief among these was Franz Eybl, in terms both of his style of painting and of the instruction he gave Pettenkofen in lithographic technique. The watercolors of Pettenkofen's friend Carl Schindler, a man barely his senior yet already marked by death, also influenced the artist. At first Pettenkofen followed his friend's technique so closely that his own work was almost indistinguishable from Schindler's.

Pettenkofen interrupted his studies to become a soldier. He spent the years 1841–3 stationed in Padua as a regimental cadet in the Second Dragoons. There he became acquainted firsthand with the military ambience that Carl Schindler (who had died in the meantime, shortly after his twentieth birthday) had portrayed so vividly.

On his return to civilian life, Pettenkofen put his experience to good use. In 1847 the firm of Leykum printed and published a series of his lithographs, *The Royal-Imperial Austrian Army*. Pettekofen's skill in lithography, as evinced in this series, meant that he was thoroughly equipped to chronicle the stormy events of the Revolution of 1848 with topical immediacy. In doing so he followed French examples, giving his work a satiricial flavor and making very personal statements in the process: Metternich is ridiculed; Prussia figures as the guiding light of Germany, and Jesuits and Redemptorists are comprehensively lampooned.

Pettenkofen's close friends included Josef Borsos, a Hungarian painter working in Vienna. That may have been one reason why Pettenkofen took part, as a war artist, in the 1849 Austrian campaign against Hungary. The result was an outstanding series of lithographs based on some exceptionally spirited working drawings in watercolor.

Pettenkofen's experiences in Hungary and the impressions he gleaned there brought about a decisive change in his work. He saw the wretched plight of the refugees, witnessed the poverty of the gypsies, and came to appreciate their natural dignity. He was fascinated by their brownskinned girls, their young women and children, and the itinerant life-style of gypsy families.

As a result, Pettenkofen returned to this delightful world in October, 1851, and paid his first visit to the town of Szolnok on the River Tisza. It was the beginning of a special relationship that was to continue for decades. Here Pettenkofen discovered his true aim in life and evolved the specific conception of nature that his luminous, *plein-air* style of painting made possible. Here Pettenkofen found the subject matter that suited him in the very life of the people.[28]

Szolnok became a kind of Hungarian Barbizon. Pettenkofen—otherwise a shy, unsettled, and awkward person—brought his painter friends there to join him. One who deserves special mention was Johann Gualbert Raffalt (1836–65), another very talented artist who died tragically young.

In the following year—1852—Pettenkofen made the first of several visits to Paris to study what was happening in painting there. From that time on, it became clear that the achievement of this artist lay in his having outgrown a tradition that had long since strayed down false paths such as genre-type anecdotal painting, or deliberately imposing portraits. Yet Pettenkofen never abandoned objective statement nor gave up his link with the visible world in favor of purely atmospheric mood painting. In that respect he showed himself to be an artist in the true Austrian tradition. "Conversant with the best of the art of past and present and blessed with exquisite taste and a keen discernment, he himself formed the yardstick by which he measured himself and others. He may have learned from abroad, but he never renounced his Austrianness," wrote Pettenkofen's biographer Arpad Weixlgärtner.[29]

After the 1860s Pettenkofen spent more and more time in Italy, mainly in Venice. The subject matter of his later years increasingly reflected this. When Pettenkofen and his friend Leopold Carl Müller (1834–92) traveled south to Naples and Sicily in 1872, the former's bright watercolors, drenched in light, reached a personal climax that was also a climax for Austrian art as a whole.

Soon after that Pettenkofen changed his palette again; he started to use duller colors, densely applied, in

124   August von Pettenkofen. *Two Gypsy Boys.* c. 1865

powerful paintings of interiors of the poor for the most part—farm kitchens, artisans' parlors, cobblers' workshops, and forges. Pettenkofen had entered his last creative period.

The artist led a restless and unhappy life—a *Wanderleben*, as he called it himself.[30] Undoubtedly part of the reason for this was his lifelong emotional attachment to a married woman. As a consequence, he never found the sort of security for which he longed. Though a native of Vienna, Pettenkofen never felt at home there, writing from Venice on May 5, 1875:

> I am overcome by a deep despondency at having to work there [in Vienna] in order to acquire a simple home. This is now made worse by the moral and pecuniary circumstances currently obtaining there, the depressing influence of which is even harder to escape at close quarters. Consequently I have none of that reassuring awareness of having a home that meets my professional and emotional needs. And I lack the kind of assurance and contentment that my whole being needs so badly if I am to make successful use of what experience and knowledge I have assembled, so far as it lies within my abilities to do so.[31]

Weixlgärtner summed up his account of the artist's life and work in 1916 by stating that Pettenkofen's artistic credo (coloristic Naturalism) should be seen as representing one of the high points of Viennese painting. Between the death of Hans Makart in 1884 and Pettenkofen's death in 1889, the latter was the most important painter in Vienna. Not until Gustav Klimt, claimed Weixlgärtner, was there another painter of comparable stature. Pettenkofen was "no pioneer and no leader of a school," his biographer concluded, "but a mature, rounded personality of powerful distinction, in whom Austrian art has every reason to take pride."[32]

## THE QUEST FOR NEW SUBJECTS

Few things more sharply indicated the way times were changing than the striking shift in artists' subject matter. Ludwig Hevesi, writing in 1903, expressed the belief that the year 1848 had given "art its freedom, that is to say, its right to self-determination."[33] Had this been true in any lasting sense, there would have been no need, in 1898, to inscribe on the Secession Movement's headquarters Hevesi's own battle cry for the avant-garde: TO THE AGE ITS ART, TO ART ITS FREEDOM.

Perhaps it was rather that the new age and the rising generation had hit upon a different attitude to the world, and consequently to art. Be that as it may, something exerted an uncommonly powerful attraction on artists. It may well have been that acquisition of the second half of the century: a fresh outlook on the world, open to all that was new and exotic—something Hans Aurenhammer aptly outlined as a going beyond the "near distance."[34]

The Vienna Academy had clung to the principles of Biedermeier painting too long, ignoring the fact that for years the younger generation had already been making pilgrimages to Munich and Düsseldorf and was about to set its sights—with a vengeance—on Paris.

The tragedy of someone like the artist Ferdinand Georg Waldmüller (who took his vain and possibly overviolent campaign against the bastions of academicism to self-destructive lengths) is very clear. Waldmüller's concept, the "truth of nature"—which he understood as an "immediate, seemingly primitive naturalness of life"—eventually "led him, leaving aside certain sociocritical paintings with a more literary content, to render spontaneous situations of movement and life that call to mind the quickness of film, taking him to the very limits of representational art."[35]

Without Metternich to protect him, Waldmüller had been pensioned off in 1857 to punish him for his attacks on the way the Academy was being run. This was the Austrian artist who, more than any other in his day, already enjoyed a European reputation. He had participated successfully in the Exposition Universelle in Paris in 1855, sold everything at his exhibition in London in 1856, and been decorated by the king of Prussia in 1861. Yet, despite his rehabilitation by Emperor Francis Joseph in 1864, Waldmüller died in poverty a year later.

The new quest for the exotic was also an attempt to escape the stifling influence of official art during the Ringstrasse period (as the 1870s were termed), with its air of pathos and unreality. The new art ranged from the religious romanticism of Joseph von Führich through the "Roman form and Venetian color" of the Karl Rahl school[36] to the intoxicatingly sensual compositions of Hans Makart and the whole Neobaroque tendency. In that quest, watercolor—a medium that lent itself to experiment and to the discovery of alternatives—played a special part.

A typical example of an artist working in this new trend was Alois Schönn, who left the Vienna Academy at the age of twenty-four and went to Paris to train under Horace Vernet (1789–1863). From there Schönn traveled widely in search of subjects to paint, visiting Africa as early as 1851. His experience of the light there was of fundamental importance to his work, as happened with so many artists. In fact, the light in Africa became the formative force behind Schönn's whole oeuvre and was a key element in the themes he tackled during his extensive travels in Hungary, Transylvania, Galicia, Italy, and Dalmatia.

Thomas Ender was another artist who went in search of new subjects following his dismissal from the Academy. Ender's first opportunity to do this came on an extended visit to Italy (probably a retirement bonus paid for by Archduke John[37]). Ender reported to his patron on November 8, 1853, after his return. The letter, which is the last proven instance of contact between them (the archduke died on May 11, 1859), enables us to trace the course of Ender's journey. From Trieste he

125    Alois Schönn. *Bazaar in Sarajevo, Serbia.* 1851

126   Thomas Ender. *View of the Matterhorn from the Gorner Grat.* 1854

127    Thomas Ender. *Mountainous Landscape with River.* c. 1865

Thomas Ender. *Vernill Falls, near Gallneukirchen, Tyrol.* c. 1865. Watercolor and Chinese white. Sammlungen des Regierenden Fürsten von Liechtenstein, Vaduz Castle, Vaduz (207).

traveled to Venice, Padua, Bologna, and Florence before taking ship from Livorno to Naples. The artist spent nearly three weeks working in Sorrento, then visited Capri and Ischia. Recalling his time in Rome thirty years earlier, Ender concluded, "... how rich and beautiful this country [is] in every part. It is with sadness that I leave it again. Italy is and always will be the richest and most beautiful of lands for art and artists. No other has such treasures and such a history of art to offer. Even today the life of men and women in these surroundings holds inspiration for the artist and the artlover. What a contrast with our ... modern cities, where houses and people are mere arid calculations ...."[38]

A year later, Ender was off on another extended tour, this time to Switzerland. Here he produced a particularly large number of notable watercolors; a posthumous exhibition held in 1876 included no fewer than eighty-one. The titles of these provide an idea of the route the artist followed. Starting from the Vorarlberg, he must have visited Lucerne and Lake Lucerne, St. Moritz, and Grindelwald. Ender saw the Eiger, the Mönch, the Jungfrau. He probably continued via Visp to the Matterhorn, the Rhone valley (taking in Chamonix), and the Lake of Geneva, and finished the trip with a visit to Lago Maggiore and Lugano.

In the following year—1855—Ender returned to Ischia for a longer stay. There he received a visit from Elise, the widow of his twin brother (Johann had died of typhus in 1854). "On our way back," she wrote, "we called on Uncle Thomas at his nature painting. He had set up his studio on the flat roof of a farmhouse, ... There I watched my brother-in-law paint a quite wonderful picture in which these beautiful and exotic natural surroundings were faithfully reflected."[39]

The aging but indefatigable artist made several trips, accompanying his son who was a railroad engineer. Thomas Ender visited the Tyrol (where the Brenner line was under construction), and he even went as far as Transylvania.

Unburdened by commissions and with neither obligations nor responsibilities, Thomas Ender now painted his most remarkable watercolors. Around 1865 his subject matter—the view—became wholly subordinate to a purely painterly concern with light, water in motion, and the freedom of nature. In Ender's late work he achieved a relaxed, wet technique of watercolor that used blending and glazing to bring a genuine climax to his oeuvre.

These late paintings also show undeniable shortcomings, however. Ender rarely succeeded in structuring his foregrounds with any clarity. In fact, a feature of his late work is the flat areas of broad brushstrokes that are always in front of the main motif.

Ender remained a generous human being to the last, devoting his final years chiefly to social work in the

128   Josef Kriehuber. *Forest Scene with Staffage.* 1872

Joseph Selleny. *Coconut Palms on Tahiti.* 1859. Watercolor. Graphische Sammlung Albertina, Vienna (28.969).

detract from Joseph Selleny's artistic achievement. What he recorded and portrayed must have provided a magnificent document of a most unusual expedition, for even the relatively few paintings to have survived constitute a major landmark in Viennese watercolor art.

## ITALY—THE ARTIST'S GOAL

Eternal Rome was the focus of all the arts—artists of all nations had shared this belief for centuries, and Rome had long been their principal place of pilgrimage. Various countries—led by France—had set up academies there, and generations of artists had laid the foundations of their creative work in Rome.

It is a fascinating exercise to trace the very different ways in which the city was seen, understood, and sought out over the centuries from the Middle Ages through the Renaissance and from the eras of Mannerism to the Baroque and Neoclassicism. The city was seen, in turn, as the heir to the ancient world, as the center of Christendom, as an ideal of idyllic natural beauty, or as a vibrant metropolis of the arts.

It followed almost as a matter of course that the post-1850 generation should also direct its steps toward Rome. Now, however, a radical change in the relationship of artists to the city suddenly occurred: a number of artists proceeded to settle in Rome (or Venice) on a long-term basis, installing magnificent studios and beginning to lead glittering social lives in keeping with their new prestige and success.

The south of Europe and the special quality of southern light also attracted many watercolorists. One of these was Ludwig Passini, son of the successful Viennese engraver Johann Nepomuk Passini (who had made the superb engraving of Peter Fendi's watercolor painting, *The Family Reunion*).

Ludwig Passini trained at the Vienna Academy under Joseph von Führich and Leopold Kupelwieser, though neither teacher had a great influence over him. Instead Passini became a devoted disciple of Thomas Ender, continuing Ender's watercolor style and eventually emerging as one of his best pupils. Passini was also friendly with Rudolf Alt; they had fled from riot-torn Vienna together in 1848 (Passini was sixteen and seized the opportunity to paint a brilliant portrait of Alt.[53])

In 1850, at the age of eighteen, Passini left Vienna for good. First he accompanied his parents to Trieste and then went on to Venice in 1851. The German artist Carl Friedrich H. Werner (1808–94), who had settled in Venice himself in 1832 after a travel scholarship, had just set up a "master studio for watercolor painting" there. Passini immediately became Werner's favorite pupil.

The young artist also befriended other artists studying in Venice, among them Emanuel Stöckler. Stöckler had also studied under Thomas Ender in Vienna and was now seeking to perfect his technique under Werner. Following his visit to an exhibition in Manchester on a

prehensively the description of the voyage. In 1859–60 he accompanied Archduke Ferdinand Maximilian on another voyage to Brazil. Later Selleny fell ill, and he spent the last two years of his life in the Inzersdorf private mental asylum. He died there, completely insane, on May 22, 1875.

A nine-year court battle over Selleny's estate finally ended when 768 studies were awarded to the naval authorities and the remainder to the artist's heirs. Only a fraction of Selleny's work survived the collapse of the monarchy, the dissolution of the Austrian navy, the interwar years, and two world wars. Most of it was assigned to the Heeresgeschichtliches Museum in Vienna, though Archduke Albert purchased a few works from the heirs for his own collection.

The titles and details of all the works are still known from the inventories taken on Selleny's death, from internal-revenue archives, and from the catalogue of the auction held by C.J. Wawra on February 29, 1884. All these documents were meticulously researched and published by Liselotte Popelka.[52]

Though the loss of many of his watercolors is only now appreciated for the tragedy it is, nothing can

Ludwig Passini. *A Priest on his Way to Administer Extreme Unction.* c. 1875. Watercolor over a pencil drawing. Professor Hans Fronius Collection, Perchtolsdorf.

trip to England, Stöckler devoted himself entirely to watercolor and decided to settle in Venice.

In 1852, Werner and Passini left Venice for study trips to Dalmatia, Lower Italy, and the Netherlands. Afterward Werner returned to his native Germany, though he subsequently embarked on many more study trips from Leipzig before setting up a separate department for watercolor painting at the Leipzig Academy in 1882.

As for Passini, he settled in Rome in 1855. There he began painting watercolors of buildings and interiors, but he soon turned increasingly to genre-type scenes in which priests and children in ecclesiastical settings figure prominently. His paintings of Rome enjoyed exceptional success at the Weltausstellung in Vienna in 1873. Passini moved to Berlin for a time when he married, and after 1873 he made Venice his place of residence for a while. The watercolor art of Ludwig Passini, with solid roots in the Viennese tradition, was of far more than local importance. It exerted a powerful influence on a whole generation of artists who were his contemporaries.

Many Austrian artists of the nineteenth century were destined to be forgotten—often quite undeservedly. The man who deserved it perhaps least of all was Anton Romako, another member of the group that included Werner, Passini, and Stöckler. His biographer Fritz Novotny described Romako as being "one of the most remarkable and most conflict-ridden artists of this whole period."[54] For no other Austrian artist was Italy of such crucial importance. Romako's art, however, was a kind that his generation found difficult to understand —the more so since public opinion had long ago come down clearly on the side of the "unconditionally visible" as opposed to any kind of "contemplative painting."[55] Few people collected Romako's work, and only about fifty of his watercolors have survived.[56]

As a result, this masterly aspect of Romako's oeuvre has contributed less than it should to the overall picture of his achievements. Although Romako's skill in handling the medium commands attention, the freewheeling imagination that characterized his apprehension of reality and led him to make intriguingly mysterious statements is even more impressive.

Novotny is right, incidentally, to point out that the frequent references in the literature to Romako's having suffered a typically "Austrian fate" are uncalled-for, in so far as "intellectual laziness and a lack of understanding of the unusual are not an exclusively Austrian specialty."[57]

That Romako was one of the most important artists of his generation must be considered beyond question

130   August von Pettenkofen. *Interior of a Neapolitan Farmhouse*. 1873

131   August von Pettenkofen. *Peasant Girl from Torre del Greco, near Naples.* 1873
132   Eduard Charlemont. *Portrait of a Lady: Anna.* c. 1875

133   Anton Romako. *Italian Woman Mending Nets on the Beach.* c. 1871

Anton Romako. *Donkey With a Load of Hay.* c. 1870. Watercolor. Historisches Museum der Stadt Wien, Vienna (114.139).

Anton Romako. *Cattle Drovers in the "Campagna."* c. 1865. Watercolor. Sammlungen des Regierenden Fürsten von Liechtenstein, Vaduz Castle, Vaduz (no inv. number).

That is a long way from saying—as Hans Bisanz does in the essay already cited—that their "cult of beauty" was based wholly on the "materialism of an upper-middle-class consumer society."[8] To my mind, that is naive myth-making. A deeply felt desire for beauty is firmly anchored in civilization. It is of the essence of *humanitas*. To seek to belittle it by foisting it upon the image of one's social foe is to be guilty of distorting history. In the art of the nineteenth century, the desire for beauty did not by any means suddenly appear with the rise of a purse-proud bourgeoisie; the search for the beautiful has been a solid, organic component of man's worldview.

It is a very different matter to cast doubt on whether the concept of beauty that the period put forward rightly qualifies as such. Beauty proper was now supplanted by optical attractions, by erotic wishful thinking (whether latent or overt), and by surprise effects aimed at provoking amazement through sheer size or technical brilliance. In short, artistry was very often mistaken for art.

Watercolor paintings, limited in size and less flamboyant in technique, were naturally incapable of producing such effects. Where the large-scale oil paintings of the Makart period aimed to create illusions, watercolors modestly sought to amuse.

Hans Makart. *Portrait of the Artist in Old German Dress* (study for the 1879 procession). 1879. Watercolor and pencil. Historisches Museum der Stadt Wien (13.829).

Alois Greil. *Emperor Maximilian I Entering Ghent.* 1880. Watercolor. Private collection.

procession. In literally hundreds of studies and detail drawings, he designed historical costumes for some 14,000 participants, who were to form various *tableaux vivants* from the life of contemporary Vienna, wearing Renaissance dress. There were representations of Commerce, Industry, and the Arts. There were delegations of students, gymnasts, huntsmen, clubs, fellowships, fire brigades, veterans, and singers. Leading figures in society played a prominent part everywhere, vying with one another in their chosen historical costumes.

With this triumph, Makart not only earned enormous popularity for himself; he also gave the arts importance in civic life and prestige in the eyes of the public such as they had never known before—and have scarcely encountered since. For the generation of artists that followed Makart, however, there was a heavy price to pay: they constantly felt that art should be a "treat for the eyes"; they could not imagine it otherwise.

Moritz von Schwind. *Pamina and the Three Boys from Mozart's Opera "The Magic Flute."* c. 1863. Pen and black ink and watercolors. Graphische Sammlung Albertina, Vienna (31.109).

Alois Greil. *The Putative Spy.* c. 1873. Watercolor over pencil. Graphische Sammlung Albertina, Vienna (28.791).

A genuine master of this type of work was Alois Greil. Born in Linz, Greil was "spotted" by no less a person than the author Adalbert Stifter. Stifter encouraged him to train in Vienna, where Greil became an accomplished watercolorist.

In addition to painting historical subjects—his *Emperor Maximilian I Entering Ghent* owes a debt to Makart—Greil also painted comic scenes. The latter are mostly taken from the rustic life of Greil's native Austria. They are painted with great skill. In *The Putative Spy*, an artist sits raptly painting from nature while a group of slow-witted peasants, who think he is spying, prepare to overpower him. Such scenes were doubtless

not uncommon in reality. The same thing had happened to Franz Edmund Weirotter near Gaming, back in the eighteenth century, and to Alois Schönn during the French occupation of Vienna.

In *Traveling Actors with Cart*, Greil even managed a sharply observed character study of a band of poor but proud itinerant Thespians hauling their beggarly cartload of props and belongings. Nevertheless, the painting constitutes a nadir of degeneration. In it, art is reduced to the level of a cheap joke.

What had happened to the biting satire that had underpinned the work of someone like Honoré Daumier, whose lithographs were so influential? Artists had long since stopped trying to draw attention to problems. Art no longer sought to provoke thought but rather, at best, to provide a substitute for it. Even where no actual joke is being portrayed, artists' intentions appear to be merely to divert—or to decorate.

That was the second task art was called upon to perform in this period. *Sopraporte*, lunettes, vignettes, and

136   Alois Greil. *Traveling Actors with Cart.* c. 1875

illustrations were the order of the day. Either the decorative needs of the new palaces and great public buildings dictated what was to be created, or such mammoth projects as the "Crown Prince's Work," initiated by Crown Prince Rudolph, *Austria-Hungary in Words and Pictures*. Many watercolor working drawings for the latter were commissioned from Theodor von Ehrmanns (b. 1846). None of them rose above the superficial level of illustration.

Another artist active around this time was Hans Schliessmann (1852–1920). He illustrated popular Viennese subjects for humorous magazines, working for *Humoristische Blätter* from 1874 and for *Kikeriki* and *Fliegende Blätter* from 1880. Schliessmann's original Viennese characters and scenes from everyday life gained him enormous popularity. One of his best-loved works shows the military band playing for the changing of the guard at the imperial palace.[9]

But so much had been lost by this time! The luminosity of watercolor painting that seems to come from within, the subtle beauty, and the depths—in short, everything that is associated with the medium had completely disappeared. "The glittering treasures of the watercolor painting of Old Vienna show evidence of the liveliest artistic energies," Bruno Grimschitz wrote in 1927.[10] His words reveal just how far "New Vienna"—as the city had begun to call itself meanwhile—had come since that time.

## INFLUENCES FROM THE WEST

The branch that had shown the greatest tendency to distance itself from official art—thereby evading the Philistine demand that art should entertain—was landscape painting. There was therefore every reason why it should have been the subject of the fiercest artistic debates. C. von Vincenti's contemporary account of the conflict between "old" and "young" artists has been mentioned.[11] This conflict was clearly reflected in the landscape class at the Academy, particularly after the situation had been sharply polarized by the reforms introduced by Count Leo Thun, the minister responsible, and by the appointment of some new professors.

In principle, opinions were divided on what landscape painting should and could achieve. One school continued to try to depict observed reality; the other was interested in the mood of a painting. The latter school was concerned with the intangible factor of atmosphere and above all, with the effect of light on the viewer's imagination. Rebell and Waldmüller had both traveled some way in this direction. Quite independently of them, Josef Danhauser had written these remarkable words in his diary back in the 1840s: "The painter's language is not form but the effect of light. His ABC ought to consist of optics and [color] degradation/*Luftperspektiv*], for they are the basis of the artistic illusion

through which he has to speak clearly in order to convey what paint is capable of."[12]

Not only does this sound astonishingly modern; it *was* astonishingly modern. There is no doubt at all that the same debates affected Austrian art as deeply as Impressionism did French art: artistic developments in France were reported in the Austrian press, and Austrians followed the theoretical arguments and noted the practical results. Most artists made a study trip to Paris. There they found confirmed what they had sought in Szolnok, discovered in the Italian *campagna*, or believed they had grasped in the Near East.

The intellectual theory of Pointillism, remained alien to the Austrian mind, however. The result was that Austrian artists never took the final step in the process of desubstantiation, namely negation of the subject. They too were concerned with the technical problems of atmosphere, light, and local color. But the radical, isolated stance of *l'art pour l'art* (art for art's sake) was not for them.

*Plein-air* painting had started the process that led to a clash everywhere between exponents of Naturalism and Ideal art. Out of that clash came *peinture pure*, a kind of painting that was emancipated from all nonpainterly ends. And painters everywhere followed this and other developments in France.

Emil Jakob Schindler, for example, knew about Jean-Jacques Rousseau, Charles-François Daubigny, and Camille Corot. However, although other Western artistic influences were undoubtedly on the increase as far as his generation was concerned, it would be wrong to suppose that Schindler's outstanding qualities as an artist stemmed from any source outside his native land. Emil Jakob Schindler was an unmistakable product of Austrian art. In fact, he was the true their of Ferdinand Georg Waldmüller,[13] which explains why Schindler did not, in his works, push his conclusions to the ultimate.

Austrian artists consciously avoided invalidating their subjects by negation. For them, the individual manifestation of nature took precedence over the optical phenomena associated with it. No matter how desubstantiated the image that they painted became, its natural form was always preserved. This was true even when they accepted that painting was a matter "of understanding nature and rendering its spiritual truths, of examining the *why* of appearances and drawing attention to the way in which they obey certain laws."[14]

The link with the visible world was so powerful in Austrian culture that, as a country, it avoided any wholesale abandonment of its artistic inheritance, nor would it meekly allow itself to be taken over by an alien trend at the heart of which lay a large measure of contempt for the visible world. (Remember the words of the French poet Charles Baudelaire: "I find it tedious and superfluous to portray what actually is. Nature is ugly, and I prefer the monster of my imagination to the triviality of facts."[15])

It is greatly to Makart's credit that he recognized Emil Jakob Schindler's talent and took him in. Makart placed

137    Emil Jakob Schindler. *River Landscape.* c. 1885

his second, smaller studio at the young man's disposal and encouraged and supported his efforts. It is said that, when Makart discovered that his protégé did not even own an unmended pair of shoes, he indulged in the typically lordly gesture of hiring an expensive carriage by the month, complete with driver, in which the young landscapist might have himself conveyed to whichever spot he wished to paint.[16]

The starting point of Schindler's career was the Vienna Academy, where he trained under the German landscape painter Albert Zimmermann.

The earthy bohemianism of Zimmermann's manner rather than the dramatic heroics of his paintings fired his young pupil with enthusiasm for a more progressive kind of art. Dutch painting exercised a far greater influence on Schindler, however. Its browns and grays stayed with him for a long time, and he himself said that the Prater had suddenly changed him. There he encountered the gray-green, silver-toned atmosphere that characterized his painting afterward.[17] Granted, Emil Jakob Schindler painted few watercolors, but those he did paint are some of the most superbly accomplished and beautiful works produced in the later years of the nineteenth century.

## RUDOLF ALT'S ARTISTIC TURNING POINT

No sooner had the confusion caused by the Revolution of 1848 abated in Vienna than Rudolf Alt returned to the city, determined to resume his artistic work without delay. But the Vienna he returned to was no longer the same; too much had changed. There is dramatic evidence of how Alt, whose artistic efforts during the early 1850s became increasingly frantic, showed a sharp decline in achievements.

There must have been a whole series of reasons for this decline. An obvious one was that, because of economic restrictions following the Revolution of 1848, it was no longer possible to obtain Whatman paper, the high-quality watercolor paper made by the Englishman James Whatman, which provided such an excellent support for watercolor painting. Hence the enthusiasm with which artists greeted an invention that Friedrich Gottlieb Keller had come up with in 1845: paper manufactured from woodpulp. Little did they suspect that barely a hundred years later these woodpulp papers would begin to turn brown and become brittle. A large number of watercolors have been lost as a result.

Furthermore—as became obvious right away—woodpulp paper called for a quite different technique of painting. Thicker layers of paint had to be used and applied more opaquely in the manner of gouache. This even led to white being put on the watercolors now. All these things ran counter to Rudolf Alt's supremely accomplished, pure watercolor technique.

Alt was also very short of commissions, his former clients having been forced by the unsettling events to leave Vienna. Lastly, with the city still in a state of siege, movement was severely restricted and travel completely impossible. For a landscape painter, this was nothing short of catastrophic. As a result, Alt fell back on copying his earlier studies, which contributed to his decline.

Curiously, Rudolf's father made a much better job of adapting to the new age. Old Jakob Alt set himself the task of continuing Daffinger's flower painting after the latter's death in 1849. He painted the *Altsche Herbarium*, a collection of 400 watercolors. Much of the collec-

Rudolf Alt. *Avenue in the Garden of Schönbrunn Palace.* c. 1850. Watercolor. Graphische Sammlung Albertina, Vienna (25.038).

Salzburg 6. Sept 69

138   Rudolf Alt. *View of the Castle and the City of Salzburg.* 1869

229

139   Rudolf Alt. *Lying-in-State in a Palace.* c. 1850

140   Rudolf Alt. *View of St. Stephen's Cathedral, Vienna, from the Graben.* 1872

Rudolf von Alt. *The Gardens of Teplitz Palace (Teplice, Czechoslovakia).* 1875. Watercolor. Private collection, Vienna.

viewpoints from which to paint his beloved motifs: San Marco Cathedral and the Doge's Palace. However, the consequences of decades of working out of doors in all weathers and in cold, drafty churches and castles were at last beginning to make themselves felt, and Alt's doctor recommended a course of treatment at a spa.

Teplice, which was situated in a particularly beautiful location between the Harz Mountains and the Bohemian highlands, was one of the most fashionable spas in all the Dual Monarchy.

The extensive grounds of the palace of the counts of Clary-Aldringen were open to visitors for restful walks. They became an inexhaustible fount of artistic inspiration for Rudolf Alt. Where Empress Carolina Augusta, Goethe, and Beethoven had once met and where Richard Wagner came in search of relaxation, Alt produced veritable "torrents" of his "tree portraits."

Back in Vienna, the time had come for official honors. The Academy and the Ministry of Culture decided to ask Alt to paint, annually, several views taken from the emperor's many domains. A committee was to suggest the subjects. It was a prestigious commission

Rudolf von Alt. *Anton Pilgram's Organ Base in St. Stephen's Cathedral, Vienna.* 1876. Watercolor with gouache highlights. Sammlungen des Regierenden Fürsten von Liechtenstein, Vaduz Castle, Vaduz (41).

of convention and the constraints of painting to commissions, Alt henceforth owed allegiance only to his own artistic aspirations.

The 1870s soon brought him further successes in Vienna. A shy, hardworking man, Rudolf Alt had always lived a somewhat retiring life. He now began to receive honors and decorations from the Academy and from the new Künstlerhaus. The first exhibition of Alt's works at the Society of Pictorial Artists (Gesellschaft bildender Künstler) in the autumn of 1870 was a decisive step toward greater recognition of his achievement and admiration for his work. The exhibition found an enthusiastic public, and Rudolf Alt soon came almost to personify the artistic life of Vienna.

Tirelessly Alt continued and even stepped up his traveling. In particular he paid repeated visits to Venice between 1871 and 1874. There he kept on finding new

Rudolf Alt. *The Porta Capuana in Naples.* 1867. Watercolor and gouache over pencil. Graphische Sammlung Albertina, Vienna (28.374).

Rudolf Alt. *View of Siena, Showing the Torre del Mangia.* 1871. Watercolor. Provenance: Miller-Aichholz Collection, Vienna (present ownership unknown).

144   Rudolf von Alt. *Self Portrait.* 1883

145   Rudolf von Alt. *The Imperial Tomb in the Royal Chapel, Innsbruck.* 1886

Rudolf von Alt. *The Dumba Family on an Outing near Liezen.* 1879. Watercolor. Graphische Sammlung Albertina, Vienna (36.602).

and one that paid handsomely. It occupied the artist for the next twenty years and took him all over the empire, from Trento to Cracow, as one major work after another took shape beneath his brush.

In 1877 something out of the ordinary occurred: the Academy of Fine Arts was opened in Vienna, and Rudolf Alt was commissioned to record the solemn event, with instructions to place the emperor in the center of his painting. In a large number of sketches and a quite astonishing overall panorama, the artist duly discharged this laborious and thankless task—nothing was beyond Alt's technical mastery now.

In 1879 he was invited by Nikolaus von Dumba, a wealthy businessman, prominent patron of the arts, liberal politician, and owner of one of the finest palaces on Vienna's Ringstrasse, to spend the summer in Liezen, in northern Styria. These weeks were filled with tremendous creativity. During them Alt's skill at capturing people and nature led him to produce a number of outstanding masterpieces—works that have few equals anywhere in the world, in any period of art.

Rudolf Alt was now in his late sixties, and the annual commission for the Ministry of Culture was beginning to prove something of a strain. He became particularly

aware of this when the committee informed him, on December 15, 1881, that the next batch of views (the palace in the Himmelpfortgasse and the staircase of the Upper Belvedere—both the work of the great Baroque architect Johann Bernhard Fischer von Erlach) had to be completed by March 15, 1882. Alt was suffering from gout and no longer felt up to meeting such deadlines. He had "never been afraid of heat or cold where work is concerned,"[19] but all that painting in unheated rooms in the dead of winter just seemed to be too much now. Nevertheless, not only were the paintings completed on time; they were brilliant examples of the watercolorist's art and earned him a great deal of admiration. The flowing effect of entirely intangible light was an essential ingredient of Baroque architecture, but one wonders precisely what technical means—acquired through long years of tireless searching—Rudolph Alt employed to translate it into terms of watercolor.[20]

The artist's seventieth-birthday celebrations soon provided an occasion for further honors of all kinds. None of this, however, should blind us to the fact that Rudolf Alt's life was by no means free of problems. Around this time, Alt concluded an already vigorous reply to a client who, on top of showing some reluctance to part with money, had sent him an insulting letter, with the shattering words, "… so I find myself faced with the necessity of taking my leave of you once and for all. How long do I have left to me, though, and does all suffering not come to an end? Yet our Viennese air never [provided] a good existence for me."[21]

However, in Alt's eyes, age and infirmity were no excuse for an artist to abandon his unremitting quest or curtail his creative activities. Consequently, the 1880s produced yet another body of splendid watercolors by Alt, painted on several journeys. Here was a veritable harvest of magnificent works such as might have brought any painter's career to a triumphant conclusion—indeed, they almost certainly would have done so. Amid the flood of mediocre art that characterized the period, this one old man—Rudolf Alt—was the only artist who had really carried on the Austrian tradition of watercolor painting. It seemed that the end of the tradition had occurred long before, leaving Alt a mere relic of a bygone age. But things were to turn out very differently.

# VIII  ON TO THE END

## THE ERA OF THE OLD EMPEROR

The sixty-seven-year reign (1848–1916) of Emperor Francis Joseph I was a period of momentous upheaval in Austrian history, both internally and externally. Industrial development raced ahead; science and technology advanced with giant strides, and fresh dimensions opened up on every hand. Amid all this turmoil, the emperor came to embody a huge, imposing figure holding steady as a rock through all personal and political vicissitudes, inextricably caught up in the seemingly insoluble problems associated with steering his huge empire between the Scylla and Charybdis of preservation and change.

Sigmund L'Allemand. *Crown Prince Rudolph Leading a Parade Before the Emperor in Prague.* 1881. Watercolor and gouache. Graphische Sammlung Albertina, Vienna (29.103).

From the day of his accession, the problems tended to concentrate in three areas: 1) Would the empire's three centers of gravity—in Germany, in Italy, and on the Danube—manage to hold their own? 2) Was the Hapsburg inheritance of a supranational state capable of being preserved in a climate of rampant nationalism? 3) How, in these new and very different political, economic, and cultural circumstances was government to be organized in future? Where was one to make conces-

241

sions, where stand firm? What adjustments needed to be made, what reassessments undertaken?

At first it looked as if no positive answer to any of these questions would be forthcoming. Although the uprisings in Italy and Hungary were defeated, the insurgents were by no means quelled. Meanwhile, tensions began to appear among other peoples, too—Bohemians, Moravians, Poles, Croats, Romanians, Galicians, Ruthenians, and Ukrainians.

Prompted by the rising tide of nationalism, two further questions became increasingly urgent. How would the German part of Austria—including its capital, Vienna, seat of the imperial residence—react to all this? Above all, what would its attitude be toward the other German states as the call for an emperor of all the Germans became louder and louder and as Prussia began to play an increasingly challenging role?

Moreover, the social problem, already impossible to ignore, now thrust itself more and more prominently into the foreground. What rights should government grant to the governed? How much say should they be given in the running of affairs? How was the existing structure of the nation (based on the old noble families) to be reconciled with the new rising classes that had become wealthy through industry and commerce?

The questions piled up. Ultimately they revolved around three centers of gravity too: liberalism, democracy, and nationalism. It was a matter of deciding how far freedom, codetermination, and self-awareness could be permitted to go before politically and socially destructive consequences began to ensue. At what point did liberty become anarchy, democratic consultation lead to paralysis, and national pride begin to threaten the fabric of the nation?

The entire second half of the nineteenth century may be seen in terms of a superhuman attempt to find the correct balance, a middle way. The attempt was founded on certain indispensable basic values, which included the mission implicit in Austria's political inheritance, an ethos of Christian humanity, and a deep belief in the concepts of loyalty, honor, and duty. Politically, this attempt assumed a wide variety of forms.

Very briefly, the period may be divided into five distinct sections:

1) The years from 1848 to 1857. When the new emperor acceded to the throne on December 2, 1848, the first task was to rebuild the authority of the Austrian state. This was done on foundations laid by Prince Felix zu Schwarzenberg. The New Year's Eve Patent of 1851 marked the decision to move from what was initially a parliamentary system of government back to Absolutism. Following an unsuccessful attempt on the emperor's life in 1853, the state of emergency was revoked. A Concordat concluded in 1855 under the auspices of Cardinal von Rauscher contributed to the later dominance of the Roman Catholic Church. In 1857, the city of Vienna was substantially changed by the removal of the fortifications, the start of construction on the famous boulevard called the Ringstrasse,

and the incorporation of the old "suburbs" into the city proper. A free, modern Vienna emerged from these changes.

2) In 1859, war broke out in Italy, and Austria lost Lombardy. This was the first victory of a nationalist movement over the ideal of a multinational nation; it had enormous influence. Austria moved away from Neoabsolutism. The constitution was restored, and a number of basic laws ushered in an era of Constitutionalism. Prussia, with its cabinet under a new minister-president (prime minister), Otto von Bismarck, became Austria's chief rival in the struggle for hegemony in central Europe. The year 1865 saw the opening of the Ringstrasse, a symbol of Greater Austria. The Seven Weeks' War with Prussia ended in a crushing defeat for Austria at Königgrätz (Hradec Kralové in Czechoslovakia) on July 3, 1866. The war in Italy, however, ended successfully for Austria with Wilhelm von Tegetthoff's victory over the Italian fleet off the island of Lissa (Viš, Yugoslavia) on July 21, 1866.

3) Count Richard Belcredi's federalist Cabinet was replaced in 1867, when Baron Friedrich Ferdinand von Beust was appointed imperial chancellor. The reconciliation with Hungary represented by the settlement of 1867 owed much to the personal intervention of Empress Elizabeth. With great solemnity at the coronation in Buda on June 8, 1867, the seal was set on the new Dual Monarchy of Austria-Hungary. However, the settlement led to mounting unrest among the Slavic peoples, who felt disadvantaged. There were uprisings in Dalmatia, while representatives of the Czech people refused to take their seats on the council of state. Count Gyula Andrássy, who joined the government in 1871, played an important political role. The removal of restrictions led to a tremendous economic boom, increasing political pressure from high finance and industry. The huge accumulations of wealth that merchants amassed in weaving, sugar, coal, brewing, and banking fueled anti-Semitic, German-nationalist tendencies among the middle classes. These years also saw the beginnings of a working class movement as the proletariat became increasingly organized. Groups of Christian Socialists were also formed, chiefly among craftsmen. The fifth Weltausstellung (held in Vienna in 1873) became a huge demonstration of Austria's industrial power and efficiency, a grandiose symbol of unqualified faith in progress and in the future. The dramatic crash of the stock market on May 9, 1873, not only put a damper on that euphoria; it introduced a period of grave economic difficulties.

4) With the building of the Neogothic City Hall (Rathaus), the installation of new water pipes from the mountains, and improved measures to control the Danube, Vienna slowly recovered. The Austrian North Pole Expedition returned in triumph, having discovered Franz Joseph Land. Liberal denominational laws were passed in defiance of conservative opposition. A rapprochement with Germany followed Austria's neutral stance in the Franco-Prussian War of 1870-1. In 1879,

146   Robert Raschka. *The Staircase in the Kunsthistorisches Museum, Vienna.* 1891

147  Franz Alt. *View of the Artist's Studio.* 1881

148    Ludwig Passini. *The Artist Cecil von Haanen.* 1879

however, this whole policy was reversed when Berlin was mandated to occupy Bosnia. Some difficult military operations had political consequences at home as the liberal opposition joined the entire left wing in launching an attack on the government.

The Dual Monarchy celebrated a solemn high point with the emperor and empress's silver wedding anniversary. The year 1880 brought a pronounced economic upswing, but Vienna received a major shock in December, 1881, when a fire at the Ring Theater caused appalling casualties. Politically speaking, the Triple Alliance with Germany and Italy (1882) marked the end of this period.

5) The political situation became increasingly polarized. The Hainburg Conference of 1888–9 united the left under the banner of Social Democracy. Its leader, a doctor by the name of Viktor Adler, who worked with the poor, founded and managed the *Arbeiterzeitung*, a newspaper devoted to labor interests. The Christian Socialists under Karl Lueger brought the liberal period in Vienna to an end. On January 29, 1889, Crown Prince Rudolph and his mistress Baroness M. von Vetsera committed suicide in a bloody drama played out in Mayerling, just outside Vienna. In 1897, the Social Democrats entered parliament for the first time. In 1898, Austria staged magnificent celebrations to mark the fiftieth jubilee of the postrevolutionary government. On September 10, 1898, the anarchist Luigi Lucheni murdered Empress Elizabeth on the street in Geneva. The heir to the throne, Crown Prince Francis Ferdinand, was urging political and military reforms. The turn of the century ushered in the final period of Emperor Francis Joseph's reign. This culminated in the dramatic assassination in Sarajevo of the crown prince and his wife Duchess Sophie of Hohenberg—the incident that triggered the First World War. It was a period that was "experimenting with the end of the world," as the satirist Karl Kraus said. Others characterized it—perhaps more aptly—as the suicide of Europe.

These fateful and dramatic decades found rich expression in every field of the arts: the highs and lows, the splendors and shams, the fears and hopelessness, which culminated in the interminable ordeal of the war, were all faithfully reflected in the mirror of culture. Of course in Vienna, the top place—as ever—was accorded to music. But the wealthy ruling classes now provided a plentiful source of patronage and one that completely altered the position of the artist in society.

For example, the Austrian-born Dutch artist Cecil von Haanen (1844–1914) comes to mind; his portrait was painted by Ludwig Passini in Venice in 1879. Writing in 1903, Ludwig Hevesi had this to say of Passini: "Particularly in the 1870s, he was able to stand comparison with the more elegant genre masters of the Second Empire. Such paintings as his *Ventian Women Mounting Pearls* reach beyond the [kitsch of the] 'Ninetta style,' despite the fact that this whole world, geared to bourgeois taste, smacks of *palette* and—come to that—of *métier*."[1]

Cultivating art and being capable not only of responding to its magic but also of making conversation about it had become *de rigueur* in Viennese society. The most sumptuous and magnificent expression of this was the plan to erect the new Hofmuseum on the Ringstrasse. Together with Maria Theresa Square and the Maria Theresa Monument, the Kunsthistorisches Museum, and the New Hofburg (the Imperial Palace), it was meant to form a grandiose complex of buildings (which were never completed, in fact). The two buildings comprising the Hofmuseum were designed to set each other off. Both built by Karl von Hasenauer and the German architect Gottfried Semper, who had been summoned to Vienna in 1871, the buildings were the intellectual crown, so to speak, of the whole Ringstrasse project. They were meant to be treasure houses of Austria's artistic and scientific patrimony.

The staircase of the Kunsthistorisches Museum became an important example of the whole so-called Ringstrasse style. It was a *Gesamtkunstwerk* (a synthesis of the arts, which was a leading idea of Historicism) that Hevesi reckoned "one of the most colossal and magnificent in the world;" he called it "a brightly colored jewel box of true Hasenauer extravagance."[2]

The lush, yet somehow pedantic watercolor by Robert Raschka conveys all the splendor of the colored marble with its plethora of gilt—bronze ornamentation, the *grande-antique* of the column shafts, the onyx marble of the door frames, and Makart's superb lunettes. From our point of view, the only interesting thing about Raschka's painting is how it compares with Alt's watercolor of the staircase in the Upper Belvedere. The comparison highlights all that distinguished a true master from his contemporaries.

The Viennese *veduta*, embodiment of so much skill and sophistication, was already well past its prime. Of the artists active in this field, the most successful was Erwin Pendl (1875–1945). Kept very busy by the imperial court and much sought after by foreign buyers, Pendl was represented at the Exposition Universelle in Paris in 1900.

Another painter of *vedute* was Ernst Graner (1865–1943), also a highly popular and successful artist and, without question, an assiduous professional. In fact, Graner may be described as the last representative of a whole period, and possibly even of his whole branch of art.

The only other artist whom we need consider in any detail as a watercolorist practising in the latter part of the century is Franz Alt, Jakob Alt's second son and Rudolf's younger brother. Franz Alt never emerged from his brother's shadow, even though there were times when he enjoyed greater esteem in aristocratic circles and among art collectors. Being nine years younger than Rudolf, Franz grew up in very much more ordered circumstances. Academy-trained (he was also gifted musically and had a musical training), Franz rejected Rudolf's advice that he should concentrate on portraiture.

Franz Alt. *Studio in the Makart Style.* c. 1880. Watercolor on a photograph. Graphische Sammlung Albertina, Vienna (37.132).

Franz Alt acccompanied his father to Italy for the first time in 1844. Soon after that he found a patron—Count Casimir Esterházy—who was to change the whole course of his life. From then on Franz Alt's career followed a quite different pattern from that of Rudolf Alt. A charming, affable man with an excellent all-round education, Franz Alt moved for the most part in elegant aristocratic circles. He was invited to stay on his friends' country estates, which is how he came to give lessons in watercolor painting (from 1849) to a young woman who was to become one of Austria's best-loved novelists, Baroness Marie von Ebner-Eschenbach (1830–1916). In 1852–3 Franz Alt spent some time working in Venice with his friend, the artist Ludwig Passini. Whether on his extensive travels or at home in Salzburg, Franz Alt moved in the most select social circles. Archduke Louis Victor, that very valuable artlover and collector, became his principal patron.

Franz Alt's work was of the highest quality. His output was perhaps rather less even than that of his brother, but he was without question a subtle and delightful artist. However, he came nowhere near his brother's achievement; his work lacks the tireless searching (and occasional despair), the intuitive exploration of all visible being that characterized the work of Rudolf.

After a prolonged stay in St. Petersburg, Franz Alt settled in Vienna in 1869. There, apart from occasional study trips to Italy or France, he led a serene and somewhat secluded existence. This atmosphere of quiet harmony is reflected in a painting of his studio, a work that conveys all his charm and skill.

Nothing more clearly illustrated the changing times —indeed, the coming of a new era—than the way in which so many areas that had previously been the province of art were taken over by photography. Here too, Vienna played an important role.

Back in 1839, when Louis Daguerre (1789–1851) had announced the details of his process in Paris, the farsighted Metternich had sent to Paris a delegation of the top men available in the technological sciences. Very soon Austrians were introducing fundamental improvements on the daguerreotype process. In that same year Professor Josef Petzval developed a totally new kind of highspeed lens, and in the following year Friedrich Voigtländer manufactured it. In 1841, Professor Joseph Berres discovered photogravure; Paul Pretsch achieved international fame with photogalvanography, and Karl Klić made a crucial breakthrough by inventing the process of heliogravure, which enabled such men as Hans Watzek, Heinrich Kühn, and Hugo Henneberg to bring art photography to an early climax.

It was inevitable that someone would make use of the new medium in conjunction with painting. That is exactly what Franz Alt did in his *Studio in the Makart Style,* brilliantly overpainting a photograph and producing what is, in effect, a striking symbol of the end of an epoch. Technology had scored a temporary victory, and the art of watercolor painting, after exactly a century, was temporarily at an end.

## CHANGING TIMES—THE FINALE

For the artists of Vienna, the 1850s were a time of deep despair. In 1903, Ludwig Hevesi described how even such artists' associations as Eintracht (Harmony) and

37  F. Novotny, in exh. cat. Essen, 1960, p. 59.
38  H. Kaut, in exh. cat. Laxenburg, 1968, pp. 64 ff.
39  Quoted by H. Bisanz, in exh. cat. Vienna, 1969 a, p. 24: "Archduke John was able to combine dream *[Traum]* and reality."
40  Handwritten note dated June 1, 1811, in Vienna, archives of the Akademie der Bildenden Künste. For a translation of the full text, see our Chapter II, p. 60–1.
41  Geramb, 1959, p. 118.
42  Koschatzky, 1978, p. 15, note 14, with sources.
43  Exh. cat. Graz, 1959, p. 19, with source.
44  Koschatzky, 1978, p. 31.
45  Statutes of the Joanneum; see Geramb, 1959, p. 18.
46  Koschatzky, 1978; p. 27, note 26, diary 1820.
47  Ibid., p. 157.


IV  FROM THE CONGRESS OF VIENNA TO THE REVOLUTION OF 1848:  BIEDERMEIER AND PRE-MARCH ERAS

1  Bietak, 1931.
2  For the term "Pre-March," see esp. Valjavec, 1944, pp. 92 ff., where the author talks about the beginnings of radicalization, movements against the privileges of nobility and clergy, mounting emphasis on German national feelings, and differences between social groups; an additional factor was the shifts in the economic structures of the age of capitalism brought about by factories and machines.
3  Valjavec, 1944, p. 6: "... the consequences of intellectual chains of development: the longing for balance, which leads to the attitude of circumspection."
4  Bietak, 1931, pp. 85 ff.: "Biedermeier becomes the quintessence of the Austrian character."
5  Ibid., p. 88.
6  Ibid., p. 90.
7  Ibid., p. 129.
8  Ibid., pp. 22 f.; "Concerning enthusiasm in the Romantic era."
9  Ibid., p. 133.
10  Ibid., p. 130.
11  Ibid., p. 129: "How happiness depends on a person's character."
12  Kralik and Schlitter, 1912.
13  Hevesi, 1903, p. 13.
14  However, Wurzbach, 1888, vol. XX (1869), p. 422, states that he was a natural son of Field Marshal Baron von Welden.
15  The corner house later rebuilt by Adolf Loos on the Michaeler Platz.
16  See Koschatzky, 1979, pp. 52 f.
17  Kralik and Schlitter, 1912, p. 635.
18  Grimschitz, 1928, pp. 70 ff.
19  Ibid., p. 75.
20  Exh. cat. Vienna, 1965 b, cat. nos. 218/I–XVI, pp. 68 ff.
21  Pirchan, 1943, p. 24.
22  All the Grillparzer quotations in this section are taken from *Grillparzers Werke*, 2 vols., Salzburg, 1958, vol. I, pp. 284 ff.
23  Exh. cat. Vienna, 1963, cat. no. 11.
24  Zimmermann, 1923, pp. 9 ff.
25  Grünstein, 1915, pp. 381 ff.
26  Exh. cat. Essen, 1960, p. 46.
27  Quoted in Adolph, 1951, p. I/16.
28  H. Adolph, in exh. cat. Vienna, 1963, p. 12.
29  Adolph, 1951, p. I/52.
30  Grünstein, 1915, p. 381; Adolph, 1951, p. I/26.
31  Adolph, 1951, pp. I/26; III/244 (no. A 101).
32  Leixner, 1906, vol. II, p. 713.
33  Adolph, 1951, p. I/27; quoted in Corti, 1950, p. 94.
34  Adolph, 1951, pp. I/28 f.
35  Exh. cat. Vienna, 1973, cat. no. 117.
36  Ibid., cat. no. 132.
37  Exh. cat. Vienna, 1963, cat. no. 35: *Morning Prayer*, but Adolph, 1951, p. III/209, no. A/66: *Evening Prayer*.
38  See H. Adolph, in exh. cat. Vienna, 1963, p. 13.
39  Jakob Gauermann's diaries, Neue Galerie am Landesmuseum Joanneum, Graz; quoted by W. Koschatzky, in exh. cat. Graz, 1959, p. 30.
40  Kisch, 1888; quoted in exh. cat. Graz, 1959, p. 64.
41  Feuchtmüller, 1962, p. 59.
42  Vienna: Akademie der Bildenden Künste, Gemäldegalerie; see exh. cat. Gutenstein-Miesenbach, 1963, cat. nos. 824–97.
43  Baron von Sacken, in *Katalog des Wiener Künstlerhauses*, 1878.
44  Feuchtmüller, 1962, p. 152, notes from "Anmerkungen."
45  Vienna: Stadtbibliothek (inv. no. 6529).
46  Feuchtmüller, 1962, p. 148.
47  Ibid.
48  See the biography of Gauermann in ibid., p. 147.
49  R. Baumstark, in exh. cat. Vaduz, 1983, p. 94.
50  W. Koschatzky, in exh. cat. Graz, 1959, cat. nos. 147 and *passim*.
51  Ibid., cat. nos. 148–9.
52  Ibid., p. 59.
53  Ibid., p. 53.
54  For a detailed account of sources, routes, and motives, see Koschatzky, 1982 a, pp. 54 ff. and the Topographical Index, pp. 189 ff.
55  O. Benesch, in Foreword to exh. cat. Vienna, 1955, p. 6.
56  Hevesi, 1911; Münz, 1954; Koschatzky, 1973; idem., in exh. cat. Vienna, 1984.
57  Koschatzky, 1973, ill. 29, p. 21.
58  Nebehay and Wagner, 1983, vol. I, p. 24, no. 22.
59  Ibid., p. 38, no. 34.
60  Koschatzky, 1973, p. 49.
61  Hevesi, 1911, p. 24.
62  Koschatzky, 1986.


V  A WORLD STILL INTACT, AND THE NEW PRE-MARCH SPIRIT

1  Exh. cat. Vienna, 1978, p. 69.
2  Ibid., pp. 75 f.
3  Feuchtmüller, 1975, pp. 78 ff.
4  Ibid., p. 89.
5  W. Koschatzky, in exh. cat. Vienna, 1978, p. 76.
6  Published in ibid., pp. 87–110.
7  Koschatzky, 1982, p. 86.
8  Ibid., p. 87.
9  Ibid., p. 94.
10  Ibid., p. 104.
11  Ibid.
12  Quoted from Adolph, 1951, p. 32.
13  In Dorotheum, 362nd art auction in Vienna, January, 1922, p. 59.
14  From Zimmermann, 1923, p. 17, to H. Kaut, in exh. cat. Laxenburg, 1968, p. 69.

15 Zimmermann, 1923, p. 5; quoted from A. Schopenhauer, *Sämtliche Werke* (ed. by J. Frauenstädt), Leipzig, 1922, Vol. I, book 3: *Die Welt als Wille und Vorstellung (The World as Will and Idea)*.
16 R. Eitelberger, *Kunst und Künstler Wiens der neueren Zeit*, Vienna, 1879, vol. I, p. 46.
17 Ibid., vol. I, p. 189.
18 Jurek, 1978.
19 Ibid., p. 43.
20 Zimmermann 1923, p. 16.
21 Ibid.
22 Grimschitz, 1928, p. 35.
23 In 1815, for the publisher J. Schönberg, military fly-sheets; in 1819–20, the lithographic series *Portrayal of the Royal–Imperial Austrian Army*; c. 1825, for Artaria, working drawings for a series of *Illustrations of Austrian Troops*, etc.
24 *Mandlbögen* were sheets *(Bögen)* of printed figures *(Mandl* = manikin) that were cut out and glued in a standing position on a ground plan that came with them.
25 Haberdiztl and Schwarz, 1930, p. 21.
26 Ibid., no. 121 (our Pl. 100); formerly in the collections of the prince of Liechtenstein, now in the Graphische Sammlung Albertina, Vienna (inv. no. 31.189); working drawing for the oil painting in the Österreichische Galerie (inv. no. 353).
27 Graphische Sammlung Albertina, Vienna (inv. no. 25.882); our Pl. 101.
28 Written on August 25, 1821, to Jean and Charles Vesque of Püttlingen; Stadtbibliothek, Vienna, no. 30.952.
29 Obituary by F. C. Weidmann, in *Wiener Allgemeine Theaterzeitung* (ed. by Adolf Bäuerle), 35th year, 1842, no. 204, p. 907.
30 Files of the Akademie der Bildenden Künste, Vienna, no. 450/1850; see exh. cat. Vienna, 1986, p. 143, from which much of what follows was taken.
31 Exh. cat. Vienna, 1986, p. 58.
32 Ibid.
33 Ibid., p. 57.
34 Albertina facsimile D105/1948; see also exh. cat. Vienna, 1973a, pp. 78ff.
35 Reproduced in Grünstein, 1923, plate XLVI.
36 Exh. cat. Vienna, 1986; Leo Grünstein was the first to refer to this passage (Grunstein, 1923, pp. 54f.).
37 Novotny, 1948.
38 Dossi, 1982, p. 210.
39 U. Jenni, in exh. cat. Vienna, 1986, p. 50.
40 Ibid.
41 J. W. von Goethe, *Sämtliche Werke*, jubilee edition, Stuttgart and Berlin, n. d., Vol. 33: *Schriften zur Kunst*, part 1, pp. 205ff., 214.
42 J. W. von Goethe, letter to Johann Heinrich Merck, "Bei Übergabe einer Zeichnung"; quoted from exh. cat. Nuremberg, 1966, p. 2.
43 Ibid.
44 J. W. von Goethe, *Sämtliche Werke*, (see note 41 above), vol. 33, p. 175: "Man, however, is not merely a thinking but also a feeling creature. He is a whole, a oneness of many intimately connected forces. And it is the whole [man] that the work of art must address; it must satisfy that rich unity, that singular multifariousness within him."
45 Wurzbach, 1888, "Daffinger" article, in volume for 1858, p. 128.
46 Pirchan, 1943, p. 101.
47 Exh. cat. Vienna, 1986, pp. 48ff.
48 R. Wagner, in exh. cat. Vienna, 1986, p. 25.
49 The etching is in the Daffinger omnibus volume, p. 7, Graphische Sammlung Albertina, Vienna (inv. no. ÖK XIX, no. 7).
50 Pirchan, 1943, p. 103.
51 Erroneously given by R. Wagner, in exh. cat. Vienna, 1986, p. 25, as "1912" instead of "1921" (Auktionshaus Miethke, Vienna).
52 Quoted from exh. cat. Vienna, 1973a, pp. 25f.
53 Grimschitz, 1928, p. 80.
54 Prince Metternich had been kept in very close touch with the latest advances by the Austrian ambassador Count Anton Apponyi. When the time came, therefore, Metternich was able to send to Paris the most able scientist in this field, Andreas von Ettingshausen, professor of physics at Vienna University. Ettingshausen's perceptions as a scientist (he also recognized the shortcomings of Daguerre's process) led immediately to decisive advances being made in Vienna. See W. Koschatzky, *Die Kunst der Photographie*, Salzburg, 1984, pp. 54ff.
55 *Wiener Zeitung*, September 30, 1839: "Der Österreichische Zuschauer."
56 See exh. cat. Vienna, 1973a, p. 178 and cat. no. 59.
57 Grimschitz, 1928, pp. 80ff.
58 H. Schwarz, in exh. cat. Vienna, 1973a, p. 128.
59 P. Pötschner, in exh. cat. Laxenburg, 1968, p. 60.
60 Ibid., p. 61.
61 W. Koschatzky, in exh. cat. Vienna, 1973a, p. 90.
62 P. Pötschner, in exh. cat. Laxenburg, 1968, p. 60.
63 C. Bodenstein, in exh. cat. Vienna, 1895, introduction.
64 For the precise route, see Koschatzky, 1982, p. 124.
65 Ibid.
66 See Koschatzky, 1982a, letter of 1847, quoted on p. 147; all in the Steiermarkisches Landesarchiv, Graz; Meran family archives, *Briefe Enders* (Ender's letters).
67 Letter of 1842; quoted in Koschatzky, 1982a, p. 124.
68 Ibid.
69 U. Thieme and F. Becker, *Allgemeines Lexikon der bildenden Künstler von der Antike bis zur Gegenwart*, (ed. by H. Vollmer), 37 vols., Leipzig, 1907–50, vol. XII, 1928, p. 145.
70 Schwarz, 1924.
71 F. Novotny, in exh. cat. Essen, 1960, p. 56.
72 Diaries of Archduke John, November 1, 1837; Steiermarkisches Landesarchiv, Graz: Meran family archives.
73 The parish of St. Leonhard, Graz, was able to purchase the entire estate with sketchbooks from these years for the Historisches Museum der Stadt Wien, Vienna.
74 See V. Birke, in exh. cat. Vienna, 1983, pp. 9ff.
75 Ibid., nos. 34–6.
76 Ibid., p. 12.
77 Exh. cat. Vienna, 1978, p. 84.
78 Ibid., p. 110.
79 Kralik and Schlitter, 1912, p. 641.
80 Ibid., p. 640.
81 Quoted from Tietze, 1925, p. 101.
82 Ibid.
83 Gutzkow, 1845, vol. II, pp. 285ff.
84 Quoted from Bietak, 1931, p. 2, note 1.
85 Theiss, 1958, p. 58.

VI  Change and Reorganization

1   All the quotations in this paragraph are from Count Karl Friedrich von Vitzthum von Eckstädt, "Berlin und Wien, 1847–1852"; reprinted in *1848: Der Vorkampf deutscher Einheit und Freiheit*; quoted from Tietze, 1925, p. 101.
2   Quoted in Kralik and Schlitter, 1912, p. 687.
3   Ibid.
4   Ibid., p. 666.
5   Ibid.
6   Ibid.
7   Exh. cat. Vienna, 1969 a, cat. nos. 642–708.
8   Koschatzky, 1975, pp. 99 ff.
9   Ibid.
10  Ibid.
11  Ibid.
12  Koschatzky, 1982 a, pp. 148 ff.
13  Ibid.
14  Ibid.
15  Ibid.
16  Ibid., pp. 149 f.
17  K. F. von Vitzthum von Eckstädt, "Berlin und Wien", (see note 1 above), p. 101.
18  Kralik and Schlitter, 1912, p. 680.
19  Ibid.
20  Quoted from Tietze, 1925, pp. 114 ff.
21  Grimschitz, 1963, p. 9.
22  Ibid., p. 10.
23  Ibid., the entire text.
24  Aurenhammer, 1975–6, pp. 77 ff.
25  Ibid., p. 78.
26  Karl Konrad Polheim, "Die wirkliche Wirklichkeit: Adalbert Stifters 'Nachkommenschaften' und das Problem seiner Kunstanschauung," in *Festschrift für Benno von Wiese*, Berlin, 1972, pp. 385 ff.
27  To Dr. A. Fournier in Paris; quoted from Weixelgärtner, 1916, vol. I, p. 8.
28  Aurenhammer, 1975–6, p. 79.
29  Weixlgärtner, 1916, vol. I, p. 235.
30  Ibid., vol. I, p. 196, letter of November 15, 1895.
31  Ibid., vol. I, p. 235, letter of May 5, 1875.
32  Ibid., vol. I, p. 238.
33  Hevesi, 1903, p. 115.
34  Aurenhammer, 1975–6, pp. 77 ff.
35  F. Novotny, in exh. cat. Essen, 1960, pp. 83 f.
36  Hevesi, 1903, p. 201.
37  Koschatzky, 1982 a, p. 152.
38  Ibid.
39  Archives of the city of Vienna: Elise Ender's travel diary, 1855, (inv. nos. 118.743/Ia; 127.459).
40  C. Bodenstein, in exh. cat. Vienna, 1895, p. 26.
41  Hevesi, 1903, p. 251.
42  Wurzbach, 1888, vol. 13, 1865, pp. 219 ff.; see also idem., *Josef Kriehuber: Katalog der von ihm lithographierten Portraits*, Munich, 1902.
43  Vincenti, 1876, pp. 349 ff.
44  Ibid.
45  Popelka, 1964.
46  Ibid., p. 15.
47  Ibid.
48  Ibid., p. 20.
49  Quoted from ibid., p. 17, note 24.
50  Ibid., p. 28.
51  Ibid.
52  Ibid., pp. 35 f., 82 ff.
53  Koschatzky, 1975, p. 100.
54  Novotny, 1954, pp. 5 ff.
55  Novotny, 1956, p. 69.
56  See Novotny, 1954, list of works, pp. 77 ff.; see also idem., 1956, p. 5.
57  Novotny, 1954, p. 5.
58  Novotny, 1956, p. 5.
59  Letter of January 29, 1850; quoted in Novotny, 1954, p. 11; see also exh. cat. Vienna, 1973 a, p. 152.
60  Novotny, 1954, p. 68.

VII  Historicism and the Late Nineteenth Century

1   H. Bisanz, in exh. cat. Vienna, 1973 b, pp. 14 ff.
2   G. Düriegl, in exh. cat. Vienna, 1973 b, pp. 7 ff.
3   Kralik and Schlitter, 1912, p. 714
4   Leitich, 1942, pp. 99 ff.
5   Hevesi, 1903, p. 203.
6   Ibid.
7   Ibid. p. 204
8   Exh. cat. Vienna, 1973 b, p. 19
9   The painting by H. Schliessmann (1852–1920) is called *Die Bergmusik (The Palace Band).*
10  Grimschitz, 1928, p. 19.
11  Vincenti, 1876, pp. 349 ff.
12  Quoted from Leisching, 1926, p. 210.
13  Grimschitz, 1928, p. 87.
14  Karl Schultz quoted in ibid., p. 88.
15  Koschatzky, 1975, p. 212.
16  Quoted from Leitich, 1942, p. 112.
17  Hevesi, 1903, p. 255.
18  Münz, 1954, p. 8 (unpaginated).
19  (Inv. no. St. W. Hs. 22.104), December 30, 1881.
20  Koschatzky, 1975, p. 186.
21  Österreichische Nationalbibliothek, Vienna: Manuscript Collection, autographs 123/71 ff., May 22, 1882.

VIII  On to the End

1   Hevesi, 1903, p. 236.
2   Ibid., p. 146.
3   Ibid., p. 200.
4   Koschatzky, 1975, p. 217.
5   Ibid.
6   Ibid., p. 218.
7   Hevesi, 1898, p. 14.

# Descriptive Captions to the Color Plates

Where bibliographic references in the captions are given in abbreviated form, full details will be found in the Selected Bibliography (p. 268).

1  Charles-Joseph Roettiers. *The Austrian Monarchy (Monarchia Austriaca*; from the teaching plates for Archduke Ferdinand). 1769. Watercolor with gold highlights on card, c. 520 × 315 cm. Österreichische Nationalbibliothek, Vienna, manuscript collection, Cod. min. 33 a.
    See Unterkirchner, 1959, p. 129; Mraz, 1979, pp. 180 ff., 258 f., 351, 353; exh. cat. Vienna, 1908, p. 55, no. 360; exh. cat. Vienna, 1980, no. 38,01.

2  Charles-Joseph Roettiers. *Systematic Index (Index Systematicus*; from the teaching plates for Archduke Ferdinand). 1769. Watercolor with gold highlights on card, c. 520 × 315 cm. Österreichische Nationalbibliothek, Vienna, manuscript collection, Cod. min. 33 a.
    See Unterkirchner, 1959, p. 129; Mraz, 1979, pp. 180 ff., 258 f., 351, 353; exh. cat. Vienna, 1908, p. 55, no. 360; exh. cat. Vienna, 1980, no. 38,01.

3  Friedrich Heinrich Füger. *Archduchess Marie Christine and Duke Albert of Saxe-Teschen Showing Their Family the Art Treasures They Acquired in Italy.* 1776. Tempera miniature on parchment, 342 × 390 cm. Signed and dated on the base of the vase: "H.F. Füger pinx. 1776." Österreichische Galerie, Vienna (2.296).
    See A.M. Schwarzenberg, "Studien zu F.H. Füger," Ph.D. dissertation, University of Vienna, 1974, pp. 35 ff.; exh. cat. Vienna, 1969 b, p. 68; exh. cat. Vienna, 1980, no. 46,04.

4  Martin von Molitor. *Rocky Landscape with a Flock of Goats.* c. 1785. Gouache on blue paper, 445 × 588 cm. Graphische Sammlung Albertina, Vienna (18.055).
    See C. Reinwetter, "Studien zu Martin von Molitor (1759–1812): Mit besonderer Berücksichtigung seiner Zeit," Ph.D. dissertation, University of Vienna, 1981, no. 48; exh. cat. Vienna, 1973 a, no. 13.
    Corresponding sketch: *Double Waterfall.* Black and white crayon on blue paper, 286 × 385 cm. Graphische Sammlung Albertina, Vienna (16.748).

5  Lorenz Janscha. *View of Vienna from Cobenzl.* c. 1796. Watercolor, 267 × 411 cm. Graphische Sammlung Albertina, Vienna (6.940).
    See Pötschner, 1978, no. 16; May, 1980, no. 49, plate 45.
    The working drawing for J. Ziegler's colored print entitled *Second View from Reisenberg Looking Toward the City*, published by J. Cappi, Vienna.

6  Jakob Gauermann. *Miss Louise von G.* 1799. Watercolor and Chinese white over pencil, 215 × 139 cm. Signed and dated, top right: "den 7tn Juny 1799/gezt: J. Gauermann." Galerie & Auktionshaus W. Hassfurther, Vienna.
    A portrait study with detailed indications for revision in the artist's own hand.

7  Carl Schütz. *St. Michael's Church and the Hofburg Theater.* c. 1790. Watercolor, 278 × 385 cm. Graphische Sammlung Albertina, Vienna (6.864).

8  Carl Schütz. *Stock-im-Eisen Square*, Vienna. 1779. Pen and grey ink, watercolor, 280 × 420 cm. Inscribed, bottom left: "Nach der Natur gezeichnet von C. Schütz 1779 (Drawn from nature by...)." Graphische Sammlung Albertina, Vienna (28.635).
    See May, 1980, no. 34, ill. plate 31; exh. cat. Vienna, 1969 b, no. 28.
    The working drawing for C. Schütz's 1779 colored print, no. 4 in the collection of views of Vienna that Artaria began publishing in 1784 (first edition).

9  Johann Ziegler. *Building the Drawbridge near the Red Tower Gate in 1780.* 1780. Pen and watercolor, 310 × 447 cm. Later inscribed, bottom left: "Schütz del." Graphische Sammlung Albertina, Vienna (25.974).
    See Schwarz, 1914, no. 36; May, 1962, no. 15; exh. cat. Vienna, 1973 a, no. 27, ill. p. 191.

10  Friedrich August Brand. *Langenzersdorf, near Vienna.* c. 1780. Watercolor and gouache with white highlights, 339 × 520 cm. Inscribed on back: "Langenzersdorf, Ausblick gegen den Leopoldsberg (Langenzersdorf, looking toward the Leopoldsberg)." Historisches Museum der Stadt Wien, Vienna (41.488).
    See exh. cat. Vienna, 1973 a, no. 6, ill. p. 53.

11  Lorenz Janscha. *The Roman Ruins in the Gardens of the Pleasure Palace at Schönbrünn.* c. 1785. Watercolor and gouache, 267 × 411 cm. Inscribed, bottom left: "Dessiné d'après Nature par L. Janscha (Drawn from nature by...)." Graphische Sammlung Albertina, Vienna (6.877).

12  Lorenz Janscha. *In Erlaa Park, Outside Vienna.* (formerly entitled, *View of the Temple and the Grove from the English Promenades in Erlaa Gardens, Austria*). c. 1790. Watercolor, 268 × 412 cm. Graphische Sammlung Albertina, Vienna (6.887).
    See exh. cat. Vienna, 1973 a, no. 32.
    Erlaa Park near Hiezing, just outside Vienna, was laid out

by Georg Adam von Starhemberg in 1766–70. It was an early example of the new English style of landscape gardening.

13   Lorenz Janscha. *The Artist Drawing in the Adlitz Rift, near Schottwien.* c. 1800. Watercolor, 275 × 416 cm. Signed, bottom right: "L. Janscha." Graphische Sammlung Albertina, Vienna (6.935).
   See Koschatzky, 1982b, ill. on front and back endpapers.
   The working drawing for the colored print *A Part of the Haidbach Rift* by Janscha and J. Ziegler.

14   Friedrich Heinrich Füger. *Portrait of Archduchess Maria Clementina of Austria, Royal Princess of Naples.* 1795. Miniature in watercolor and gouache on ivory; circular: diameter 146 cm. Signed and dated: "Füger p. 1795."
   Maria Clementina was born in 1777, the daughter of Emperor Leopold II and sister of Emperor Francis I (II) and Archduke John. She was married by proxy to King Francis I of the Two Sicilies, in Vienna in 1790, and the marriage was consummated at Foggia in 1797. In the following year, the princess gave birth to a daughter – Carolina, who later became Duchess of Berri; Maria Clementina died prematurely in 1801.
   The miniature (see A. Stix, *H.F. Füger*, Vienna, 1925, no. 56, plate XLIX) was formerly in the Figdor Collection. It was auctioned on behalf of a private owner by Sotheby's of London in March, 1986; when it fetched the unusually high price of £ 47,300.

15   Friedrich Heinrich Füger. *Portrait of a Young Man in a Brown Coat.* 1785. Gouache with white highlights on ivory; oval: 118 × 85 cm. Signed and dated, bottom right: "Füger, p. 1785." Formerly in the Bourgoing Collection, Vienna; now in the Historisches Museum der Stadt Wien, Vienna (132.025).
   See Laban, 1905, catalogue no. 82, plate VI, no. 2; Leisching, 1907, no. 35, plate I; exh. cat. Vienna, 1905, no. 957; exh. cat. Vienna, 1965b, no. 155; exh. cat. Vienna, 1973a, no. 18, ill. p. 89.

16   Carl Philipp Schalhas. *Trees and Rocks.* c. 1785. Watercolor and Chinese white, 130 × 176 cm. Signed, bottom right: "C. Schallhas." Graphische Sammlung Albertina, Vienna (4.822).

17   Carl Schütz. *Belvedere Palace (Schloß Belvedere), Vienna.* 1784. Pen and watercolor, 275 × 421 cm. Inscribed and dated, bottom left: "Nach der Natur gezeichnet von C. Schütz. 1784." Graphische Sammlung Albertina, Vienna (28.632).
   See Schwarz, 1914, no. 42; exh. cat., Vienna, 1969b, no. 29; exh. cat. Vienna, 1973a, no. 28, ill. p. 171.
   The working drawing for C. Schütz's 1785 colored print.

18   Matthäus Loder. *Twelve Designs for Playing Cards with German Color Suits.* c. 1818. Watercolor over pencil, each c. 83 × 53 cm. Historisches Museum der Stadt Wien, Vienna (left to right and top to bottom: 167.902/28, 2, 10, 19, 3, 29, 20, 11, 6, 23, 24, 32).
   See Witzmann, 1986.
   The date can be deduced from the 1818 etching series *Zerrbilder menschlicher Torheiten (Caricatures of Human Follies)*.
   The author is grateful to Dr. Reingard Witzmann for her kindness in placing these newly discovered works by Matthäus Loder at his disposal.

19   Matthäus Loder. *View of Vienna from the Theresian Bridge.* c. 1810. Watercolor, pen and ink over pencil, 325 × 470 cm. Graphische Sammlung Albertina, Vienna (5.821).
   See Tietze, 1925, ill. p. 19; May, 1980, no. 53, ill. plate 49; Wietersheim, 1982, no. 164; exh. cat. Graz, 1959, no. 92; exh. cat.Vienna, 1954, no. 17; exh. cat. Vienna, 1973a, no. 97; exh. cat. Vienna, 1978, no. 34.

20   Matthäus Loder. *Banquet in a Baronial Hall.* c. 1807–8. Watercolor and gouache, pen and grey ink over pencil, 203 × 321 cm. Signed, bottom left: "Loder." Graphische Sammlung Albertina, Vienna (5.819).
   See Wietersheim, 1982, no. 151; exh. cat. Vienna, 1973a, no. 98; exh. cat. Vienna, 1978, no. 36.

21   Johann Nepomuk Hoechle. *The Battle of Aspern.* 1809. Pen and watercolor, 290 × 398 cm. Inscribed on back: "La Bataille d'Aspern la soirée du 20 [Mai] a 9 heure et Demi les Francais avancent les Autrichien les repoussent, la partie… (The Battle of Aspern on the evening of [May] 20 at 9:30 p.m. the French advance, the Austrians repulse them, the engagement…)." Graphische Sammlung Albertina, Vienna (26.383).
   See Tietze, 1925, plate 10; exh. cat. Vienna, 1973a, no. 40.

22   Joseph Rebell. *View of Lake Como.* 1811. Watercolor, 282 × 418 cm. Signed and dated, bottom right: "Jos. Rebell 1811." Graphische Sammlung Albertina, Vienna (b. 243).

23   Johann Nepomuk Hoechle. *Emperor Francis I Welcoming Czar Alexander I of Russia and King Frederick William III of Prussia Outside Vienna.* 1814. Watercolor and pen and ink, 259 × 345 cm. Signed and dated, bottom left: "Höchle 1833. Februar"; inscribed, bottom center: "Seine Majestät Kaiser Franz I. bewilkomt vor dem Anfang des grossen Einzuges die beyden Majestäten Alexander I. Kaiser von Russland und Friedrich Wilhelm König von Preussen ausser dem Tabor zwischen der ersten und zweyten Brücke. den 25 September MDCCCXIIII (Prior to the start of the great entry procession, His Majesty Emperor Francis I welcomes their twin majesties Alexander I, czar of Russia, and Frederick William, king of Prussia, between the first and second bridges to Tabor [on the Danube] on September 25, 1814"; inscribed, bottom left: "Geschehen den 25. September 1814 (Took place on…)." Graphische Sammlung Albertina, Vienna (22.675).
   See exh. cat. Vienna, 1965a, III/no. 69; exh. cat. Vienna, 1969a, no. 128; exh. cat. Vienna, 1973a, no. 43.
   The working drawing for no. 12 in the 1833 lithographic series *Great Moments in the Life of His Majesty Emperor Francis I of Austria, Apostolic King.*

24   Johann Nepomuk Hoechle. *Emperor Francis I Entering Vienna Through the Carinthian Gate.* 1814. Watercolor, 210 × 284 cm. Signed, bottom left: "Höchle"; inscribed, at bottom: "Feyerlicher Einzug Seiner Majestät Kaiser Franz I vor der Triumphpforte am äusseren Kärtner Thor zu Wien den 16ten Juny 1814… (Formal entry of His Majesty Emperor Francis I in front of the triumphal arch at the outer Carinthian Gate in Vienna on June 16, 1814…)." Graphische Sammlung Albertina, Vienna (22.674).
   See exh. cat. Vienna, 1965a, VII/no. 22; exh. cat. Vienna, 1969a, no. 127; exh. cat. Vienna, 1973a, no. 42.
   The working drawing for no. 11 in the 1833 lithographic series *Great Moments in the Life of His Majesty Emperor Francis I of Austria, Apostolic King.*

25 Johann Adam Klein. *Mounted Uhlans at Emperor Francis I's Entry into Vienna*. 1814. Watercolor over pencil, 128 × 195 cm. Signed, dated, and inscribed, top right: "A.K. fec. Wien 1814 bei dem Einzug des Kaisers." Graphische Sammlung Albertina, Vienna (28.553).
See exh. cat. Rotterdam, 1964, no. 86; exh. cat. Vienna, 1965a, VII/no. 30; exh. cat. Vienna, 1973a, no. 39, ill. p. 109.

26 Jakob Gauermann. *Pastoral Scene*. 1817. Gouache, 253 × 349 cm. Signed and dated, bottom left: "J. Gauermann f. 817." Private collection, Vienna.
See Marko, 1980, no. 361; exh. cat. Innsbruck, 1970, no. 34, ill. 34.
Entered under this title in Gauermann's autograph list of his works.

27 Jakob Gauermann. *Pürgg at the Foot of the Grimming*. 1816. Watercolor, 413 × 608 cm. Inscribed and dated: "May 30, 1816 Grimming." Private collection (E.J. 108).
See Marko, 1986, no. 339; W. Skreiner, *Steiermark in alten Ansichten*, Salzburg, 1978, plate 63/no. 123, p. 323; exh. cat. Graz, 1959, no 76.

28 Jakob Gauermann. *Archduke John Climbing the Hochwildstelle on August 25, 1819*. 1819. Watercolor, 285 × 225 cm. Private collection (E.J. 84).
See Marko, 1980, no. 391; exh. cat. Gutenstein-Miesenbach, 1962, p. 170, no. 233; exh. cat. Graz, 1959, no. 85.

29 Jakob Alt. *View of the Lake of Traun*. 1817. Watercolor and gouache, 366 × 545 cm. Signed and dated, bottom right: "J. Alt. 1817." Graphische Sammlung Albertina, Vienna (4.942).
See exh. cat. Vienna, 1973a, no. 173.

30 Thomas Ender. *View of Oberdöbling, near Vienna*. 1814. Watercolor over pencil, 240 × 340 cm. Signed, bottom right: "Tho. Ender"; inscribed and dated, bottom center: "1814 Ober-Döbling." Historisches Museum der Stadt Wien, Vienna (45.357).
See Koschatzky, 1982a, no. 13; exh. cat. Vienna, 1969a, no. 405.

31 Thomas Ender. *View from the Corcovado, near Rio de Janeiro*. 1817–18. Watercolor over pencil, 324 × 472 cm. Akademie der bildenden Künste: Kupferstichkabinett, Vienna (13.201).
Cf. the corresponding painting: Ferrez, 1958, p. 70; Koschatzky, 1982a, no. 30; copperplate engraving from the print by J.N. Passini and J. Axmann.

32 Thomas Ender. *The Austrian Chamberlains on Their Way to São Paolo*. 1818. Pencil with watercolor, 400 × 525 cm. Inscribed, bottom center: "No 582 die österreichischen Kammer Herrn auf der Reise nach St. Paul." Akademie der bildenden Künste: Kupferstichkabinett, Vienna (13.824).
See Koschatzky, 1982a, no. 29; exh. cat. Vienna, 1964, no. 89 (ill.); exh. cat. Vienna, 1973a, no. 48.

33 Balthasar Wigand. *Vienna Seen from Grinzing*. c. 1825. Watercolor and gouache with traces of pencil, 124 × 197 cm. Signed, bottom left: "Wigand"; inscribed: "Wien von Grinzing zu Sehen." Graphische Sammlung Albertina, Vienna (29.617).
See exh. cat. Vienna, 1977, no. 86.

34 August Wilhelm Rieder. *Portrait of Franz Schubert*. 1825. Watercolor over pencil on card, 197 × 247 cm. Signed and dated, bottom left: "W. Rieder May 825"; inscribed, bottom left: "Nach der Natur von Wilh. Aug. Rieder 1825"; inscribed, bottom right: "Franz Schubert [the composer's own signature] gestorben den 19. November 1828 (died…) [added in a different hand]." Historisches Museum der Stadt Wien, Vienna (104.170).
See exh. cat. Vienna, 1969a, no. 457.

35 Leopold Kupelwieser. *Franz Schubert on an Outing in the Country, Pictured on the Way from Atzenbrugg Castle to the Mill in the Mead (Aumühle)*. 1820. Watercolor and gouache, 237 × 388 cm. Signed and dated, bottom right: "Kupelwieser 1820." Historisches Museum der Stadt Wien, Vienna (18.751).

36 Ferdinand Georg Waldmüller. *Old Soldier with Three Children*. 1827. Watercolor, 315 × 266 cm. Signed and dated, bottom right: "Waldmüller 1827." Graphische Sammlung Albertina, Vienna (34.723).
See Grimschitz, 1957, no. 213.

37 Matthäus Loder, *Archduke John Taking Leave of Anna Plochl near the Town of Aussee*. 1825–6. Watercolor over pencil, 310 × 370 cm. Private collection (E.J. 265).
See Koschatzky, 1978, p. 94; Wietersheim, 1982, no. 876; exh. cat. Graz, 1959, no. 131; exh. cat. Vienna, 1973a, no. 94; exh. cat. Vienna, 1978, no. 71.

38 Matthäus Loder. *Archduke John at the Foot of the Ankogel, near the Village of Gastein*. 1827. Watercolor and gouache over pencil, 268 × 370 cm. Signed and dated, bottom right: "Loder 1827"; inscribed with title on gold shield. Private collection (E.J. 280).
See Koschatzky, 1978, ill. 40; Wietersheim, 1982, no. 893; exh. cat. Graz, 1959, no. 140; exh. cat. Vienna, 1973a, no. 93, ill. p. 125; exh. cat. Vienna, 1978, no. 85, ill. p. 39.

39 Matthäus Loder. *Huntsman Jörgl in Winter Gear*. c. 1820. Watercolor over pencil, 365 × 240 cm. Private collection (E.J. 355).
See Mautner-Geramb, 1932–9, ill. 218; Wietersheim, 1982, no. 479; exh. cat. Graz, 1959, no. 118; exh. cat. Gutenstein-Miesenbach, 1962, no. 241; exh. cat. Vienna, 1973a, no. 92; exh. cat. Vienna, 1978, no. 58, ill. p. 24; exh. cat. Stainz, 1982, no. 19/36.

40 Matthäus Loder. *The Ascent to Consecrate the Cross on the Erzberg*. 1823. Watercolor over pencil, 280 × 365 cm. Private collection (E.J. 269).
See Mautner-Geramb, 1932–9, ill. 68 (detail); Wietersheim, 1982, no. 850; exh. cat. Graz, 1959, no. 141; exh. cat. Vienna, 1978, no. 97.

41 Matthäus Loder. *Waterfalls in Full View of the Ice in the Joiner's Cirque (Tischlerkar), near the Village of Gastein*. 1826–7. Gouache and watercolor over pencil, 275 × 355 cm. Inscribed and dated, bottom right: "Loder 1827" (in gold ink). Private collection (E.J. 335).
See Wietersheim, 1982, no. 908; exh. cat. Graz, 1959, no. 145; exh. cat. Vienna, 1978, no. 86, ill. p. 36.

42 Matthäus Loder. *Copper Smelting in Kalwang, Styria*. c. 1825. Watercolor over pencil, 382 × 254 cm. Inscribed, bottom center, with title. Private collection (E.J. 310).

See Wietersheim, 1982, no. 717; exh. cat. Dortmund, 1958, no. 307; exh. cat. Graz, 1959, no. 115; exh. cat. Gutenstein-Miesenbach, 1962, no. 243; exh. cat. Vienna, 1965a, XXIV/no. 22, ill. 72; exh. cat. Vienna, 1973a, no. 96; exh. cat. Vienna, 1978, no. 52.

43   Leopold Fischer. *Portrait Study of a Young Couple.* c. 1830. Watercolor miniature on paper, 294 × 200 cm. Private collection, Vienna.

44   Johann Nepomuk Hoechle. *The Duke of Reichstadt Lying in State.* July 1832. Watercolor, 375 × 505 cm. Graphische Sammlung Albertina, Vienna (38.398).
     The working drawing for a lithograph.

45   Eduard Gurk. *The Imperial Residence in Baden, near Vienna.* 1833. Watercolor, 443 × 565 cm. Signed and dated, bottom center: "Gurk ad nat. f. 1833." Graphische Sammlung Albertina, Vienna (22.613).
     See exh. cat. Vienna, 1978, no. 109.

46   Jakob Alt. *The Artist's Wife Reading near Stiebar Palace, Gresten, Lower Austria.* 1834. Watercolor and gouache, 452 × 559 cm. Signed and dated, bottom right: "J. Alt 1834"; inscribed, on the mount: "Gresten in Österreich." Österreichische Nationalbibliothek, Vienna (Pk 502/18).
     See Koschatzky, 1975, watercolor cat. no. 9, peep-show series 5; exh. cat. Vienna, 1973a, no. 104.

47   Four portrait miniatures, c. 1835:
     a) Emanuel Thomas Peter (copy after Daffinger). *Empress Marianne of Austria.* c. 1835. Watercolor miniature on ivory, 90 × 72 cm. Signed, bottom right: "Em. Peter." Formerly in the collection of Archduchess Alice of Tuscany (present ownership unknown).
     Empress Marianne (or Maria Anna; 1803–84) was a daughter of King Victor Emanuel I of Sardinia. She married Crown Prince Ferdinand of Austria (who became emperor in 1835) on February 26, 1831, and following his abdication in 1848, lived in Prague.
     See Liesching, 1907, plate 171; Grünstein. 1923, plates XIV, XXV, XLV; L. Schidlof, *La Miniature en Europe,* Graz, 1964, p. 188 ["*un des chefs-d'œuvre de l'artiste*"].

     b) Moritz Michael Daffinger. *Portrait of a Lady [Princess Löwenstein?].* c. 1835. Watercolor miniature on ivory, 92 × 72 cm. Formerly in the collection of Dr. E. Ullmann, Vienna (present ownership unknown).
     c) Moritz Michael Daffinger. *Portrait of Marie Daffinger, the Artist's Wife.* c. 1833. Watercolor miniature on ivory, 135 × 106 cm. Formerly in the collection of C. Castiglione. Vienna (present ownership unknown).
     d) Moritz Michael Daffinger. *Portrait of Marie Daffinger, the Artist's Wife.* 1828. Watercolor miniature on ivory, 120 × 94 cm. Marion Hinteregger-Pierer Collection, Vienna.
     See Pirchan, 1943, ill. 98; Koschatzky, 1982b, no. 125; exh. cat. Salzburg, 1967, no. 13, plate 12; exh. cat. Vienna, 1973a, no. 74, ill. p. 63.

48   Moritz Michael Daffinger. *Portrait of Marie Daffinger, the Artist's Wife.* c. 1827. Watercolor on ivory, 156 × 102 cm. Formerly in the collection of C. Castiglione, Vienna (present ownership unknown).
     See Grünstein, 1923, plate XLIV; L. Schidlof. *La Miniature en Europe.* Graz, 1964, p. 188 ["*excellente*"].

49   Moritz Michael Daffinger. *Portrait of the Dramatist Franz Grillparzer.* 1827. Watercolor over pencil, 355 × 261 cm. Signed and dated, bottom right: "Daffinger 827." Historisches Museum der Stadt Wien, Vienna (33.911).
     See Pirchan, 1943 plate XIV; exh. cat. Vienna, 1973a, no. 69.

50   Peter Fendi. *The Wedding Morning from Schiller's Poem "The Lay of the Bell."* 1832. Watercolor and gouache over pencil, 240 × 316 cm. Inscribed and dated, bottom right: "Fendi. 1832." Sammlungen des Regierenden Fürsten von Liechtenstein, Vaduz Castle, Vaduz (283).
     See Adolf, 1951, A 101 (where the date is given as 1828).
     Accompanies the passage: "*Lieblich in der Bräute Locken / Spielt der jungfräuliche Kranz / Wenn die hellen Kirchenglocken / Laden zu des Festes Glanz!* (Lovely, thither are they bringing, / With her virgin wreath, the Bride! / To the love feast clearly ringing, / Tolls the church bell far and wide! [tr. Edward Bulwer-Lytton])."

51   Peter Fendi. *The Son's Homecoming from Schiller's Poem "The Lay of the Bell."* 1833. Watercolor over pencil, 235 × 314 cm. Inscribed, bottom right: "Fendi f." Sammlungen des Regierenden Fürsten von Liechtenstein, Vaduz Castle, Vaduz (282).
     See Adolf, 1951, A 271.
     Accompanies the passage: "*Fremd kehrt er heim in's Vaterhaus / Und herrlich in der Jugend Pranden / Wie ein Gebild aus Himmels Höh'n, / Mit züchtigen verschämten Wangen / Sieht er die Jungfrau vor sich steh'n* ([He] seeks, stranger-like, the Father Home. / And, lo, as some sweet vision breaks / Out from its native morning skies, / With rosy shame on downcast cheeks, / The Virgin stands before his eyes [tr. Edward Bulwer-Lytton])."

52   Peter Fendi. *Returning from the Fields (Ave Maria) from Schiller's Poem "The Lay of the Bell."* 1833. Watercolor over pencil, 244 × 318 cm. Inscribed and dated, bottom right: "Fendi. 1833." Sammlungen des Regierenden Fürsten von Liechtenstein, Vaduz Castle, Vaduz (281).
     See Adolf, 1951, A 272.
     Accompanies the passage: "*Holder Friede / Süsse Eintracht / Weilet, weilet, / Freundlich über dieser Stadt / Möge nie der Tag erscheinen / Wo des rauhen Kriegers Horden, / Dieses stille Thal durchtoben* (… Peace and Concord sweet! / Distant the day. Oh! distant far. / When the rude hordes of trampling War / Shall scare the silent vale [tr. Edward Bulwer-Lytton])."

53   Peter Fendi. *The Thunderstorm.* 1836. Watercolor, 213 × 268 cm. Signed and dated, center right: "Fendi. 1836." Sammlungen des Regierenden Fürsten von Liechtenstein, Vaduz Castle, Vaduz (263).
     See Adolf, 1951, A 97; Spitzmüller, 1955, ill. plate 60; exh. cat. Gutenstein-Miesenbach, 1962, no. 806; exh. cat. Vienna, 1963, no. 80; exh. cat. Vienna, 1973a, no. 144.
     Cf. another painting in watercolor and the 1837 oil painting (Österreichische Galerie, Vienna [1.374]).

54   Peter Fendi. *A Peasant Woman and Child Beside a Statue of the Virgin Mary.* c. 1840. Watercolor over pencil, 159 × 127 cm. Graphische Sammlung Albertina, Vienna (35.898 [recently acquired]).
     See exh. cat. Vienna, 1973a, no. 146.

55   Peter Fendi. *Young Woman and Child Beside a Hen Coop.* 1836. Watercolor over pencil, 225 × 268 cm. Signed and dated, bottom right: "Fendi. 1836." Sammlungen des Regierenden Fürsten von Liechtenstein, Vaduz Castle, Vaduz (262).
    See exh. cat. Gutenstein-Miesenbach, 1962, no. 807; exh. cat. Vienna, 1963, no. 79; exh. cat. Vienna, 1973a, no. 122.

56   Peter Fendi. *Two Princesses of Liechtenstein with Their Governess.* 1838. Watercolor over pencil, 196 × 234 cm. Signed and dated, bottom left: "Fendi. 1838." Graphische Sammlung Albertina, Vienna (31.016).
    See Adolf, 1951, A 55; exh. cat. Vienna, 1963, no. 47; exh. cat. Vienna, 1973a, no. 152, ill. p. 7.
    The two princesses are Elise, who later married Prince Hugo of Salm-Reifferscheid-Raitz, and her sister Fanny, who later married Prince Robert Arenberg. The governess is Mlle Verneuille (later Mme Amiot), who had long held that position in the Liechtenstein household.

57   Peter Fendi. *Illustration for Schiller's Poem "The Fight with the Dragon."* 1835. Watercolor and gouache, 237 × 318 cm. Signed and dated, bottom left: "Fendi. 1835." Sammlungen des Regierenden Fürsten von Liechtenstein, Vaduz Castle, Vaduz (274).
    See Adolf, 1951, A 283 or 284.

58   Peter Fendi. *Illustration for Schiller's Poem "The Fight with the Dragon": "Dich hat der eitle Ruhm bewegt...."* ([... thou hast] dared thy sacred sword to wield / For fame in a forbidden field [tr. Edward Bulwer-Lytton])." 1835. Watercolor and gouache, 238 × 314 cm. Signed and dated, bottom right: "Fendi. 1835." Sammlungen des Regierenden Fürsten von Liechtenstein, Vaduz Castle, Vaduz (275).
    See Adolf, 1951, A 283 or 284.

59   Peter Fendi. *Illustration for Schiller's Poem "The Cranes of Ibycus."* 1834. Watercolor and gouache, 236 × 316 cm. Signed and dated, bottom right: "Fendi 1834." Sammlungen des Regierenden Fürsten von Liechtenstein, Vaduz Castle, Vaduz (277).
    See Adolf, 1951, A 295 or 296.

60   Peter Fendi. *A Visit to the Nun.* 1839. Watercolor, 168 × 204 cm. Signed and dated: "Fendi. 1839." Private collection, Vienna.
    See exh. cat. Vienna, 1963, no. 57.

61   Peter Fendi. *Pilgrims' Halt.* 1842. Watercolor and pencil, 84 × 108 cm. Private collection, Munich.

62   Peter Fendi. *Gypsy Encampment.* 1840. Watercolor, 162 × 237 cm. Signed and dated, bottom right: "Fendi 1840." Graphische Sammlung Albertina, Vienna (25.470).
    See exh. cat. Vienna, 1973a, no. 125.

63   Peter Fendi. *Family Reunion of the Imperial House of Austria in the Autumn of 1834.* 1834. Watercolor, 380 × 530 cm. Signed and dated, bottom left: "Fendi. 1834." Erzherzog Franz Ferdinand Museum, Artstetten Palace.
    See Adolf, 1951, A 15; exh. cat. Vienna, 1963, no. 36 (with refs.), ill. 3; exh. cat. Vienna, 1973a, no. 138.
    Engraved by Johann Nepomuk Passini, together with a cephalogram of those portrayed.

64   Peter Fendi. *Album Flyleaf for Prince Clemens Lothar Metternich, Chancellor of State.* 1837. Watercolor over pencil, 205 × 250 cm. Signed and dated, bottom center: "Fendi. 1837." Graphische Sammlung Albertina, Vienna (28.409).
    See Adolf, 1951, A 68; exh. cat. Vienna, 1963, no. 69; exh. cat. Vienna, 1973a, no. 156.

65   Peter Fendi. *Evening Prayers.* 1839. Watercolor and pencil, 269 × 363 cm. Signed and dated, bottom left: "Fendi. 1839." Graphische Sammlung Albertina, Vienna (28.334).
    See Haberditzel-Grimschitz, 1922, pp. 21, 30, sheet 12; exh. cat. Vienna, 1924, no. 99, ill. p. 51; Adolf, 1951, A 66; exh. cat. Düsseldorf, 1959, no. 43; exh. cat. Vienna, 1963, no. 35; exh. cat. Munich, 1972, no. 208, plate 162; exh. cat. Vienna, 1973a, no. 132; exh. cat. Vienna, 1979, no. 13.
    Commissioned by Archduchess Sophie in 1839 as a Christmas gift for her husband Archduke Francis Charles.

66   Thomas Ender. *The Passage Through the Urtelstein in the Helenen Valley, near Baden.* c. 1830. Watercolor with Chinese white and scraped highlights, 148 × 218 cm. Signed, bottom right: "Tho. Ender." Galerie & Auktionshaus W. Hassfurther, Vienna.
    Cf. the corresponding engraving: Graphische Sammlung Albertina, Vienna (79.483) [see exh. cat. Vienna, 1964, no. 109] and (79.485), a second state (141 × 219 cm) signed, bottom left in the plate: "Tho. Ender fec."

67   Josef Höger. *Hallstadt*, from an album with views of Ischl commune. 1836. Watercolor over pencil, 249 × 326 cm. Sammlungen des Regierenden Fürsten von Liechtenstein, Vaduz Castle, Vaduz (no inv. number).

68   Josef Höger. *The Road to the Lake of Gosau*, from an album with views of Ischl commune. Watercolor, 305 × 244 cm. Sammlungen des Regierenden Fürsten von Liechtenstein, Vaduz Castle, Vaduz (no inv. number).

69   Thomas Ender. *Archduke John with his Wife and Companions at the Top of the Gamskarkogel, a Hill near the Village of Gastein, August 24, 1829.* 1829. Watercolor, 273 × 456 cm. Signed, bottom left: "Thom. Ender"; inscribed on back: "Gamskarkogel bei Hof-Gastein." Private collection (E.J. 572).
    See Koschatzky, 1982a, no. 63; exh. cat. Vienna, 1964, no. 125.

70   Thomas Ender. *The Artist at Work Opposite the Grossvenediger.* c. 1835. Watercolor, 250 × 355 cm. Signed, bottom right: "Thom. Ender." Private collection (E.J. 595).
    See Koschatzky, 1982a, no. 154 (with ill.).

71   Thomas Ender. *View of the Glacier Looming Above Kaprun.* c. 1830. Watercolor, 235 × 374 cm. Signed, bottom left: "Thom. Ender." Private collection (E.J. 609).
    See Koschatzky, 1982a, no. 66 (with ill.); exh. cat. Vienna, 1895, no. 358; exh. cat. Vienna, 1964, no. 208; exh. cat. Vienna, 1973a, no. 205.

72   Thomas Ender. *The Grossglockner, the Highest Point in Austria, with the Pasterze Glacier and Mount Johannes.* 1832. Watercolor, 263 × 380 cm. Signed, bottom right: "Thom. Ender." Private collection (E.J. 613).
    See exh. cat. Vienna, 1895, no. 352; exh. cat. Vienna, 1964, no. 211.

73 Jakob Alt. *View from the Artist's Studio in the Alser District of Vienna Looking Toward Dornbach.* 1836. Watercolor over pencil, 512 × 415 cm. Signed and dated, bottom right: "J. Alt 1836." Graphische Sammlung Albertina, Vienna (28.336).
See Tietze, 1925, p. 43; Grimschitz, 1928, p. 50, ill. 42; Grimschitz, 1961, no. 48; Koschatzky-Haiböck, 1970, no. 24; May, 1980, no. 95, plate 90; exh. cat. Essen, 1960, no. 6; exh. cat. Munich, 1972, no. 203, plate 161; exh. cat. Vienna, 1973a, no. 191, ill. p. 2.

74 Rudolf Alt. *Self Portrait.* 1835. Watercolor, 183 × 132 cm. Signed, bottom right: "R. Alt"; inscribed, bottom left: "das bin ich (that's me)." Historisches Museum der Stadt Wien, Vienna (116.761/2).
See Rœssler, 1909, plate 10; Hevesi, 1911, ill. p. 39; Koschatzky, 1975, watercolor cat. no. 35/01, ill. 46; exh. cat. Vienna, 1976, no. 112, ill. 16; exh. cat., Vienna, 1984, no. 25.

75 Jakob Alt. *Italian Port.* 1835. Watercolor, 250 × 372 cm. Signed and dated, bottom left: "J. Alt 1835." Graphische Sammmlung Albertina, Vienna (28.383).
See exh. cat. Vienna, 1973a, no. 201.

76 Jakob Alt. *View of the Church of San Giovanni in Laterano, Rome.* 1835. Watercolor, 411 × 515 cm. Signed and dated, bottom right: "J. Alt 1835." Graphische Sammlung Albertina, Vienna (22.556).
See Koschatzky, 1975, peep-show series 33 (where the date is erroneously given as 1838).

77 Rudolf Alt. *Eisgrub Palace (Schloss Eisgrub) Before its Reconstruction.* Before 1845. Watercolor, 137 × 194 cm. Sammlungen des Regierenden Fürsten von Liechtenstein, Vaduz Castle Vaduz (28).

78 Rudolf Alt. *The Bay of Cattaro in Dalmatia.* 1840. Watercolor, 289 × 390 cm. Inscribed and dated, bottom right: "Cattaro 23ᵗ October 1840"; inscribed on back: "No. 80 Rud. Alt. Dalmatien. Bocca di Cattaro, Studie. 23. Octob. 1840." Private collection, Vienna.

79 Rudolf Alt, *The Solar Eclipse over Vienna on July 8, 1842.* 1842. Watercolor, 307 × 440 cm. Signed, dated, and inscribed, bottom left: "Wien am 8ᵗ Juli 1842 / R. Alt." Historisches Museum der Stadt Wien, Vienna (105.390; Arthur Roessler Bequest).
See Roessler, 1909, pp. 33 f.; Koschatzky, 1975, watercolor cat. no. 42/27, ill.83; exh. cat. Vienna, 1912, no. 44; exh. cat. Vienna, 1955, no. 74; exh. cat. Vienna, 1969a, no. 411; exh. cat. Vienna, 1973a, no. 235; exh. cat. Vienna, 1976, no. 124, ill. 2; exh. cat. Vienna, 1984, no. 67.

80 Leander Russ. *The Solar Eclipse over the Marchfeld Plain on July 8, 1842.* 1842. Watercolor and gouache, 425 × 575 cm. Signed and dated, bottom right: "Leander Russ 1842"; old inscription: "Das Marchfeld während der Sonnenfinsternis am 8. VII 1842 vom Felsenkeller oberhalb Nussdorf (The Marchfeld [Plain] during the solar eclipse on July 8, 1824, from the rock cellar above Nusstorf)." Graphische Sammlung Albertina, Vienna (22.783).
See exh. cat. Vienna, 1973a, no. 234; exh. Bawag (no cat.), 1983.

81 Rudolf Alt. *View of Vienna from the Spinner at the Cross, a Medieval Wayside Shrine.* 1841. Watercolor and gouache with scraped highlights, 380 × 591 cm. Signed and dated, bottom left: "Rudolf Alt 1841" [last figure barely legible]. Historisches Museum der Stadt Wien, Vienna (56.389).
See Hevesi, 1911, p. 71; Koschatzky, 1975, watercolor cat. no. 43/40, ill. on jacket; May, 1980, no. 58, plate 54; exh. cat. Vienna, 1955, no. 73 (where the date is given as 1841); exh. cat. Vienna, 1969a, no. 410 (date: 1841); exh. cat. Vienna, 1976, no. 133 (date: 1843); exh. cat. Vienna, 1984, no. 70 (date: 1843).

82 Rudolf Alt. *The Prince of Liechtenstein's Study in Rasumovsky Palace on the Landstrasse, Vienna.* 1842. Watercolor, 293 × 373 cm. Signed and dated, bottom right: "R. Alt. 1842." Sammlungen des Regierenden Fürsten von Liechtenstein, Vaduz Castle, Vaduz (58).
See exh. cat. Lucerne, 1950, no. 20.

83 Rudolf Alt. *The Garden Room in Rasumovsky Palace in Vienna.* 1845. Watercolor, 305 × 393 cm. Signed and dated, bottom left: "Rudolf Alt 1845." Sammlungen des Regierenden Fürsten von Liechtenstein, Vaduz Castle, Vaduz (2.355).
See exh. cat. Lucerne, 1950, no. 24; exh. cat. Vienna, 1984, no. 79.

84 Rudolf Alt. *View of Dürnstein in the Wachau.* 1843. Watercolor, 280 × 357 cm. Signed and dated, bottom left: "R. Alt 1843." Graphische Sammlung Albertina, Vienna (34.921).
See Koschatzky-Haiböck, 1970, no. 31; exh. cat. Munich, 1972, no. 205; Exh. cat. Vienna, 1973a, no. 223.

85 Jakob Alt. *View of the Dachstein Mountains in the Salzkammergut.* 1840. Watercolor, 420 × 525 cm. Signed and dated, bottom right: "J. Alt 1840." Graphische Sammlung Albertina, Vienna (22.584).
See Koschatzky-Haiböck, 1970, no. 34; exh. cat. Vienna, 1973a, no. 105.

86 Rudolf Alt. *View from the Lake of Aussee Looking Toward the Trisselwand.* 1859. Watercolor, 266 × 370 cm. Signed, dated, and inscribed, bottom left: "R Alt Alt-Aussee 1859"; inscribed on back: "Adalbert R v. Lanna Prag Rudolfinum." Dr. Rudolf Leopold Collection, Vienna.

87 Eduard Gurk. *Markt Mödling on the Pilgrimage to Mariazell, from "Scenic Trip" (Malerische Reise);* no. 2 ("The First Day"). 1833–4. Watercolor, 255 × 310 cm; on a mount 326 × 425 cm. Niederösterreichisches Landesmuseum, Vienna (6.536/2).
See Feuchtmüller, 1975, pp. 78 ff.

88 Eduard Gurk. *Glassworks near Türnitz on the Pilgrimage to Mariazell, from "Scenic Trip" (Mahlerische Reise);* no. 18 ("The Second Day"). 1833–4. Watercolor, 260 × 340 cm. Niederösterreichisches Landesmuseum, Vienna (6.536/18).
See ref. under Pl. 87 above; exh. cat. Vienna, 1978, no. 132.

89 Eduard Gurk. *View from Annaberg Looking Toward the Ötscher on the Pilgrimage to Mariazell, from "Scenic Trip" (Mahlerische Reise);* no. 22 ("The Second Day"). 1833–4. Watercolor, 261 × 340 cm. Niederösterreichisches Landesmuseum, Vienna (6.536/22).
See ref. under Pl. 87 above; exh. cat. Vienna, 1978, no. 134.

90 Eduard Gurk. *View of Mariazell on the Pilgrimage to Mariazell, from "Scenic Trip" (Mahlerische Reise);* no. 34 ("The

Third Day"). 1833–4. Watercolor, 328 × 426 cm. Niederösterreichisches Landesmuseum, Vienna (6.536/34).
See ref. under Pl. 87 above.

91  Joseph Gerstmeyer. *Emperor Francis I and Empress Carolina Augusta Entering Mariazell.* Before 1835. Watercolor, 307 × 395 cm. Graphische Sammlung Albertina, Vienna (25.001).

92  Eduard Gurk. *The Royal Castle and Archbishop's Palace on the Hradčany in Prague.* c. 1836. Watercolor, 448 × 588 cm. Inscribed on back, on the mount (former title): "Die k.k. Burg und der Erzbischöfliche Pallast am Hradschin zu Prag." Graphische Sammlung Albertina, Vienna (22.644).
See exh. cat. Vienna, 1973a, no. 109; exh. cat. Vienna, 1978, no. 123.

93  Thomas Ender. *The Propylaea on the Acropolis of Athens.* 1837. Watercolor, 243 × 365 cm. Private collection (E.J. 1085).
See Koschatzky, 1982a, no. 99 (with ill.); exh. cat. Graz, 1959, no. 177; exh. cat. Vienna, 1964, no. 171.

94  Carl Schindler. *Soldiers on the March.* 1840. Watercolor over pencil, 183 × 230 cm. Signed and dated, bottom right: "Schindler Carl 6. Juny 1840." Österreichische Nationalbibliothek, Vienna: portrait collection and picture archives (Pk 3050,18).
See S. Kehl-Baierle, "Carl Schindler—Leben und Werk," Ph.D. dissertation, University of Vienna, forthcoming.
The author is grateful to Sabine Kehl-Baierle for drawing his attention to this newly discovered painting.

95  Carl Schindler. *Ascending for the Baptism of the Bell.* 1840. Watercolor, 203 × 275 cm. Inscribed and dated, bottom right: "Schindler 1840." Österreichische Nationalbibliothek, Vienna: portrait collection and picture archives (Pk 3050, 17).
Certain stylistic peculiarities—figures like the blacksmith pushing the wagon (cf. Graphische Sammlung Albertina, Vienna [25.986]) or the horse drawing it (cf. Graphische Sammlung Albertina, Vienna [25.104])—suggest the hand of Johann Friedrich Treml in this picture, which would make it a typical example of the close collaboration that existed between these two artists, who almost formed a workshop.
See S. Kehl-Baierle, "Carl Schindler—Leben und Werk," Ph.D. dissertation, University of Vienna, forthcoming.
The author is grateful to Sabine Kehl-Baierle for drawing his attention to this newly discovered painting and to its significance.

96  Carl Schindler. *The Generous Vineyard Keeper.* c. 1840. Watercolor and Chinese white, 144 × 166 cm. Galerie & Auktionshaus W. Hassfurther, Vienna.
See Haberditzl-Schwarz, 1930, no. 58, plate 26; exh. cat. Vienna, 1927, no. 94.
One of a total of three variants of this subject; the other two —also watercolors—are dated 1841.

97  Johann Friedrich Treml. *The Distribution of Gifts on St. Nicholas's Day.* 1844. Watercolor, 209 × 242 cm. Signed and dated, bottom right: "Treml 1844." Graphische Sammlung Albertina, Vienna (28.353).

98  Carl Schindler. *Battle Scene from the Wars of Liberation.* c. 1840. Watercolor over pencil, 200 × 250 cm. Graphische Sammlung Albertina, Vienna (28.331).

See Grimschitz, 1928, ill. 20; Haberditzl-Schwarz, 1930, no. 92, ill. plate 76; exh. cat. Vienna, 1927, no. 109.

99  Carl Schindler. *Cuirassier Officer Beside the Body of a Comrade from an Infantry Regiment.* c. 1841. Watercolor over pencil, 175 × 238 cm. Graphische Sammlung Albertina, Vienna (25.471).
See Haberditzl-Schwarz, 1930, no. 123, ill. p. 19; exh. cat. Vienna, 1927, no. 113; exh. cat. Vienna, 1928, no. 138; exh. cat. Essen, 1960, no. 152; exh. cat. Rotterdam, 1964, no. 100; exh. cat. Vienna, 1973a, no. 164.

100  Carl Schindler. *The Wedding Party out Driving with Guests.* 1841. Watercolor over pencil, 142 × 225 cm. Graphische Sammlung Albertina, Vienna (31.189).
See Haberditzl-Schwarz, 1930, no. 121, frontispiece; exh. cat. Vienna, 1927, no. 127; exh. cat. Rotterdam, 1964, no. 102, ill. 9; exh. cat. Vienna, 1973a, no. 158.
A squared variant of Schindler's 1841 oil painting (Österreichische Galerie, Vienna).

101  Carl Schindler. *On the Dance Floor.* 1840. Watercolor and pencil, 186 × 227 cm. Signed and dated, bottom right: "C. Schindler 1840." Graphische Sammlung Albertina, Vienna (25.882).
See Koschatzky, 1982a, no. 126, ill. p. 241; exh. cat. Rotterdam, 1964, no. 101; exh. cat. Vienna, 1973a, no. 157.

102  Moritz Michael Daffinger. *Orchid.* c. 1840. Watercolor, 302 × 222 cm. Signed, bottom right: "Daffinger." Graphische Sammlung Albertina, Vienna (5.097).
See Munich exh. cat., 1972, no. 108 (with ill.); exh. cat. Vienna, 1973a, no. 81.

103  Moritz Michael Daffinger. *Stemless Primrose.* c. 1840. Watercolor, 289 × 204 cm. Inscribed, bottom right: "Primula veris acaulis L. / Primula acaulis Jacq." Akademie der bildenden Künste: Kupferstichkabinett, Vienna (7.622).
See Grünstein, 1923, plate LV.; Pirchan, 1943, plate XXVIII; Koschatzky, 1982b, ill. 96; exh. cat. Essen, 1960, no. 37, plate 3; exh. cat. Lübeck, 1965, no. 29c; exh. cat. Vienna, 1973a, no. 78; exh. cat. Vienna, 1986, no. 19, plate 18.

104  Josef Höger. *The Radhausberg, near Gastein.* 1831. Watercolor, 232 × 299 cm. Inscribed and dated: "Rathausberg bey Böckstein Gastein 1831." Sammlungen des Regierenden Fürsten von Liechtenstein, Vaduz Castle, Vaduz (1613).

105  Thomas Ender. *View of Clam Castle (Burg Clam).* c. 1835. Watercolor and pencil, 237 × 394 cm. Inscribed, bottom center: "Schloss Clam", and bottom right: "Nr. 65." Sammlungen des Regierenden Fürsten von Liechtenstein, Vaduz Castle, Vaduz (187).
See Koschatzky, 1982a, no. 49 (with ill.).

106  Johann Fischbach. *View of Salzburg with the Kapuzinerberg.* 1840. Watercolor over pencil, 313 × 364 cm. Signed and dated, bottom right: "Johann Fischbach 1840." Graphische Sammlung Albertina, Vienna (14.107).
See Koschatzky-Haiböck, 1970, no. 38; exh. cat. Vienna, 1973a, no. 227, ill. p. 83.
An oil painting of the same subject but with different scenery in the left foreground was executed in 1844 (Residenzgalerie, Salzburg).

107 Franz Barbarini. *View of Salzburg from the Kapuzinerberg.* c. 1840. Watercolor, 222 × 317 cm. Signed bottom right: "Fr. Barbarini." Graphische Sammlung Albertina, Vienna (4.998).
See exh. cat. Essen, 1960, no. 30.

108 Josef Höger. *Wooded Landscape with Stag and Deer.* c. 1840. Watercolor, 326 × 443 cm. Sammlungen des Regierenden Fürsten von Liechtenstein, Vaduz Castle, Vaduz (301).
See exh. cat. Lucerne, 1950, no. 153.

109 Franz Alt. *The Tiefer Graben in Vienna.* 1843. Watercolor over pencil, 265 × 183 cm. Signed and dated, bottom left: "Franz Alt 843." Graphische Sammlung Albertina, Vienna (28.265).

110 Thomas Ender. *The Highest Point on the New Road over the Wormser Joch.* 1843. Watercolor, 278 × 404 cm. Private collection (E.J. 741).
See Koschatzky, 1982a, no. 125; exh. cat. Vienna, 1895, no. 340; exh. cat. Vienna, 1964, no. 251.
This pass is now known as the Stilfser Joch, or Passo dello Stelvio.

111 Thomas Ender. *Mountainous Landscape in the Tyrol.* c. 1844. Watercolor, 157 × 224 cm. Signed, center left on the rocks: "Tho. Ender." Private collection (E.J. 685).
See Koschatzky, 1982a, no. 127.

112 Thomas Ender. *The Ruins of Wolkenstein in Southern Tyrol.* 1845. Watercolor, 376 × 260 cm. Private collection (E.J. 700).
See Koschatzky, 1982a, no. 138; exh. cat. Vienna, 1964, no. 261.

113 Thomas Ender. *Ponte di Colombano, near Rovereto.* 1847. Watercolor, 362 × 327 cm. Private collection (E.J. 760).
See Koschatzky, 1982a, no. 139; exh. cat. Vienna, 1895, no. 173; exh. cat. Vienna, 1964, no. 284.

114 Emanuel Stöckler, *The Cliffs (Faraglioni) of Capri.* c. 1840. Watercolor, 371 × 503 cm. Inscribed and signed, bottom left: "CAPRI / E. Stöckler." A. Storm Collection, Vienna.

115 Franz Barbarini. *View of Vienna from Sievering.* c. 1840. Watercolor, 166 × 248 cm. Inscribed and signed, bottom left: "F. Barbarini Wien." Private collection, Vienna.
For a long time, this work was thought to be by Thomas Ender.

116 Josef Höger. *Mill, near Golling.* 1842. Watercolor, 350 × 452 cm. Signed and dated, bottom right: "J. Höger 1842." Graphische Sammlung Albertina, Vienna (14.710).
See exh. cat. Vienna, 1973a, no. 211, ill. p. 105.

117 Leander Russ. *Allegory of Emperor Ferdinand I's Reign.* 1843. Watercolor and gold paint, 361 × 464 cm. Signed and dated, bottom right: "Leander Russ 1843"; inscribed: "RECTA TUERI. / 1831. / AERE. 1841 / WIEN 1830. / AUSTRIA / 1838. / AMNESTIE. / 1843." Graphische Sammlung Albertina, Vienna (22.776).
From the series made for Emperor Ferdinand I's peep show.

118 Leander Russ. *Emperor Ferdinand I Opening the Newly Constructed Road over the Semmering Pass.* 1842. Watercolor,

325 × 474 cm. Signed and dated, bottom right: "Leander Russ 1842." Graphische Sammlung Albertina, Vienna (22.784).
From the series made for Emperor Ferdinand I's peep show.

119 Leander Russ. *The Unveiling of the Emperor Francis Monument in Graz.* 1842. Watercolor, 430 × 580 cm. Signed and dated, bottom right: "Leander Russ 1842." Graphische Sammlung Albertina, Vienna (22.771).
See exh. cat. Vienna, 1973a, no. 107.
From the series made for Emperor Ferdinand I's peep show.

120 Leander Russ. *Emperor Ferdinand I Visiting the Schlossberg in Graz.* 1842. Watercolor and Chinese white, 345 × 445 cm. Signed and dated, bottom right: "L. Russ 1842." Graphische Sammlung Albertina, Vienna (22.788).
From the series made for Emperor Ferdinand I's peep show.

121 Josef Kriehuber. *Emperor Francis Joseph I of Austria.* 1851. Watercolor, 390 × 300 cm. Signed and dated, bottom left: "J. Kriehuber 851"; inscribed, bottom left: "Franz Joseph." Private collection.
See Koschatzky, 1982b, no. 127.

122 Josef Kriehuber. *Count Günther Stolberg zu Stolberg in the Uniform of a Cavalry Captain.* 1850. Watercolor over pencil, 300 × 221 cm. Signed and dated, bottom left: "Kriehuber 850." Private collection, Vienna.

123 Josef Kriehuber. *Field Marshal Prince Felix zu Schwarzenberg.* 1852. Watercolor over pencil, 367 × 272 cm. Signed and dated, bottom right: "Kriehuber 852." Graphische Sammlung Albertina, Vienna (26.707).
See exh. cat. Vienna, 1979, no. 15.

124 August von Pettenkofen. *Two Gypsy Boys.* c. 1865. Watercolor, 195 × 244 cm. Signed, bottom left: "a.p." Jenö Eisenberger Collection, Vienna.
See Weixlgärtner, 1916, III/718.

125 Alois Schönn. *Bazaar in Sarajevo, Serbia.* 1851. Watercolor and pencil, 438 × 597 cm. Signed, bottom right: "Schönn." Graphische Sammlung Albertina, Vienna (28.849).

126 Thomas Ender. *View of the Matterhorn from the Gorner Grat.* 1854. Watercolor, 333 × 503 cm. Graphische Sammlung Albertina, Vienna (36.935).
See Koschatzky, 1982a, no. 149.

127 Thomas Ender. *Mountainous Landscape with River.* c. 1865. Watercolor, 280 × 387 cm. Národni Galeri, Prague (K 4.271).
See exh. cat. Vienna, 1964, no. 312.

128 Josef Kriehuber. *Forest Scene with Staffage.* 1872. Watercolor over pencil, 283 × 497 cm. Signed and dated, bottom right: "Kriehuber 872." Graphische Sammlung Albertina, Vienna (29.167).

129 Johann Nepomuk Passini. *Mountain Landscape with Two Hikers.* c. 1856. Watercolor, 348 × 274 cm. Graphische Sammlung Albertina, Vienna (36.912).

130 August von Pettenkofen. *Interior of a Neapolitan Farmhouse.* 1873. Watecolor, 371 × 277 cm. Signed, bottom left:

## JOHANN AUGUST HEINRICH
b. Dresden, 1794; d. Innsbruck, 1822

Admitted to the Dresden Academy in 1810; traveled to Vienna in 1812, where he trained at the Academy under J. Mössmer and gained admittance to the circle of German Romantics working in the Vienna (the Olivier brothers, J. Schnorr von Carolsfeld); returned to Dresden in 1818 for health reasons; enjoyed great success there; visited Salzburg in 1820, painting landscape sketches; received the backing of the king of Saxony; on a trip to Italy financed by the king, Heinrich got no farther than Innsbruck, where his early death deprived the nineteenth century of potentially one of its more important landscape painters.

G. Krämer. *Der Maler und Zeichner A. Heinrich*, Karlsruhe, 1979.

## JOHANN NEPOMUK HOECHLE
b. Munich, 1790; d. Vienna, 1835

Son of the painter Johann Baptist Hoechle; trained initially under Ferdinand Kobell; moved to Vienna with his father in 1800 and studied at the Academy until 1808 under M. Wutky and F. H. Füger; fought in a number of engagements, including the Battle of Aspern in 1809, and gained a great reputation as a battle painter; attended the Congress of Vienna, 1814–15, as a member of the emperor's retinue; visited Rome and Naples in 1819; took part in the great military manoeuvers in Hungary in 1820; produced lively, relaxed portrayals of landscape; later turned to folkloric genre painting. Hoechle is also important for his lithographic series depicting the Austrian army and key moments in the life of Emperor Francis.

## JOSEF HÖGER
Vienna, 1801–1877

After finishing the gymnasium, trained at the Academy under J. Mössmer and J. Rebell; was professor at the Academy from 1849–51; his friendship with the Albertina director Franz Rechberger gave him access to the works of the Old Masters; preferred clear, unmixed colors when painting in watercolor; under the influence of Jakob Gauermann, turned to portraying nature; undertook long journeys and walking tours with his brother-in-law Friedrich Gauermann (in the Alps, to Venice) and painted a large number of watercolors, many of which were subsequently lithographed: *Watercolor Tutor, Landscape Studies for Beginners, Tree Studies in Pictures* (Höger was dubbed *Bäume-Raffael*—"the Raphael of trees").

## LORENZ JANSCHA
b. near Radmannsdorf, Carniola (now Radovljica, Slovania), 1749; d. Vienna, 1812

Trained at the Vienna Academy from 1770 under F. E. Weirotter and J. C. Brand; continued to work there after completing his studies until he assumed the position of "corrector" in the landscape class in 1797 on the death of C. P. Schalhas; took over the landscape-drawing class on the death of F. A. Brand in 1806; effected the transition from the Rococo landscape with its staffage to a realistically apprehended landscape *veduta*, accomplishing this particularly in watercolor; collaborated with C. Schütz and J. Ziegler from 1785–95 on a series of views of the city and environs of Vienna; also painted land-

*Lorenz Janscha*
by Johann Adam Klein

scapes of the Alpine regions, the Rhine, and the Danube, which were widely disseminated as series of colored etchings. Janscha's new, realistic approach to landscape had a major influence on the next generation of artists.

## VALENTIN JANSCHA
b. near Radmannsdorf, Carniola (now Radovljica, Slovania), 1743; d. Vienna, 1818

Brother of the painter Lorenz Janscha; trained at the Vienna Academy; appointed to the staff of the Ore-blending and Manufacturers' College in 1788; appointed second assistant to Hubert Maurer at the Academy in 1801. Valentin was a far less important artist than his brother.

## JOHANN ADAM KLEIN
b. Nuremberg, 1792; d. Munich, 1875

Trained at Nuremberg Art College under Ambrosius Gabler from 1802–5; was much encouraged to go on walking tours and study nature; modeled himself on Wilhelm von Kobell; moved to Vienna in 1811 and befriended the artists Bartsch, Füger, and Molitor, among others; moved back to Nuremberg in 1815; returned to Vienna with his friend J. C. Erhard in 1816; won wide recognition and received many commissions, including one from Prince Metternich for studies of horses on Hungarian stud farms; went on joint trip with Erhard, Welker, and the Reinhold brothers to the Salzkammergut and Salzburg in 1818; traveled via Switzerland to Italy in 1819; joined the group that had formed around J. A. Koch in Rome; spent the years 1821–39 in Nuremberg; lived in Munich from 1839. Klein, who achieved an important synthesis of sensitive observation of nature and lively Realism, had a strong influence on the developments in Vienna.

C. Jahn. *Das Werk des J. A. Klein*. Munich, 1863; W. Schwemmer. *J. A. Klein: Ein Nürnberger Meister des 19. Jahrhunderts.* Nuremberg, 1966; R. Freitag-Stadler: *Bestandskatalog der Stadtgeschichtlichen Museen Nürnberg: J. A. Klein, Zeichnungen und Aquarelle.* Nuremberg, 1975.

## JOHANN KNAPP
b. Vienna-Hundsthurm, 1778; d. Schönbrunn, 1833

Son of a modest winegrower; studied flower painting at the Academy under J. B. Drechsler; spent three years working in a

277

wallpaper factory, then returned to the Academy to produce patterns for teaching purposes; was appointed flower and fruit painter in the emperor's Dutch garden at Schönbrunn; gave painting lessons to the Viennese nobility and in court circles, one of his pupils being Archduke Charles's wife Henriette; was made a freeman of the city of Vienna in 1803 and painter by appointment to Archduke Anthony in 1804, with a commission to paint mushrooms and plants; his 300 watercolors of a wide variety of Alpine plants, painted for Archduke John, were published as prints in 1808. Knapp's principal work is a painted tribute to the botanist Baron Nikolaus Joseph von Jacquin (1727-1817), *Jacquin's Memorial* (1822; Vienna: Österreichische Galerie).

## JOHANN KNIEP
Vienna, 1779–1809

Trained at the Vienna Academy from 1793 (in F. A. Brand's landscape class); accompanied Archduke John when he climbed the Schneealp in 1802, subsequently becoming painter by appointment to the archduke and painting numerous watercolors with colorful portrayals of landscapes over monochrome groundwork drawn with a pen or pointed brush; Kniep's oil paintings were more rooted in the Ideal landscape tradition (modeled on Claude Lorraine).

## JOSEPH ANTON KOCH
b. Obergiblen near Elbingenalp, Lechtal, Tyrol, 1768; d. Rome, 1839

A herdboy in his childhood, Koch received his early art training at the Karlsschule in Stuttgart; rebelling against Academism in 1781, he fled to France; traveled in Switzerland from 1792–4, painting idyllic Alpine landscapes; spent several years in Rome with the generous backing of an Englishman named Nott; befriended by Bertel Thorwaldsen, E. Wächter, and G. A. Wallis; spent 1812–15 in Vienna, where he knew the Romantics grouped around the philosopher and critic Friedrich von Schlegel; returned to Rome in 1815 and became a key figure in the artistic life of that city. Although not one of the true Viennese watercolorists, Koch had a particularly powerful and enduring influence on them and on other contemporaries.

O. R. von Lutterotti. *J. A. Koch*. Innsbruck, 1944.

## MARIE KRAFFT
b. Vienna, 1812; d. Villach, 1885

Daughter of the painter Johann Peter Krafft, who was her first teacher; subsequently studied watercolor painting under Thomas Ender, lithography under N. Dewerth; in 1840 married National Bank official Franz Troll and from then on devoted herself exclusively to copying Old Masters. Her early watercolor portraits show evidence of great skill and are typical products of the Viennese Biedermeier era.

## JOSEF KRIEHUBER
Vienna, 1800–1876

Son of a saloonkeeper in the Josefstadt district; received drawing instruction at a very early age; trained at the Academy from 1813–18; spent the years 1818–22 in Poland as drawing teacher to Prince Sanguszko; returned to Vienna in 1822 to continue his studies, earning his living doing lithographs for the firm of J. Trentsensky; in 1825 turned exclusively to portraiture, initially under the influence of F. Lieder; received a wide variety of commissions as a society portraitist, painting watercolor landscapes in the summer months; the arrival of photography in 1839 brought a big drop in Kriehuber's portrait commissions and led to severe financial hardship; made an honorary member of the Academy in 1866, and taught drawing at the Theresianum. The man who had once been the busiest portrait painter in Vienna died a pauper. Kriehuber was very important both as a portrait lithographer and for his lithographs after drawings in the Albertina.

W. von Wurzbach. *J. Kriehuber, der Porträtlithograph der Wiener Gesellschaft*. Vienna, Zurich, 1954; idem. *J. Kriehuber, Katalog der Porträtlithographien*. Vienna, 1955.

## LEOPOLD KUPELWIESER
b. Piesting, Lower Austria, 1796; d. Vienna, 1862

Entered the Vienna Academy in 1809; absorbed the Viennese Neoclassicism of Johann Peter Krafft; visited Rome in 1824 with the Russian nobleman Alexander Beresin; quarreled with the Nazarenes there (Josef von Führich) but found inspiration in the works of Fra Angelico; on his return to Vienna, worked initially as a portraitist, receiving many commissions and earning wide recognition; accepted appointment as "corrector" at the Vienna Academy in 1831 and professor in 1836 (succeeding J. Redl); received commissions for altarpieces in Vienna and Lower Austria, including a painting on the theme of the rosary for the high altar of the Dominican church in Vienna (1837); switched to fresco painting in 1845; produced his most important work in the 1850s, including the dome and transept decorations in Vienna's Alt-Lerchenfeld Church (1855). Kupelwieser's patrons and benefactors included Empress Carolina Augusta, Archduchess Sophie, and the Brandis family.

R. Feuchtmüller. *L. Kupelwieser und die Kunst der österreichischen Spätromantik*. Vienna, 1970.

## SIGMUND L'ALLEMAND
Vienna 1840–1910

Nephew and pupil of the battle painter Friedrich L'Allemand; attended the Academy under Christian Ruben and Karl Blaas, succeeding to the latter's chair in 1833; continued his uncle's work as a painter; completed many studies on the Schleswig-Holstein campaign in 1864 and on the Italian campaign in 1866; concentrated on portrait commissions from the imperial family and the nobility after 1880, when he was one of the most sought-after portraitists of his day; also painted the occasional costume genre piece.

## MATTHÄUS LODER
b. Vienna, 1791; d. Vordernberg, Styria, 1828

Entered the Academy in 1797; studied flower painting at first, then turned to architecture, and eventually, under the influence of Füger, took up landscape drawing (his open-air studies show a predilection for ruins, waterfalls, and rocky outcrops); was awarded a Rome scholarship in 1808 but turned it down for family reasons; worked as drawing teacher to Archduchess Marie Louise; was made painter by appointment to Archduke John in 1816; became the archduke's favorite painter because Loder best captured John's ideas of the beauty of unspoiled nature and of the costumes, customs, and the way of life of country people; accompanied the archduke on all his trips, painting his landscapes to precise instructions; died of pulmonary disease in 1828. For a long time Loder remained unknown, because his entire oeuvre was in Archduke John's private collection; however, today, he has a firm place among the leading watercolorists of his time.

M. T. von Wietersheim [née Meran]. "Von der Ritteridylle zum Bilddokument: M. Loder, ein Kammermaler des Erzherzogs Johann von Österreich." Ph. D. dissertation, University of Munich, 1982.

## FRIEDRICH LOOS
b. Graz, 1797; d. Kiel, 1890

Trained in the landscape class at the Vienna Academy under J. Mössmer, M. Leybold, and J. Rebell; visited what is now Burgenland (then part of Hungary) in 1823; worked in Leipzig in 1825; moved to Salzburg in 1826 and collaborated on a panorama of the city; spent the years 1835–40 in Vienna, moving toward a highly individual, pre-Impressionist style of painting; subsequently spent eleven years in Rome; visited Bremen, Oldenburg, Hamburg, and Copenhagen in 1851–3; made a study trip to Norway in 1856; taught drawing at Kiel University from 1863 until his death. Loos was the first Austrian painter in whose work the achievements of German Romanticism became visible in depth.

## MARTIN VON MOLITOR
Vienna, 1759–1812

Trained at the Vienna Academy under Johann Christian Brand; received particular encouragement from Prince Kaunitz; already a member of the Academy in 1784; turned down the offer of the chair left vacant by Brand's death in 1795; commissioned by the newly established Agency for Art and Industry in 1802 to provide *Views from the Tyrol*; formed a close friendship with Jakob Gauermann. Molitor's approach to landscape had a profound effect on the younger generation of artists; most of his work consisted of watercolors, gouaches, and drawings.

C. Reinwetter. "Studien zu Martin von Molitor (1759–1812): Mit besonderer Berücksichtigung seiner Zeit." Ph. D. dissertation, University of Vienna, 1981.

## JOSEF MÖSSMER
Vienna, 1780–1845

Received initial instruction from his father Johann Mössmer, an engraver living in Vienna; trained at the Academy from 1796 under Friedrich August Brand; was strongly influenced by Martin von Molitor; befriended by Franz Rechberger, director of the Count Friess Gallery and subsequently of the Albertina; traveled round Austria in 1810–11; deputized for the ailing Lorenz Janscha at the Academy from 1808 and succeeded him in 1815; suffered a crippling stroke in 1842. Mössmer's own artistic standing was never very high, but his advocacy of working in the open air set an example to generations of students in the first half of the nineteenth century.

## JOHANN NEPOMUK PASSINI
b. Vienna, 1798; d. Graz, 1874

Studied landscape at the Vienna Academy under Carl Seipp from 1813–24; trained under Johann Georg Mansfeld, a designer and engraver at the court Cabinet of Antiques, from 1814–18; executed all the oustanding orders following Mansfeld's death and earned a reputation as an engraver, notably for his copies of Thomas Ender's Brazilian watercolors and Peter Fendi's *Family Reunion* (see Pl. 63); formed friendships with Fendi, Jakob and Rudolf Alt, and Moritz von Schwind; traveled in the Vienna region and visited Salzburg and Upper Austria, producing numerous watercolor landscapes; became head of the art institute of the Austrian Lloyd's in Trieste in 1850 and produced lithographs, watercolors, and oil paintings of the local landscape; moved to Graz in 1852, and in 1855 took the job of freehand-drawing teacher at the high school there; produced series of lithographs (including his Schlossberg album and the Gleichenberg suite) while his drawing and painting, whether in watercolor or oils, became steadily more important. Passini's work, predominantly graphic in his early years, became increasingly painterly in structure as he matured. Nature in his landscapes started out broad and deep, but toward the end of his career he adopted a more detailed approach. Figures and animals continued to function as staffage.

Gertrude Celedin. "J. N. Passini, Leben und Werk." Ph. D. dissertation, University of Graz, 1982; "J. N. Passini, Gemälde und Grafik," exh. cat. Graz: Neue Galerie und Stadtmuseum, 1983.

## LUDWIG PASSINI
b. Vienna, 1832; d. Venice, 1903

Son of the engraver and painter Johann Nepomuk Passini; trained at the Academy under Leopold Kupelwieser and J. von Führich; influenced by Thomas Ender, who molded his watercolor style; moved to Trieste in 1850, then to Venice; visited Dalmatia, the Netherlands, and Italy with Karl Werner in 1852; spent the years 1855–64 in Rome, painting watercolors of architecture and interiors, and subsequently genre pictures featuring mainly clerics and children; had a wide circle of friends, which included Anton Romako; married and moved to Berlin in 1864; had a studio in Venice from 1873; participated in the 1873 Weltausstellung in Vienna with his paintings of Rome (which conditioned his contemporaries' view of that city); as recognition for his artistic achievements was awarded the *Pour-le-Mérite* Order by Emperor William II of Germany. Passini's watercolors, rooted in Viennese art, were of supraregional importance in terms of style and subject matter.

## EMANUEL THOMAS PETER
b. Jägerndorf, Silesia (now Krnov, Czechoslovakia), 1799; d. Vienna, 1873

After training in his native Silesia as a stonemason and architect, he attended the Vienna Academy from 1818–21, initially in the architectural-drawing class; became an admirer and pupil of Moritz Michael Daffinger, making superbly accurate copies of his master's work before striking out on his own, though still very much in Daffinger's style (L. Schidlof calls him "a bourgeoisified edition of Daffinger"); lived in Vienna from 1830, and from around 1842 was Daffinger's legitimate and much sought-after successor in the field of the portrait miniature, though his output declined sharply after 1860.

L. Schidlof. *La Miniature en Europe.* Graz, 1964, vol. 2, p. 645.

## AUGUST VON PETTENKOFEN
Vienna, 1822–1889

Trained at the Academy under Leopold Kupelwieser from 1834–40; spent the years 1841–3 in the army in Padua (officer rank); continued his art training under Franz Eybl, who had some influence on him, though the great exemplar of his early years was Carl Schindler; Peter Fendi's watercolor technique helped to mold him as an artist; spent 1848–9 painting military scenes and illustrating Austrian military history; took part in the Hungarian campaign as a military painter; made several trips to Paris from 1852 onward and was one of the first Austrian artists to have close contracts with the Barbizon School, as painterly elements displaced graphic elements in his art and the overall impression of what was seen came to matter more than the faithful depiction of every detail; combined his newly acquired style with Hungarian subject matter (gypsy life, peasants and animals in the landscape) during frequent stays in the Hungarian puszta (at the artists' colony in Szolnok); became a member of the Vienna Academy in 1866, of the Munich Academy in 1872, and was ennobled in 1876; spent his last years shunning human company and traveling restlessly. Pettenkofen's watercolors represent the apogee and, at the same time, the culmination of Viennese watercolor art, anticipating the dawn of a new era in which Vienna was no longer the focus of artistic interest.

A. Weixlgärtner. *A. Pettenkofen.* Vienna, 1916.

## FRANZ XAVER PETTER
Vienna, 1791–1866

Studied flower painting at the Vienna Academy under J.B. Drechsler and S. Wegmayr; became "corrector" for the flower painting class in 1814; named professor at the College of Manufacturing Design in 1832, and academic councilor and director of the latter institution in 1835. Together with his son Theodor (1822–1874) and with Drechsler, Knapp, Wegmayr, and Nigg, Petter numbered among the leading representatives of Viennese flower painting, which was a particularly important constituent in the manufacture of the city's famous porcelain. Very much in the spirit of the Biedermeier era, the plant kingdom, as part of the given world, was made an object of special study, in which maximum fidelity to nature was combined with a delight in beauty. The resultant symbiosis proved exemplary for several generations of artists.

## MATHIAS RANFTL
Vienna, 1805–1854

Trained at the Academy under Johann Peter Krafft from 1817–25; liked landscape painting but turned to genre painting, taking most of his subjects from his own environment in Vienna; visited Russia in 1826–7, enjoying success as a portraitist in St. Petersburg and Moscow; visited London and Paris in 1836. Ranftl was considered a powerful Viennese original and was a friend of many important artists; he died in the cholera epidemic.

## ROBERT RASCHKA
b. Bucharest, 1847 (place and date of death unknown)

Trained at the Zurich Polytechnic and at the Vienna Academy under Friedrich von Schmidt, qualifying as an architect; worked as an architect (he designed the parliament building in Brno in 1870) and a painter of architectural subjects.

## JOSEPH REBELL
b. Vienna, 1787; d. Dresden, 1828

Trained at the Vienna Academy, studying architecture under Louis de Montoyer, then landscape painting under Michael Wutky (whence Rebell's predilection for such "special effects" as nighttime paintings and volcanic eruptions); visited Switzerland in 1809, Milan and Upper Italy in 1810; spent the years 1813–15 in Naples, painting thirteen views of the city; lived in Rome from 1815–24, where his work was pointed out to the visiting Emperor Francis I at an exhibition in the Caffarelli Palace; subsequently appointed by the emperor to succeed Füger as director of the Imperial Art Gallery; appointed to the Academy council in 1826; became titular professor of landscape painting at the Academy in 1828; died suddenly on a visit to Dresden in the same year. Drenched in light, Rebell's landscapes had a great influence on the way in which landscape painting developed in Vienna.

## AUGUST WILHELM RIEDER
b. Döbling, near Vienna, 1796; d. Vienna, 1880

Son of the composer Ambrosius Rieder; entered the Academy in 1812 and trained under Hubert Maurer; received a commission from Interior Minister Count Saurau to copy certain paintings in the imperial collection; turned to portraiture; taught at the Academy of Engineering; taught at the Military Academy in Wiener Neustadt in 1856; spent the years 1857–78 as curator of the Imperial Art Gallery in the Belvedere; collaborated with Franz Eybl; became a member of the Vienna Academy in 1870. Rieder's watercolor portrait of Franz Schubert is probably his best-known work.

## CHARLES-JOSEPH ROETTIERS
Paris, 1692–1779

Important engraver (at the Paris Mint), draftsman, book illustrator, and chronicler working in Paris; was ennobled in 1757, appointed councilor at the Académie Royale in 1776; enjoyed close relations with the French court (design for the Royal Revels for Louis XV); received the particular patronage of Madame de Pompadour. In 1769 Roettiers executed (in watercolor with gold highlights) a total of ninety-nine instructional plates on a wide variety of subjects, taking in every discipline of intellectual and physical education, as drawn up by Philipp von Rottenberg, the tutor to the young archdukes.

"Maria Theresia und ihre Zeit," exh. cat., Vienna: Schloss Schönbrunn, 1980, nos. 38.01–03.

## ANTON ROMAKO
b. Atzgersdorf, near Vienna, 1832; d. Döbling (Vienna), 1889

Entered the Vienna Academy in 1847 to train under Waldmüller; trained at the Munich Academy under Wilhelm von Kaulbach in 1849–50; returned to Vienna in 1850 to train in

K. Rahl's private studio for monumental painting; worked in Karl Werner's masters' studio for watercolor painting in Venice in 1854–5; visited Spain; moved to Rome in 1857 and became the favorite painter of the foreign colony there; his villa on the Monte Mario served as a rendezvous for artists and others (Liszt and Feuerbach, for example); returned to Vienna in 1876 after suffering various personal reverses, but found the competition there (Hans Makart) too strong; visited Salzburg and Gastein in 1877 and Paris in 1878; spent some time working in Geneva in 1882, and his final years in poverty and sickness in the Döbling district of Vienna. Romako's highly realistic and, at the same time, eerily profound expressiveness was misunderstood by many of his contemporaries with the result that he had no following as such, though he is now regarded as a pioneer of modern art in Austria.

F. Novotny. *Der Maler Anton Romako*. Vienna, Munich, 1954.

### FERDINAND RUNK
b. Freiburg im Breisgau, 1764; d. Vienna, 1834

Entered the Vienna Academy in 1785; worked for Archduke John from 1800 (the archduke's series of the "... finest picturesque localities in the Tyrol...," among other things); became court painter to Prince Schwarzenberg besides working for other nobles; befriended Jakob Gauermann, to whom he gave substantial assistance at the start of the latter's artistic career in Vienna.

"Die Kammermaler um Erzherzog Johann," exh. cat., Graz: Neue Galerie am Landesmuseum Joanneum, 1959, nos. 55 f.

### CARL RUSS
Vienna, 1779–1843

Trained at the Academy from 1793 under Johann Christian Brand (landscape) and Hubert Maurer (history painting); graphic training under J. B. Beckenkamp and J. E. Mansfeld; became painter by appointment to Archduke John in 1810; traveled with the archduke through the Alpine region, painting landscapes and a series of costume pictures in watercolor; also produced numerous works dealing with the history of the Hapsburgs; was appointed curator of the Imperial Art Gallery in the Belvedere in 1818; also purchased works for Prince Salm's Raitz Castle in Moravia; moreover, worked as an etcher and lithographer. The artistic charm of Russ's costume paintings, in which the figures are reminiscent of dressed-up puppets and the landscapes have the look of stage sets, lies chiefly in the freshness of their colors.

E. Melly. *Carl Russ, Umriss eines Künstlerlebens*. Vienna, 1844; "Die Kammermaler um Erzherzog Johann," exh. cat., Graz: Neue Galerie am Landesmuseum Joanneum, 1959, pp. 30 ff.

### LEANDER RUSS
b. Vienna, 1809; d. Kaltenleutgeben, near Vienna, 1864

Son of the artist Carl Russ, whose studio was a center of artistic life in Vienna; trained at the Academy from 1823–9; traveled in Italy; made a crucial trip to the Middle East with Baron Anton Prokesch-Osten, which marked the beginning of his interest in cultural history; produced many works for the imperial court.

### CARL PHILIPP SCHALHAS
b. Bratislava, 1767; d. Vienna, 1797

Trained privately under Johann Christian Brand from 1781; entered the Academy in 1787 and was awarded a court prize; produced a series of eighteen colored etchings of the Vienna region *(Landscapes Painted and Etched from Nature)* around 1791 and followed it with a series of various Austrian views; became a "corrector" at the Academy under Friedrich August Brand in 1795; died young of consumption. A talented member of the generation that began the transition from the late Baroque manner to Biedermeier art, Schalhas rejected all staffage and foreground mystification and developed a new feeling for space and color, exploiting the transparency of watercolor.

### ALBERT SCHINDLER
b. Engelsberg, Austrian Silesia, 1805; d. Vienna, 1861

Spent his childhood years as a poor farm boy in Silesia, where he was discovered by Peter Fendi, who took him back to Vienna with him; trained at the Academy from 1827–32; a pupil and friend of Fendi, Schindler eventually became his professional partner in 1828; made many copies of his teacher's works, showing a preference for genre subjects; made lithographs of Fendi's works based on Schiller's poem *The Lay of the Bell*; was appointed to succeed Fendi as craftsman and engraver at the Imperial Coin and Antiques Cabinet in 1842; then ceased to practice as a genre painter in the Fendi manner; also painted portrait miniatures.

### CARL SCHINDLER
b. Vienna, 1821; d. Laab im Walde, near Vienna, 1842

Son of the drawing teacher Johann Josef Schindler; entered the Academy in 1836 to train under Leopold Kupelwieser; had to break off his studies several times for health reasons; became Peter Fendi's best pupil (from 1837) as well as his friend; much influenced by Fendi; himself influenced his colleagues in the Fendi circle (Johann Friedrich Treml, Albert Schindler, and the young August von Pettenkofen); showed a preference for military subjects (prompted by his father's work as an illustrator of manuals of military science, the influence of such French military lithographers as J. L. H. Bellangé and A. Raffet, and his own observations of military manoeuvers on the nearby glacis, made from the family home in the Laimgrube); received a commission in 1838 to produce a series of illustrations of Austrian army uniforms, though only two were lithographed; in 1840 produced drawings for Trentsensky's lithographic series *War in Vivid Portrayals*, though these were much changed in transferral; had shown an oil painting in the 1839 Academy exhibition (all his oil paintings were carefully prepared in drawings and watercolor sketches); also painted numerous watercolors for their own sake; did no traveling except to visit his grandparents in St. Pölten a few times; died prematurely of pulmonary consumption. Carl Schindler's mature talent—notwithstanding his short life—is seen most clearly in his free, relaxed, almost Impressionistic watercolors.

F. M. Haberditzl and H. Schwarz. *Carl Schindler: Sein Leben und sein Werk*. Vienna, 1930.

## EMIL JAKOB SCHINDLER
b. Vienna, 1842; d. Westerland, Sylt, 1892

Trained at the Academy under A. Zimmermann from 1860–9; studied the seventeenth-century Dutch masters and the masters of the Barbizon School (Théodore Rousseau, C. Corot, C.F. Daubigny); made his first trip to Dalmatia in 1874; visited Venice and the Netherlands in 1876–7; spent the summers of 1882–4 in Goisern (Salzkammergut); settled in Plankenberg in the forest near Vienna (Wienerwald) in 1885; wintered in Dubrovnik and Corfu in 1887–8. Schindler combined a poetical view of nature with close observation of the natural world.

H. Fuchs. *Emil Jacob Schindler: Zeugnisse eines ungewöhnlichen Künstlerlebens* [work catalogue]. Vienna, 1970.

## JACOB MATTHIAS SCHMUZER
Vienna, 1733–1811

Studied architecture at the Academy; worked as an architectural draftsman and painter in Bratislava; took up copperplate engraving at an early age; was sent to Paris in 1762 at the instigation of Prince Kaunitz, to train under Johann Georg Wille; returned to Vienna in 1766 and founded an Academy of Engravers under his own direction; a new approach to nature inspired by his experience abroad (studying nature "in full light") molded the next generation of landscape painters and furnished the starting point for a new Realism in art; appointed court engraver in 1767, and in 1771 named principal of the training colleges for art teachers in the crown lands.

## ALOIS SCHÖNN
b. Vienna, 1826; d. Krumpendorf, near Klagenfurt, 1897

Trained at the Vienna Academy under Josef von Führich and Carl Russ; spent some time in Paris in 1850–1; visited Africa in 1851; made study trips to Hungary, Transylvania, Galicia, Italy, Sicily, Dalmatia, and Tunis; became a member of Vienna's Künstlerhaus in 1861; worked as a genre, landscape, and portrait painter and also as an etcher and lithographer. Schönn was an important *veduta* painter in Vienna.

## CARL SCHÜTZ
b. Ljubljana, 1745; d. Vienna, 1800

Son of a painter who moved his family to Vienna; trained under the architect Johann Hetzendorf von Hohenberg, acquiring the skills needed to produce urban *vedute* (accurate rendition of architecture in perspective and proportion) as well as a facility for staffage; worked on the *Collection de 50 vues de la ville de Vienne*, a series of views of Vienna published by Artaria & Co., over the period 1779–98; produced a variety of architectural views of cities, castles, country mansions, and ruins, also many individual drawings of commemorative coins, classical allegories, historical events, festive occasions, costumes, and uniforms; served as "master of drawing" at the Imperial Academy of Engineers from 1795–1800. Schütz introduced into Austria the "Aberli style" of contour print (named after the Swiss draftsman, painter, and etcher Johann Ludwig Aberli), in which the landscape was etched only in outline and then washed or hand-colored (in three colors).

## MORITZ VON SCHWIND
b. Vienna, 1804; d. Munich, 1871

Son of Johann Franz von Schwind, an imperial court secretary and legation councilor; attended the Schotten School in Vienna; studied philosophy at Vienna Unviersity; attended the Academy from 1821–3; earned his living by doing casual work in the art field; numbered Schubert, Lenau, Grillparzer, Kupelwieser and the Olivier brothers among his friends; concentrated initially on romantically religious subject matter (under the influence of Julius Schnorr von Carolsfeld) then switched to Realism under the influence of Johann Peter Krafft, combining it with a greater contemporary relevance; moved to Munich in 1828 and turned to fairytale scenes; appointed professor at the Munich Academy in 1847 and received important commissions from the Bavarian court; helped to decorate the new opera house on Vienna's Ringstrasse in 1863–7.

E. Kalkschmidt. *Moritz von Schwind: Der Mann und das Werk*. Munich, 1943; "Moritz von Schwind und seine Vaterstadt Wien," exh. cat., Vienna: Historisches Museum der Stadt Wien, 1954; G. Pommeranz-Liedtke. *Moritz von Schwind: Maler und Poet*. Vienna, Munich, 1974.

## JOSEPH SELLENY
b. Meidling, Vienna, 1824; d. Inzersdorf, near Vienna, 1875

Trained at the Vienna Academy under Thomas Ender and Franz Steinfeld, winning nine prizes; won the Academy's Rome Prize in 1854–5 to study in Italy; soon revealed a particular talent for portraying nature and landscape, notably in his studies of trees and plants; was patronized by Archduke Ferdinand Maximilian; obtained permission to accompany the frigate *Novara* on her transatlantic expedition in 1857 and brought back some 2,000 sketches; became a member of Vienna's Künstlerhaus in 1861; had a retrospective exhibition at the Künstlerhaus in 1875–6 with 450 pictures from the *Novara* expedition; spent his final years in a private mental asylum at Inzersdorf.

L. Popelka. *Ein österreichischer Maler segelt um die Welt: Joseph Selleny und seine Aquarelle von der Weltreise der Novara 1857–1859*. Graz, Cologne, 1964.

## ANDREAS STAUB
b. Marialach, Alsace, 1806; d. Vienna, 1839

Entered the Vienna Acdemy in 1825; took part in Academy exhibitions from 1830–9; worked mainly as a lithographer around 1835; produced lithographs after portraits by F. von Amerling and T. Ender, among others; died by his own hand.

L. Grünstein. *Moritz Michael Daffinger und sein Kreis*. Vienna, 1923, pp. 87, 95 ff.

## EMANUEL STÖCKLER
b. Nikolsburg (now Mikulov, Czechoslovakia), 1819; d. Bolzano, Italy, 1893

Entered the Vienna Academy in 1837 to train under Ender and Mössmer; spent some time in Switzerland and Italy in 1839 and visited the Middle East with Ender, producing many studies; visited Rome and Paris; visited an exhibition in Manchester in 1857, an event that crucially influenced his decision to specialize in watercolor painting; moved to Venice and became friends with Ludwig Passini; settled at the Russian court in 1875 under the patronage of Czarina Maria Alexandrovna; returned to Austria in 1880 and took up permanent residence near Aussee in the Salzkammergut.

## JOSEF EDUARD TELTSCHER
b. Prague, 1801; d. Piraeus, Athens, 1837

Trained as a lithographer in Brno and Vienna; studied at the Vienna Academy from 1823; was on friendly terms with Franz Schubert and his circle; often also worked in Graz during the years 1829–32; visited Greece in 1837 and died while swimming at Piraeus. Teltscher's miniatures, with their delicate, hatched brushstrokes, sometimes look as if they are painted on porcelain; they often bear a resemblance to the portrait miniatures of Moritz Michael Daffinger. Teltscher was one of the most highly regarded portraitists and lithographers in Vienna.

## ROBERT THEER
b. Johannisberg, Austrian Silesia, 1808; d. Vienna, 1863

Son of the gemcutter Joseph Theer and brother of Adolf and Albert Theer; trained at the Vienna Academy under Josef Klieber; took part in the Academy exhibitions from 1828–46, showing portrait miniatures on ivory or enamel, portrait lithographs, and copies of Old Masters. Theer's early works were done in small formats (mounted in bracelets, medallions, or brooches) with strong flesh tones, while in his mature period he absorbed influences from M.M. Daffinger. They also reproduced some of Daffinger's portrait miniatures lithographically.

## JOHANN FRIEDRICH TREML
Vienna, 1816–1852

Son of Friedrich Treml, scenic director at Vienna's Hofburg Theater; began training at the Vienna Polytechnic but soon switched to the Academy; was a pupil and close friend of Peter Fendi and was much influenced by another member of the Fendi circle, Carl Schindler; married Fendi's niece in 1842; showed a preference for genre subjects featuring soldiers, peasants, and craftsmen; began to receive commissions from the imperial family in 1849. Treml achieved popular recognition through lithographic reproductions of his works. His artistic strength is particularly in evidence in his relaxed, sketch-like watercolor studies.

U. Jurek. "Das Werk Friedrich Tremls." Ph. D. dissertation, University of Vienna, 1978.

## FERDINAND GEORG WALDMÜLLER
b. Vienna, 1793; d. Hebenstreitmühle, Hinterbrühl, near Baden, 1865

Left home in 1807; entered the Academy to train under H. Maurer and J.B. Lampi; worked as a miniaturist in Bratislava in 1811; summoned to Zagreb as a drawing teacher by Count Gyulay; married the singer Katharina Weidner and worked for a while as a scene painter, accompanying his wife on her engagements in Prague, Brno, and Baden; started painting in oils and copying Old Masters; visited Italy in 1825; visited Dresden, Leipzig, and Munich in 1827; became curator

*Ferdinand Georg Waldmüller* by Josef Danhauser

of the Imperial Art Gallery in 1829; became a professor at the Academy and, in 1835, a member of its council; first visited Paris in 1830; concerned himself with theoretical problems and, from 1840, with writing polemics criticizing the "stylisticists" at the Academy; forced into semi-retirement in 1864 as a result. Waldmüller was rehabilitated by Emperor Francis Joseph later in the same year; received international recognition and enjoyed major successes with his portraits, genre paintings, and landscapes (he sold all 31 oil paintings exhibited in London in 1856, and was decorated by the Prussian king in 1861 and by the Austrian emperor in 1863), but spent his final years in embittered poverty.

B. Grimschitz. *F.G. Waldmüller, Leben und Werk.* Salzburg 1957; M. Buchsbaum. *F.G. Waldmüller.* Salzburg, 1976.

## BALTHASAR WIGAND
b. Vienna, 1770; d. Felixdorf, near Vienna, 1846

A painter of miniature *vedute* of Vienna depicting historical events (the emperor's departure from the Hofburg, processions during the Congress of Vienna, etc.) with staffage of tiny but well-characterized figures; particularly fond of portraying horses; principle mediums gouache and watercolor; highly esteemed even in his lifetime; headed a workshop producing pictures for jewel boxes, paperweights, lampshades, and suchlike objects with emphasis on views of Vienna and its environs.

"Balthasar Wigand," exh. cat., Vienna: Historisches Museum der Stadt Wien, 1977.

## JOHANN ZIEGLER
b. Meiningen, Saxony, 1749; d. Vienna, 1802

Trained at the Vienna Academy under J. Schmuzer; learned drawing from nature and from the technique of copperplate engraving; began collaborating with Carl Schütz and Lorenz Janscha on the series *Collection de 50 vues de la ville de Vienne* published by Artaria & Co. in 1779; completed the first edition of 36 prints in 1784; completed the remaining prints (57 in all) in 1798, working from his own and other people's drawings; produced engravings after Lorenz Janscha, Martin von Molitor, and Ferdinand Runk; captured new views of the environs of Vienna and the Alpine regions on extensive walking tours. Ziegler is important as one of the chief masters of *vedute* of Old Vienna.

# Acknowledgments

# Photo Credits

The author wishes to thank the following people and institutions for the extensive encouragement and help he received while working on the present book: Sabine Kehl-Baierle and Dr. Ulrike Gaisbauer, for compiling the biographical data and the captions; the collections of the prince of Liechtenstein in Vaduz, and especially their director Dr. Reinhold Baumstark, for being particularly obliging; the Historisches Museum der Stadt Wien, Vienna, and its director Dr. Robert Waissenberger (†); the Österreichische Nationalbibliothek, Vienna, above all the portrait collection and the photo archives, and its director Dr. Walter Wieser; as well as the Winterstein Collection in Munich; Count Franz von Meran, Bad Homburg; Professor Dr. Rudolf Leopold; Galerie Hassfurther, Vienna, and the library and Kupferstichkabinett of the Akademie der bildenden Künste, Vienna, and its direktor Dr. Robert Wagner, as well as Dr. Ulrike Jenni.

Since the author was firmly resolved to give the technical quality of the color reproductions his closest attention, almost all the watercolors were rephotographed in a uniform manner. This job was undertaken with great vigilance and personal engagement by the photographer Peter Ertl, Vienna.

Finally, the author is extremely grateful to his publisher Office du Livre S.A., Fribourg, and its collaborators, especially its director Mr. Jean Hirschen, who had the original idea for a book on this subject, and Emma Staffelbach for her excellent, perceptive design.

Vienna, June, 1987                    Walter Koschatzky

# INDEX

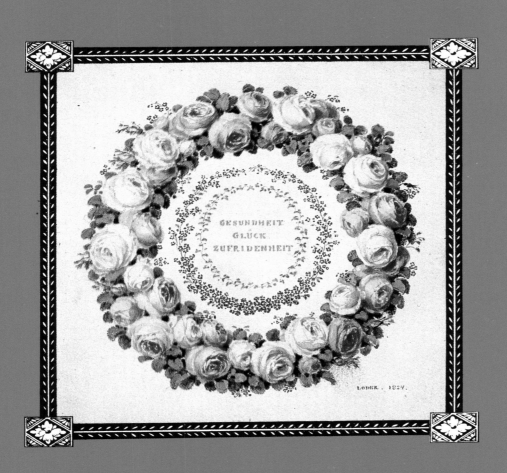

GESUNDHEIT
GLÜCK
ZUFRIDENHEIT

LODER . 1827.